CROOKED ROAD

The Story of
the Alaska Highway

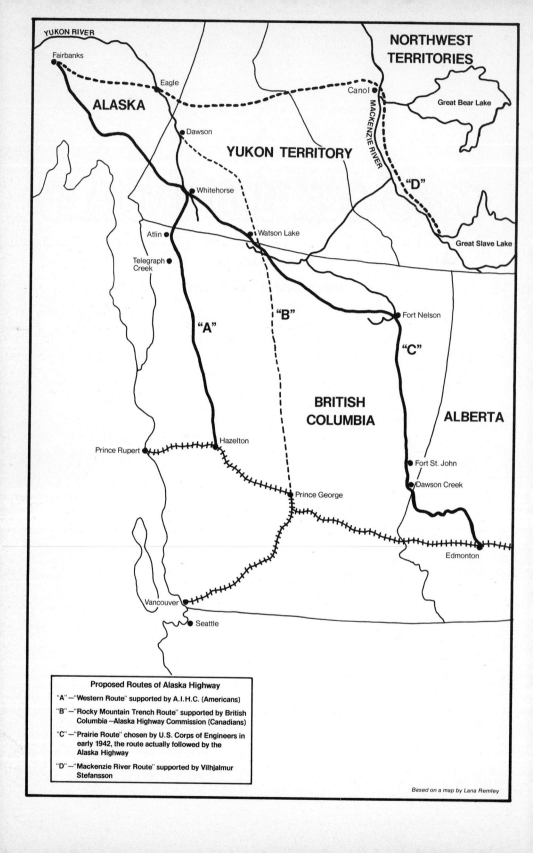

YUKON RIVER

Fairbanks

Eagle

ALASKA

Dawson

**NORTHWEST
TERRITORIES**

Canol

Great Bear Lake

MACKENZIE RIVER

YUKON TERRITORY

"D"

Whitehorse

Great Slave Lake

Atlin

Watson Lake

Telegraph
Creek

"B"

Fort Nelson

"A"

"C"

**BRITISH
COLUMBIA**

ALBERTA

Hazelton

Prince Rupert

Fort St. John

Dawson Creek

Prince George

Edmonton

Vancouver

Seattle

Proposed Routes of Alaska Highway

"A" — "Western Route" supported by A.I.H.C. (Americans)

"B" — "Rocky Mountain Trench Route" supported by British
  Columbia — Alaska Highway Commission (Canadians)

"C" — "Prairie Route" chosen by U.S. Corps of Engineers in
  early 1942, the route actually followed by the
  Alaska Highway

"D" — "Mackenzie River Route" supported by Vilhjalmur
  Stefansson

Based on a map by Lana Remley

CROOKED ROAD

The Story of
the Alaska Highway

by
DAVID A. REMLEY

McGRAW-HILL BOOK COMPANY

New York   St. Louis   San Francisco   Düsseldorf

London   Mexico   Sydney   Toronto

123456789KPKP79876

Library of Congress Cataloging in Publication Data

Remley, David A
    Crooked road: the story of the Alaska Highway.

    Bibliography: p.
    Includes index.
    1. Roads—Alaska—History.   2. Alaska—History.
I. Title.
HE356.A4R45   388.1'09798'6   75-23239
ISBN 0-07-051872-6

For Larry Lancashire, Russel B. Nye,
and William E. Wilson,
who never met each other,
but should have.

Preface

THIS IS a book of many memories. I first spent a winter in the North twenty years ago and have been back three or four times since. I will probably go again. My first trip there was a journey backward in time, and so have been the other ones. In search of certain old and little explored places in myself and in the North and its people, I returned again and again, never quite finding what I sought, but having rich times anyway.

One of the things that interested me a long time ago was the Alaska Highway itself. When I first drove it in 1964, I could not help wondering about the men who had built it. Who were they? How had they done it? Had they known anything of road building in the North, where winter is a world of freezing and crackling white things everywhere? What had they known of bridging glacial, braided rivers, of corduroying bottomless muskegs, of building road on permafrost? What happened? Who were the seven Corps of Engineers regiments, the civilian engineers, and the contractors who had cut the pioneer road through nearly fifteen hundred miles of bush in the short summer months of 1942? Why had they done it? Where were those men today? What were their memories?

I was just as interested, perhaps more so, in the local people themselves, the northerners. What had they been like before the Alaska Highway traversed their summer-green, winter-white space? How had the road changed their daily lives, their values, their outlook? They had previously hunted, trapped, fished, and traveled by dog team or packhorse across endless blue distance. How had the highway changed that? How did they feel now about what had happened to them and their land? And what of the land itself? The North of Canada and Alaska is the last of that vast continental wilderness that gave European men the illusion of unlimited space, time, and natural wealth. The North is a museum of a wild land that once extended from Florida swamps to Alaska barrens, from Hudson's Bay shores to Baja's dry reaches, from Virginia's damp woodlands to California's High Sierra and her rolling blue sea. Partly because of the Alaska Highway and the transportation revolution it and other roads brought into the North, the last great wild place presently goes under to men educated in technology and driven by the motives of profit and progress. In the 1950s and the 1960s I watched while history moved toward the close of the white man's 450-year tangle with American wilderness.

In my trips north I thought too of the people who drove the highway—truckers, soldiers, tourists, migrants to both east and west, nearly as varied and colorful an assortment of men and women as ever forked horse or rode wagon over the westward trails of the nineteenth century. Who were these people? Why were they going east or west? What were they after? What did they actually find? What were their disappointments? All of them, whatever particular reason they gave for driving the Alaska Highway, seemed restless. What did their restlessness mean? Was it the same compulsion to wander and seek that moved the emigrants through Cumberland Gap, down the Ohio, up the Missouri, the Arkansas, the Platte, toward Oregon or California or the mysterious Spanish land of New Mexico and Santa Fe? Was it the urge that drove men toward mountain gold fields, silver mines, the Klondike? Could it be the same as the spirit that American literature had for so long recorded—the restlessness, the spiritual journey, of an Ishmael, a Huck Finn, a Boone Caudill, or in recent writing, of a Jack Kerouac, an Edward Abbey, a John Graves?

In writing this book I have tried mainly to discover the facts, and then to tell the story they revealed as well as I could. Often I have allowed the people whom I talked with and taped to tell their own stories in their own voices. This I did in order to preserve their language itself, their phrasing and their images, all of which express the fabric, the texture, of their thought and feeling. I wanted to capture for a book the color, the breath if possible, of the lives of the people who have connected themselves in one way or another with the Alaska Highway; the stories of those people would compose the drama of humanity when a new technological society met, came in conflict with, and began to subsume an old northern community which was in many ways medieval. To make such a record, the gathering and use of oral history seemed to me essential. Oral history, since it is the stuff of memory, is often unreliable as to the cold facts of an historical event, but unlike those cold facts, it reveals human attitude, a changing thing. Oral accounts come close to giving the shape of the character and the temper of the people of a special time and place, their soft spots and their crusts, their estimations, their derisions, their admirations.

But the cold facts are just as important. Indeed, having the facts correct is a duty in the writing of history, and seeking them out a pleasure. The search for factual truth calls out the curiosity. It brings all the problem-solving instincts to full life. Digging out the facts, especially when they are hard to get at, is a hell of a lot of fun.

I remember one of many instances. There is an old log bridge at Canyon Creek, mile 996.3 on the Alaska Highway. It is known as the Aishihik River bridge, and the local people say that the Jacquot brothers built it early in this century for the wagon road from Whitehorse to Kluane Lake. So certain are they of being right that some years ago the Yukon tourism department put up a sign at Canyon Creek commemorating the work of the Jacquots and their A-frame bridge. I too assumed that the local people were probably correct. But an engineer, a good friend of mine, who works for the Canadian Department of Public Works examined the bridge and told me that the bolts and the other steel parts used in its construction could not possibly have been available in the early 1900s. He believed that someone must have built the bridge much later, probably that the U.S. Army Corps of Engineers had done it in 1942.

In 1975 a student of mine at the University of New Mexico introduced me to her father, a man who had worked on a Public Roads Administration location party surveying line for the Alaska Highway in April 1942. His party had started at Canyon Creek and had camped there for a while. He showed me some pencil sketches and watercolors he had made of an A-frame bridge the Corps was building over the Aishihik River while he was there. The sketches are unquestionably of the same log bridge still standing at mile 996.3.

Such a piece of factual information will not change the flow of history, but solving the problems of getting at it and the excitement of making the discoveries are hard to beat for pleasure. Perhaps it is an excitement akin to that of finding real gold or fresh beaver streams when the continent was new, when life in North America was young and hopeful, when mineral wealth, timber, fish, big game, and land resources seemed endless. Now these things are gone, or nearly so. We are left with our history, all the pains and the pleasures of probing it.

The Aishihik River bridge, rapidly deteriorating, is, incidentally, the last of the original Corps of Engineers bridges still standing along the Alaska Highway. All the others long ago went the way of rotting wood in rain and snow and spring runoff, and it will no doubt soon go, too. A new steel bridge already carries the highway across the Aishihik, and men talk of paving the Alaska Highway, of making it a modern highway designed for fast traffic. That would be a good thing, they say, for the northern economy, especially for Alaska's economy. The truck companies would like it because it would save tires and equipment breakdowns. The tourists would not have to eat dust. Sight distances over hills and around curves would be greatly lengthened. Migrants could easily make the trip one way in three days or less. All those things are no doubt true. By comparison with modern roads in the urbanized areas of Canada and in the United States, the Alaska Highway is a slow road. Most of it is still a gravel road, dusty, gritty, crooked. For myself, I hope they leave it the way it is.

Contents

CROOKED ROAD

The Story of
the Alaska Highway

T HE LURE of the North! It is a strange and a powerful thing. More than once I have come back from the great frozen spaces, battered and worn and baffled, sometimes maimed, telling myself that I had made my last journey thither, eager for the society of my kind, the comforts of civilization and the peace and serenity of home. But somehow, it was never many months before the old restless feeling came over me. Civilization began to lose its zest for me. I began to long for the great white desolation, the battles with the ice and the gales, the long, long Arctic night, the long, long Arctic day, the handful of odd but faithful Eskimos who had been my friends for years, the silence and the vastness of the great, white, lonely North. And back I went accordingly, time after time, until, at last, my dream of years came true.

> *Robert E. Peary, who reached the North Pole April 6, 1909, in the company of Matthew Henson, Seegloo, Egingwah, Ootah, and Ooqueah. From* The North Pole *(London: Hodder and Stoughton, 1910), p. 24.*

The North Needs Your Young

"Lots of young Americans are coming here. I like them. They are decent. They care about the things that matter. They come here because they do not like the things that are happening to America."

A car salesman, Prince George,
British Columbia, 1973

IT IS AUGUST 28, 1973. The blueberries are nearly gone on the road to Atlin. A few currants and raspberries remain. The Black Cottonwood have already turned to gold, and the aspen and birch are quickly going yellow. A strong wind blows in off the lake. It will turn very cold tonight.

A young Canadian woman in the hotel at Atlin pours herself a cup of coffee. She has come with her husband from Ontario. He cooks for a fall hunting party from the States. She works in the kitchen at the lodge. They have children. "There are a lot of young people coming north now," she says. "They come to get away from the cities, from the hassle back there. Work is hard to find. Often there is none. You take whatever you can get. It works out." She rises, returns to the kitchen. Her blonde hair is drawn tightly back. Her hazel eyes are sharp, with intelligence and resignation.

Dan is a young American from Alamogordo. He might be from Kokomo or Akron. He came to Canada several years ago because he did not believe in fighting the war in Vietnam. From Vancouver he went to Whitehorse—old city of the Yukon—where he has wintered two years. He thinks this year he may go back to Vancouver or Victoria, though he has found Whitehorse good to him. There is a coffeehouse for the homeless. There are odd jobs around town. He does not talk much. He smiles often and withdraws his hands. He cannot go home, but he says he is not bitter. He writes to his parents.

Paul is a hitchhiker. His mother lived, when he last saw her, in Denver. He got to Anchorage in eight rides on the Alaska and

Glenn highways from Dawson Creek. He started back Outside, but customs officials would not let him cross the border because he had no money, so he returned to Anchorage. A few days later, Paul turns up in Kenai—still hitchhiking. He wears a brown wool jacket with a tan hood. He keeps seeing a large snake and an iguana staring at each other. Sometimes he sees a broken golden pot. He thinks if he could get a dog, a gun, and some blankets, he could move into an abandoned cabin in the bush and make it there. He has never wintered in the North and has no idea what its cold can do. Before he gets out of the car, he asks, "Could you lay a dollar on me for pie and coffee, Man?" Probably, winter will find him in the Southwest where it is warm and there is much sunshine.

Jason and Carol came to Alaska from southern Wyoming. Jason had spent the previous winter in a cabin not far from Slana, after guiding sheep hunters in the fall for a local master guide. He returned to Wyoming and brought Carol back with him. Near a coffee stop on the Glenn Highway beyond Mentasta Pass they found an old cabin and repaired it. Jason fixed the windows and the roof. Friends gave them a stove. Carol cans jellies made from blueberries and currants. Both of them work at the coffee stop. Jason does odd jobs and runs the gas pump; Carol serves coffee and breakfast to travelers. Jason is confident about himself, but he knows the winter will be hard for Carol. "I am trying to get her ready for it. I help her all I can. She will be lonely." Jason can take care of himself. By next winter, Carol should be better at it.

In their twenties, Sarah and Melissa quit college and left home. They have hitchhiked the Alaska Highway and are headed south on the Haines Road to take the ferry to Ketchikan where they will meet a friend of a friend. He will help them locate a cabin for the winter. I find them a few miles below Haines Junction, at a coffee stop where they have been stuck for two days. It has rained almost constantly this summer. They have been using their tent, and their belongings are damp. They carry all their things in their back packs. The girls take things as they come, but they are happy for the ride.

A young doctor brings his wife from Denver. They are sick of the city—its noise, its dirt, its tight schedules. They hope to find a small town in British Columbia or maybe the Yukon where he can practice medicine, where he can get to know his patients, a place where the people will appreciate him. He is bearded. The two dress in washed-out Levis and drive an old VW bus. They have already filled out immigration papers.

Chip Thomas is a Cat skinner for the Alaska Highway Department. He is probably twenty-four. He came from the lower Forty-eight and lives alone in a trailer not far from Gakona. Lucinda moved to Wrangell from Nevada three years ago. Her parents are wealthy. Though she likes them, she cannot live their way. At Wrangell, she has worked in the cannery and has operated a cash register at one of the groceries. She is hitchhiking to Nevada for a visit. When she returns to Wrangell in the fall, she hopes to take over the job of reading the electric meters for the light company. She will drive a company pickup truck. Her time schedule will be her own.

Many other travelers drive the Alaska Highway and all the roads of the far north each year. Thousands come in truck campers and big cars pulling trailer homes. Hundreds drive large motor vans. Most of these are older people, some on two- or three-week vacations, others retired with time on their hands. Those with short vacations beat the highway. Some have accidents. They are miserable because northern distances are so long. Many find it impossible to accept the North, after the security of their homes and jobs and routine lives. Its space, its distances, its rain, its dust, its mountains and rivers are simply too much for them. "Could you tell us what there is to see between here and Fairbanks?" a middle-aged woman asks a trucker at Forty-mile Roadhouse at Tetlin Junction near the border on the Alaska Highway. It is another 220 miles of driving, and they have just driven well over 1200 from Dawson Creek, most of it on gravel. They do not look squarely at the magnificent country around them. They are tired. They feel threatened by this oversized and extreme land. To the south and east on this August evening there is a purple, then blue-green alpenglow on the Mentasta and Nutzotin mountains between 6 and 9 P.M.

Forty-mile Roadhouse is a good place to get the atmosphere of the Alaska Highway. K-W and LTI freightliners stop here to gas up. The drivers have coffee and supper in the well-weathered log lodge while their rigs are serviced. Gladys, a rangy, white-haired woman with bright brown eyes, is the hostess. She wears white cotton sox rolled down to her ankles. Gladys is friendly, but crusty, straightforward. The drivers like her. She talks their language. Talk smart and you get a smart reply. Ask, and you get a straight answer. A tourist: "Why do they call this place Forty-mile?" Gladys: "It's a long story, and I ain't got time to stand here and tell you."

Another old-time roadhouse hostess on the highway told me: "A man walked in here one day, looked at the clock and said, 'Is that the right time?'

"'No,' I said. 'It's yesterday's time.'

"So he thanked me and left. I don't know if he ever did figure it out." She smiled. "I've been here twenty years," she said. "I'm old. I'm tired. I've been here too long. People I used to like I don't like anymore. I'm always mad at everybody. I'm just tired and old."

Lodges like Forty-mile or Johnson's Crossing, mile 837, which retain something of the flavor of the old North, are rapidly disappearing from the Alaska Highway. Many of those old-time lodges were built of logs with red or white painted trim around the windows. Gas pumps. An ancient diesel generator rumbles twenty-four hours a day. A sign by the door reads: "CABIN RATES. $10 FOR ONE. $12 FOR TWO. AFTER HOURS TAKE AN EMPTY CABIN." Inside is a freshly polished, small maple bar with round stools. Tables hold cans of Pacific brand condensed milk for coffee. In the summer, pint glass jars on each table hold bouquets of wildflowers, cut daily. Someone has tacked raw furs to the walls. There are a parrot in a cage, a battered upright piano, Indian beadwork in a glass case which also holds the hand-cranked till. An eight-day Regulator clock ticks on the wall, and a World War II GI barrel heating stove is still in use. Shelves hold books, mostly westerns and romantic novels mixed with how-to-fix-it and how-to-do-it manuals. A bulletin board behind the till reads: "Movies tonight at the Catholic Church. For Avgas and repairs inquire at the store." The movie notice is three weeks old.

The pies are always fresh at all these log lodges. Blueberry. Apple. Apricot. Pecan. You can have a piece barefaced, or you can have it with ice cream. The pies are juicy and thick with fruit, and the crust is always flaky. At 6 A.M. the cook has already baked the day's pies. The barrel stove pops and cracks. The door jangles. A traveler stomps in for coffee and breakfast while a man outside fills the tank with gas. The traveler might take a clean cup from a shelf, as he would see the locals doing, and go into the kitchen to pour himself a cup of coffee from the big pot on the kitchen range. There are sizzling slices of ham and open-eyed eggs. Pancakes rise.

The character of such lodges on the highway, indeed all over the North, changes fast. Painted frame houses and buildings with aluminum siding long ago began replacing the cabins, the metal huts, and the GI barracks which were converted to civilian use after the war. Fuel oil furnaces replace the wood stoves, canned fish from the store the ones you used to catch and smoke for yourself. There was a time when every man who lived in the North carried a belt knife. Now only hunters and dudes do. There was a time when every man had a cabin smell—mixed odor of raw furs, smoked fish and moose hide, wood fires, damp woolens, and the sweat of hard labor. Around the towns like Whitehorse, men now bathe daily and dress carefully before they go to work.

Even the oldest and best lodges turn about and face a plastic present. For years, Tom and Rose Mould operated Muncho Lake Lodge, mile 463. It was a popular stop for truckers, and the drivers gave autographed pictures to Rose, who placed them on the walls of her café. She hung her hootenanny back of the counter. This was a one-of-a-kind thing which looked like an oversized owl's head. Someone had made it from the skin of the butt end of a Dall Sheep and had given it a wooden beak and large buttonlike eyes. Drivers told stories about it. I sat in the café one summer day when two truckers came in and ordered coffee and apple pie. One of them looked up almost reverently at the hootenanny and began to talk.

Rose was out hunting one day in the mountains back of the lake, the veteran driver told the younger one. She shot a big bear—an old silvertip—skinned it out, and hung the hide in a tree while she went back to the lodge for the jeep to pack the hide out.

"When she got back with the jeep, here was this Great Northern owl, this hootenanny, packin' the hide off for himself. So Rose shot him and packed the both of 'em out in the jeep—it took two trips—and there hangs his head on the wall."

It was noon. The café was full of tourists. The silence of pleasure, a pleasure both in the telling and in the listening, filled the air.

Muncho Lake Lodge still has the hootenanny, but now it hangs on the wall of a cocktail lounge, an adjoining room recently added or redecorated by the new owners. Truckers and tourists still stop—the food is good—but the lodge is a different place. Modern.

The highway towns, too, are in rapid transition. Fort St. John, Fort Nelson, Whitehorse. Only a few log buildings are left. A new Hudson's Bay Company post is a modern department store with a large grocery section and a line of cash registers. There is always a Macleods with the big red M. Bright brown and yellow colors gloss the Canadian Imperial Bank of Commerce. The shiny buildings look somewhat like McDonald's hamburger stands.

New Fort Nelson is on the Alaska Highway not far from the airport built early in World War II. The old town is on the other side of the river. A very few families still live there, and the men drive off to work in the morning, probably to the new town or to the smelly refinery a few miles south down the highway. In the wintertime they trap a little, in the summertime prospect. There is mining activity all over the North. In many places choppers fly prospectors in and out. Business.

An Indian man. Probably a Slave or a Beaver along this part of the highway. Farther north, he would be a Casca or a Tlingit. I see him walking toward Fort Nelson. He uses a cane, has black hair, and his teeth are tobacco-stained. He moves unsteadily, and I stop to give him a ride. "I'm seventy-one years old," he says before getting in. "I seen that buildin'," he says, pointing at a two-story log house, "since I was a kid. My daddy, he seen it. My granddaddy, he seen it."

The old man has a daughter in Ottawa and a son in Vancouver. His son wants him to come to the city to live. "I was there three months last year. I had him put me on the bus and send me home. This is home. Here!" He points down hard with the first finger of his right hand.

"It is a good place. I am goin' to die here." He smiles, happy that he will die at home.

Now, almost everywhere along the highway, it is necessary to lock your car, then not leave it for long. There are people who steal. Barney Streeper of Fort Nelson speaks:

Well, when we come into the country there on the Peace River, we was
fifty miles [out] . . . , ten miles by canoe and the rest by road. Well, you
walked, and there was a stoppin' place on the Peace River and
you'd . . . come up and you'd send to Eaton's or Simpson's for stuff
and you left your money and your letter and stuff there, and somebody'd come along and pick it up and take it to the post office and mail
it and bring your mail back and leave it there, and you'd come in [and
get it]. Then when civilization come, when you left your money there it
was gone. . . . Well, it's gettin' more civilized now. You can't even stop
overnight down here at the . . . hotel without their breakin' into it and
takin' stuff out. . . . My God, [used to be] you'd break down here on
the highway . . . and go off and leave it, and you come back in two
weeks and it wouldn't be touched. Break down on the highway now
and you leave it an hour and you come back and you can't even find the
traces of it. It's all gone. Civilization.

Nan Streeper, Barney's wife: "There were good things about the
old days, yes, wonderful things. The way people were together!
You couldn't survive without your neighbor. You knew that. And
people got along. Now, this is opened up to civilization."

But the good hotels and lodges along the highway are nearly
always busy, at least in the summertime. One of the many kinds of
people who stay in them are the construction men, for maintenance
of this gravel road is a year-round industry. In the summer of 1973
a small crew of workers lives in one of the lodges on Kluane Lake
while they repair that sector of the highway. They eat breakfast
and supper in the dining room, the cook packs their lunches and, in
the early hours of morning, fills their steel thermos jugs with hot
coffee. One of the pleasures of the supper hour is the good food.
The other is the conversation itself, and these people practice it
well, for talk in the North has always had to do what movies and the
TV set do Outside—make the day's entertainment. Their conversation is a kind of communion, a sharing in each other's experience of
the loneliness and the frustration of the day's work. The movement
is leisurely. There are long pauses while the men chew, then create
their next remarks. A certain edginess shows in the almost constant
banter.

The men walk in. They are all young, probably in their
twenties. The door bangs. Feet shuffle. A sign by the till reads,
"WIPE YOUR FEET OUTSIDE." The cook, Thomas, opens the talk.

9

"Hello, boys. Ready to eat?"

"Just as well begin now."

The men sit down. They smile and laugh, greeting one another. Chair legs scrape on the floor. The owner has placed the table before a window looking out upon indescribably wild, light blue-green Kluane Lake.

From the kitchen Thomas talks with the men as he puts their dinners on the plates. China dishes rattle.

"What's for supper tonight, Thomas?"

"This is Chinaman's food. Rice." He pronounces the word "Chinnamon."

He lugs the plates of rice and beef chunks to the table and places them solidly one at a time before the five men.

"Coffee now, boys?"

"Yes. Please."

"I'd like a beer."

"Gotta go up to 1083 tomorrow."

"What you doin' up there?"

"Not much to do. They better give me somethin' more to do."

"You could scrape the beaver dams outta the culverts."

"Eat a beaver, save a tree."

"Every time I take a coffee break this old sea gull comes up and sits on the sand pile."

"Hell, he knows what a coffee break's for."

"There's this gull comes up and sits on a sand pile every day I eat my lunch. Gave him half of one of Thomas's sandwiches today. He took it down and dunked it in the crick."

"Hear that, Thomas?"

"What, Mackintosh?"

"Your sandwich was so tough the old gull had to take it down and dunk it in the crick."

"Go to hell, Mackintosh. I'll fix your breakfast in the morning. Gonna put arsenic in it. Will you help me, McClintock?"

"Yeh, I'll hold 'im down."

"Hey, Christasen. Wanta buy a car?"

"How much, Thomas?"

"Make an offer."

"Fifty bucks."

"Go to hell. Dirty bugger."

"What did *you* give for it?"

"Twenty-five. Guy came in here last week. Left it. I inherited a car."

"More coffee, boys?"

"Yes, please."

"Pie now?"

"No, thanks. I'll take mine about nine or ten o'clock."

The men sip their coffee silently. Two of them tip back the chairs.

"Well, gotta go saw off that bolt."

"Hell, ain't you got that done yet, Thompson?"

Mackintosh and Thompson slide back their chairs, get up, and amble out.

"Thanks, Thomas. See you at breakfast."

"I'm leavin' tomorrow, Thomas. Want me to finish up the meal sheets now?"

"Might as well."

Thomas brings out the sheets and Christasen goes over them.

"How much for Wednesday's supper?"

"Don't remember. Put down whatever you think is right. Whatever *you* think."

"O.K. I'll put down three-fifty, same as Thompson put down."

"Make it three. Three is fine."

"Is Thompson the fat guy or the thin guy?"

"Thin guy, Thomas."

"Fat guy?"

"No, thin guy."

"Oh. I thought he was the fat guy."

"Fat guy's Richardson."

Christasen adds up the sheets, thanks Thomas, and walks out.

I get up to leave, after paying for my supper.

"Thanks. You headed up, or down?"

"Up."

"Well, have a good trip."

Outside, a long-haired hitchhiker waits beside the road. An LTI diesel rig roars by, raising a pillar of dust, and a Canada jay hunts scraps the dogs have not found. On a ridge above this dusty new road, the pioneer Alcan Highway winds up over Soldiers Summit, where the ceremony officially opening the pioneer road to military traffic took place on November 20, 1942. The air is still and cold. There is no sound now that the truck has gone. Kluane waters have not changed. The lake is very cold and turning gray in the evening light. Fireweed petals have begun to fall. Soft shadows extend. I drive north looking for a place to pull off and sleep. I am car camping.

The Road Is Going to Be Built

IN ANOTHER AUGUST—thirty-one years earlier—the pioneer Alcan Highway approached completion. On February 2, 1942, a Special Cabinet Committee appointed by President Roosevelt had ordered General Crawford to report in one week on the available construction equipment and on the problems of building the road to Alaska across northern Canada from Edmonton. Crawford passed the orders immediately to Brig. Gen. C. L. Sturdevant, Assistant Chief of Engineers. He told Sturdevant that the United States Army Corps of Engineers would be assigned the task, and he requested plans for the job within a few days. Sturdevant discussed the project with the Commissioner of the Public Roads Administration (PRA), and in two days came back to the War Department with a report and a comprehensive plan. The stunning attack at Pearl Harbor less than two months before had forced the formation of the Special Cabinet Committee and its decision to build the Alaska Highway. "The route is incidental to the main fact," said Ernest Gruening of Alaska. "The road is going to be built."

Sturdevant's plan called for the necessary arrangements with the Canadian government and for an immediate allotment from the President's Emergency Fund. General Sturdevant and his staff made the important distinction between the first stage of the project (cutting the pioneer tote road) and the second stage (constructing the improved, year-round roadway). The pioneer road was to be sufficient only "to get equipment through and to permit supply of troops." Temporary bridges and strings of pontoons would make the river crossings. Planimetric maps for the country south of Whitehorse would be ready within a few weeks, the plan read, and it noted, though inaccurately, that maps for the location of the road north of Whitehorse were already "sufficient." Hundreds of miles of muskeg and the wild rivers from Whitehorse far into Alaska would require on-the-spot determination of location and later relocations of the highway line.

General Sturdevant tentatively outlined the work the Public Roads Administration was to do in cooperation with army engineers. The plan called for PRA road location parties to work north from Whitehorse and army parties to work south from there. Subsequent discussions with PRA chief Thomas H. MacDonald and subsequent orders, however, led to important changes in the plan. In actual fact, the army seems to have done most of its own locating for the pioneer road opened at the end of 1942, and the PRA most of the locating or relocating for the improved road which it completed in 1943. It is often said that there were two original roads, the army's, following the army line, and the PRA's, following the PRA location line. In fact the two lines often converged and followed each other for long distances. When disagreements occurred between army and PRA location engineers about the best route for the final highway, military headquarters in Washington firmly stated that army officers had the authority to make the choice. To do their work, parties of army or PRA locators (and sometimes both together) went into the field with local guides, mushers, packers, and bush flyers to survey out the line the road was to follow.

The PRA would also employ and manage, according to Sturdevant's plan, the private contractors whose workers were to come behind the soldiers, correcting alignment and grade, building permanent bridges and culverts, and surfacing the highway with gravel or crushed rock. "Blacktop or other surface," the general's plan optimistically stated, was "to be added after proper settlement." Clearly the Corps of Engineers' planners knew little about subarctic construction problems at the time. The intensely cold weather and the soggy muskegs would prevent the rapid finishing possible in relatively mild climates on solid ground. After the war's end, the road would be left to the Canadians in a condition suitable only for the passage of trucks and rugged military vehicles.

But Sturdevant's plan sharply outlined the objective of the Corps of Engineers on the Alaska Highway during World War II. It was an objective the Corps would refuse to compromise. "The purpose," read the plan, was "to cover the entire route with a minimum road at the earliest practicable date." The key phrases were "minimum road" and "earliest practicable date." To build a road simply passable for military supply vehicles and to do it as quickly as possible under the intense pressures of war and of weather were practical ideals. Given the characteristics of the country over which the road must pass—the mountains, the glacial rivers, the muskegs, and the distances themselves—the ideals may even seem unrealistic. The engineers of the Public Roads Administration, however, would not be happy with this military ideal, this expediency. They were scientific roadbuilders. In their assignment, to improve the road, they insisted upon higher standards. They were to argue with the men of the Corps, but they would have to compromise.

Brigadier General J. R. B. Jones, Ret.

Brigadier Jones, who lived in Edmonton and worked until recently for the University of Alberta, was Senior Highway Engineer for the Alaska Highway after the Canadian takeover. In 1957 he returned from an area command in New Brunswick to become commanding officer of the Canadian army's Northwest Highway System.

[The pioneer road] was only meant for access for contractors. Then they put the PRA people on it . . . and they had very, very high standards. . . . Easy curves. Easy gradients. Good sight distances. But it was pretty slow, so [the army] said hurry up, so they sort of dropped the standard, and they worked . . . at several places at a slightly lower standard. . . . And then [the army] said, it looks as though the war is going to finish. Sort of do the best you can and get out.

Sturdevant's report to the Special Cabinet Committee also outlined the earliest Corps of Engineers plan for the actual construction of the military highway, at first called the "Alcan" and later the "Alaska" Highway. The plan involved two survey companies for highway line location, four light ponton companies for providing the river and stream crossings, and four construction regiments for cutting road. According to the plan, the 35th Combat Engineer Regiment would move by rail to Edmonton, Alberta, and then to Dawson Creek, British Columbia, some 370 modern highway miles northwest of Edmonton. From Dawson Creek, the 35th would make a winter march another 300 miles northwest over a winter trail to Fort Nelson. Here in the spring their work was to begin. They would cut tote road from Fort Nelson west, after the thaw and runoff, as soon as the country had dried out enough to permit labor. The 35th would reach Contact Creek, 219 miles west of Fort Nelson, on September 24. Standing on the tracks of their battered Cats which sat rumbling in the cold, clear water, the men would greet the soldiers of the 340th Regiment who had punched through all the way south from Whitehorse.

The 340th General Service Regiment was to be activated immediately at Vancouver Barracks. Sturdevant's plan called for the 340th to move to Whitehorse by May 1 to build road south behind the location engineers. Their work would extend all the way to Contact Creek (actually they went from Carcross to Teslin Lake and began working south from there). Another regiment, the 341st General Service, would move from Fort Ord to Fort St. John. In the spring, the 341st was to build road from there to Fort Nelson, 250 miles away. In the meantime, the other construction regiment of the four named in Sturdevant's plan—the 18th Combat Engineer Regiment—would go to Skagway, at the end of Lynn Canal, the seaport for the Yukon and northern British Columbian interior, and from there to Whitehorse over the White Pass and Yukon Railway. From Whitehorse the 18th was to begin construction toward the Alaska border, 300 miles west.

Thus the sketch of the plan for opening the pioneer Alcan road: the four original regiments and the three which the army added later [the 93rd, the 95th, and the 97th] were to cut a path in one working season over nearly twelve hundred miles of muskeg, mountain, and river from Fort St. John, British Columbia, to the Alaska border and from there another 208 miles to Delta Junction on the Richardson Highway between Valdez and Fairbanks. These seven regiments would do most of the work of cutting the pioneer road, although they were to be heavily supported by Public Roads Administration locators and contractors who would themselves cut portions of it and make improvements elsewhere. The road would be passable by October, and the official opening ceremony would take place on a ridge above Kluane Lake on November 20. The regiments were to work under the constant pressures of war and of the coming northern winter. The speed with which they labored astounded old northerners.

C. D. MacKinnon

C. D. MacKinnon was a Canadian civilian transportation expert who worked for the American Army Corps of Engineers in 1942 and 1943. He inventoried and placed priorities upon shipments of matériel going up the line from Edmonton for the CANOL project.

I went up with the Superintendent of the Northern Alberta Railroad, and he looked at this and he said, "You know, these Americans are crazy! Look at that be-yootiful equipment."

I said to 'im . . . , "Well," I said, "let me tell you somethin'. They'll go down swingin'. You can bet your neck if this trainload of Cats, and bulldozers, and draglines are gone, and Le Tourneaus, there'll be another trainload come behind 'em."

And he said, "Well, they'll need it."

But I said, "Well, Charlie, I'll see yuh in about six months [and] we'll see what it is."

And boy they were [all over the place], and then every time you'd look up they were another fifteen or twenty miles up the road and it was tough workin'.

Norman Harlin

Norman Harlin was a Canadian trapper in the Yukon and the Northwest Territories in the 1930s. He and his brother, Jack Harlin, worked for PRA survey parties out of Whitehorse in 1942.

Wherever I stop, these tourists talk about how crooked the road is, and hell, well sure it is, it has to be. I mean, they put it through in seven months. Which is unbelievable. Fifteen hundred miles of road! [Dawson Creek to Delta Junction is 1,429 miles, modern highway mileage.] And there wasn't an axe mark anyplace except these wide places, villages. To me it was unbelievable. Course, it shows what unlimited manpower and resources can accomplish. Money was *no* object! . . . .

I was sitting at Watson Lake . . . after Pearl Harbor . . . [when the announcement came over the radio that] the Alaska Highway [would] be built and open for traffic in October this year. That was the first part of 'forty-two. And us bush apes sittin' there laughin' about this American stuff and I rode a convoy back [from Watson Lake to Teslin] on the twenty-third of October. Which to me was somethin' unbelievable.

By February 6, General Marshall and Secretary of War Stimson had approved Sturdevant's plan. On that day it went to the White House for the President's signature. There were some changes, but the directive President Roosevelt approved was essentially the master plan drawn up by General Sturdevant's staff. Exactly four days had passed since the Special Cabinet Committee had met on February 2 and instructed the army to have a report ready within a week. Five days later, on the eleventh, General Crawford received a phone call from Secretary Stimson's office. It was 2:45 in the afternoon. Mr. Schott spoke crisply: "I have discussed this matter with the President, and he approves. You are authorized to immediately proceed with the project. . . ."

Within hours of the President's approval of the plan, the army wired orders for putting its details into action. The 35th Combat Engineer Regiment under General De Witt's command at Fort Ord would have to be ready to move out by the first of March. Similar orders went to other commanders whose engineer units would be involved in the construction work. Arctic clothing and "special rations that will stand freezing" were ordered from G-4, supply. The Quartermaster General was to replace the engineer outfits' motorcycles with one-quarter-ton trucks—four-by-fours—and he must find two QMC officers and enough men to operate two railheads, the one at Dawson Creek and the other at Whitehorse. The Chief Signal Officer was to provide enough radio equipment and men to maintain communications between the widely scattered units. The Surgeon General would supply a medical staff and equipment. Even the Chief of Finance was called upon for two finance officers and their staffs.

The responsibilities of each of the two national governments had now to be spelled out as quickly as possible. Canada and the United States of America exchanged diplomatic notes on March 17 and 18. The Americans agreed to make the surveys and to build the pioneer road, to order the PRA to write contracts for the completion of the highway "without regard to whether the contractors are

Canadian or American," to maintain the highway until six months after the war's end, and to transfer to Canada at that time "that part of the highway which lies in Canada . . . subject to the understanding that there shall at no time be imposed any discriminatory conditions" upon the use of the road by American civilians. Prime Minister King agreed to "acquire" the rights-of-way, to "waive" duties or transit charges on all through shipments between the United States and Alaska, to "waive" duties, taxes, and license fees upon all equipment and supplies used by the Americans and upon the personal effects of the workers, to "remit" income tax of Americans and American corporations employed on the project, to facilitate the entry of American construction workers, with the understanding that they were not to be repatriated at Canadian expense, and to allow the use of the local timber, gravel, and rock needed for the construction.

The two notes also allowed the working out of the "practical details" through "direct contact" between the Canadian and American agencies involved, subject, if necessary, "to confirmation" by further diplomatic notes. Although the fine edges still remained to be honed in conferences and notes, the two governments would manage to cooperate throughout the war on the basis of the March agreements. Severe problems had to be met at the war's end over points not covered in the March notes or in further agreements. The two most difficult were the problems of how to dispose of the millions of dollars worth of American equipment remaining in Canada, and the American fear, as the war came to its end, that Canada might close the highway. The Dominion government had not guaranteed in the March note to maintain the highway after the Americans left. Alaskans were especially worried. The new highway, built with much American money and effort, was their only overland route to the lower Forty-eight. In the historical spirit of compromise and agreement, however, the two nations would resolve these difficulties.

The Defense of Alaska Is the Defense of Canada

AT A PRESS CONFERENCE on February 17, 1942, President Roosevelt made a statement that frightened Canadians. It was what he did not say more than what he did say that was so unsettling. Asked about the American capacity to defend Alaska, he replied that he could "give no reassurance" that an attack upon Alaska was out of the question. Canadians saw in that statement a warning of approaching disaster. Bruce Hutchison wrote in the *Vancouver Province* that this "most amazing admission on defense ever made by an American President" had sounded a "warning" which ran "like an electric shock" throughout Ottawa, Canada's capital. Hutchison demanded a heavier concentration of Canadian military power on the northwest coast. Until this time, the Dominion had centered the strength of its army and air force upon the European war. She had looked eastward. Now she must think of defending the West. Alaska might be Japan's next military objective. "The defense of Alaska," Hutchison wrote, "is the defense of Canada."

Hutchison's article appeared in the *Province* on February 18. On the nineteenth the *Edmonton Journal* reported that United States Army Engineers were already in Canada to study the possibilities of building the military highway from Edmonton, the capital of Alberta, to Alaska. A commission of four Americans had just left the Alberta capital and gone up to Dawson Creek, Fort St. John, and Fort Nelson to look at the land. The *Journal* staff was pleased that the Edmonton route might be the one chosen of the four which had been proposed and seriously considered. The *Journal* had long been a proponent of this so-called "prairie route" which would tie together the air bases of the Dominion's Northwest Staging Route between Edmonton and Alaska. There would be obvious economic benefits for Edmonton and north-central Alberta. While "the precise route cannot be decided until the surveys are made," the *Journal* said, "there now seems every prospect of the project going ahead by the Alberta route." On February 25, the *Journal* reported that the Americans had returned from their trip up the line west of Edmonton. They had traveled all the way to Fort Nelson and had found the prairie route, what they had seen of it, "entirely feasible."

Four important men made up the American preliminary study commission—Col. William M. Hoge and Col. Robert D. Ingalls for the Corps of Engineers, Lt. Col. E. A. Mueller of the Quartermaster Corps, and one civilian, a Senior Highway Engineer from the Public Roads Administration, C. F. Capes. It was a select group, all men of experience. A lifelong engineer officer, Hoge would be given command of the 635 miles of construction from Dawson Creek to Watson Lake. His first command post would be at Fort St. John. Colonel Ingalls commanded the 35th Combat Engineer Regiment, the first to arrive for construction on the southern end of the new military highway. Colonel Mueller knew the problems of supply. C. F. Capes was an expert construction engineer from the Denver office of the PRA.

Colonel Hoge, the spokesman for the group, was tight-lipped. He told a *Journal* reporter that his purpose was to study the problems of building a road from Edmonton through Grande Prairie, Fort St. John, Fort Nelson, and Whitehorse and to report his findings directly to Washington. He and his group were not to decide which of the proposed routes the highway should follow (that decision had already been made in Washington, and Hoge knew it). Besides this prairie route, or Route C, three others had been proposed, two of them much farther to the west (designated Routes A and B) and the other in the far north, following the Mackenzie River Valley (Route D). Each had its strong political and commercial proponents. So far as Hoge knew, he said, the army had not yet selected any of these four routes.

The colonel recognized that one of the most difficult problems of making a precise study of the prairie route was "the complete lack of 'real' maps or even of any kind of maps" of much of the area the road would have to cross. Other members of the commission also admitted that building the military road from Dawson Creek would be a "huge job." The journalists realized this fact too. Peter Elliott of the *Edmonton Journal* wrote that "there are roaring streams and rivers that swell their banks in the spring" and "stretches of deep, soggy muskegs; there are mountain passes to be traversed, and canyons to be bridged." But Elliott asserted that the "vast plains, rolling river valleys, almost treeless tundras, and some stretches already marked with roadbeds" should make the job at least possible. He was optimistic. Most of the rivers would be very difficult to bridge; the "roadbeds" beyond Fort St. John, where they existed at all, were only winter trails. These were passable in the winter, but the warm spring days and summer sunlight turned them into soggy ditches along which even pack-horses found it difficult to pick their way.

By the sixth of March, just one month and four days after the President's Special Cabinet Committee had instructed General Crawford to order plans, the news was out that the army had decided the Alaska military highway must be built through Edmonton. By this time survey crews were already in the field, and hundreds of American soldiers were preparing for the Canadian north. The first trainload of engineer troops steamed through Edmonton on Saturday evening and arrived at end of steel—Dawson Creek—in the early hours of Monday morning. There the soldiers began, even before noon, to prepare the railhead for the thousands of troops and civilian workers who would follow them during the coming months.

Troop trains are smoky strings of cars and engines that seem always to pass in the night. They whistle in the early hours of gray mornings when only a brakeman might be up, swinging his lantern along the track. They move hearselike, steadily. Dark string follows upon string, made up of passenger cars and freights and flats carrying the equipment and supplies needed to care for the men and to keep them at work—food, tents, medicines, tools, cars, jeeps, trucks, Cats, and shovels. If the trains that slipped through Edmonton in mid-March 1942 stopped at sidings and depots, there were only brief exchanges between their men and the city's people. Engines took on water and fuel quickly. Here and there a girl might stand for moments, talking with soldiers who leaned out a window or waited on the catwalk between the cars. Then the train began slowly to move, windows closed, soldiers returned to their cars to sleep or to play cards.

Dawson Creek was a beehive. The 35th Engineers began to arrive on March 9. Company A of the 648th Topographic Battalion came in on the thirteenth, and the 74th Light Ponton Company arrived the next day. The last of the 35th were in Dawson Creek on the 16th. Officers set up temporary headquarters in a hotel, enlisted men tent-camped west of town, and the soldiers quickly completed a quarter-mile spur and a 300-foot extension to the main railway track. Trucks, many of them owned by local farmers, moved freight within hours from the railhead toward Fort St. John, the next town up the line. Supplies soon moved out from there toward Fort Nelson over the winter trail. Officers and men pushed themselves. Winter trails would become impassable within days. The streets and roads around Dawson Creek were already quagmires from the heavy traffic. Asked by a journalist about the precise route of this new highway, the Americans were nearly silent. "It's going north," said one officer. "That's all. That's about all we can say."

The PRA locators and the engineer officers in the field used their own judgment about the specific location of the roadway. When the construction troops and the PRA contractors completed the pioneer tote road in late 1942, it extended well over 1,400 total miles from the railhead at Dawson Creek to the junction with the Richardson Highway southeast of Fairbanks, near Big Delta. In the winter of 1942–1943 the men also began a branch road southward toward the sea from a point on the Alcan Highway about 100 miles west of Whitehorse. This so-called Haines Road ran nearly 160 miles from Haines Junction on the Alcan over a dizzying range of coastal mountains down to the port of Haines, Alaska, on the Lynn Canal not far from Skagway.

The locators often had trouble simply staying ahead of the construction troops. Many old-timers tell stories about that trouble.

Earl Bartlett

Earl Bartlett worked during the war as an electrical specialist, a repairman for the Royal Canadian Electrical Mechanical Engineers. He was stationed for a time at the Liard River on the Alcan Highway and, later, at Fort Nelson.

The Alaska Highway was an emergency project, . . . in places very badly engineered. But there was an urgency there, the threat of invasion from Japan of the west coast, which would probably deny the country the shipping lanes entirely . . . so time was an important thing. . . .

I was told that the . . . surveyors were in the process of surveying the highway out properly, the gentleman's way of doing things, the scientific way. The construction crews came along with their supplies all arranged for, and their work laid out for them and the [locators] were in the way. They bypassed [them], in many places went on and laid the highway out without proper survey because of the time element, and they left the surveyors behind them. At Liard River I was talking with some boys who had worked on the construction of about three miles of it from the first point of contact with the Liard around to where the bridge was, and one of these fellows told me that they just didn't have a surveyor there. Equipment was there, the road had to be done, and they sent a man out with snowshoes and an axe in the general direction of their objective, and he hacked the trees and blazed them, and the bulldozers followed along behind him.

This is the way the tote road looks in 1942. North of Fort St. John the old winter trail disappears in March thaw. Mountainous, heavily forested ground lies farther to the west, and the locators decide to open their road in the high country. As soon as the soaked earth dries out enough for heavy machinery to move, the soldiers go to work.

From the flat land around Fort St. John, the new road starts north past windy, treacherous Charlie Lake, the lake that takes the lives of several engineers. Soon it climbs ridges framed in fireweed in early June. From Pink Mountain to Trutch it stays on the ridgetops, the eastern slope of the Rockies. Along here soldiers look west up smoky blue valleys into the heart of the Rocky Mountains. The tote road crosses the Beatton River, named for an old Hudson's Bay Company factor (Frank Beaton; the mapmakers misspelled his name); the Sikanni Chief, named for an Indian; and the Buckinghorse, named for Bob Barker's villainous old horse. Past Trutch, 200 miles from Dawson Creek, it follows along the ridges on the east side of the valley of the Prophet and parallels that river to Fort Nelson.

Between Fort Nelson, 300 miles out, and Watson Lake, 635 miles from Dawson Creek, locators carefully examine two routes. It is nearly a tossup. They choose the one across Raspberry Creek and the Kledo River, past Steamboat Mountain, straight up the rocky box of Tetsa River to Summit Lake, 400 miles from Dawson Creek, at over 4,000 feet the top of the Rockies, the highest point on the Alaska Highway. Below Mount St. George, the tiny lake shimmers cold on late June mornings. There are sudden rain showers. Fireweed glows pink.

Then the line runs northwest again, down the stony canyon of MacDonald Creek, across the Racing River, up the Toad and over a divide to Muncho Lake, 460 miles out. Snow trims the mountain ranges which lie along every sky edge at Muncho. From the deep green lake, the tote road follows Trout River to the banks of the Liard, wild old northern river with its Rapids of the Drowned. Here at about mile 500 locators dispute whether the road should follow the north or south bank the rest of the 135 miles to Watson Lake. They take the north bank. The road crosses the river to Liard Hot Springs, the bathing place where all soldiers and travelers stop to wash away the dust and mud of the Alcan.

George Nelms

During World War II George Nelms, a Canadian, helped build the suspension bridge over the Peace River on the Alcan Highway near Fort St. John.

The soldiers built the first building that was put in on the hot springs, and they built it right over the hot spring so that the water ran through the middle and they could sit there on both sides . . . dangle their feet. . . .

There's two hot springs. . . . And between those two, [Tom and Rose Mould] had a garden. And it's still visible there if you know where it is, a small plot . . . and they had potatoes and carrots, and they could leave them in there all winter, dig them out as they needed them, and they never froze, on account of the hot springs themselves. . . . And the carrots were the sweetest, the nicest you ever tasted. Oh Gee they were lovely!

But then, of course, as soon as the tourists started coming through [after the war], they couldn't maintain their garden because everybody went in there. [The tourists] had to dig something up, and they just destroyed it you know. So [the Moulds] had to abandon it. But you can still tell where it is. . . . There's part of the old fence there.

DEFENSE OF ALASKA IS DEFENSE OF CANADA

Earl Bartlett

[They had a slab walkway into Liard Hot Springs, slabs from the sawmill.] Then they built—out of boards covered with tar paper—a dressing room with a do-it-yourself heating plant in it [a wood stove], so if you wanted to go in there in the wintertime, you built a fire, and it didn't take long to warm it so you had a nice warm dressing place. And then there was a covered ramp went down into this pool—the pool had a floor in it then, a wooden floor, and the pool was covered with a building screened in . . . against flies, which of course wouldn't bother you in the wintertime. . . . And the most thrilling experience was to dive in under this sidewall of this building and come out in the pool outside, and could be thirty-five or forty below zero, with frost crackling on the trees, and a bright moonlight night, deep snow, and you had to pinch yourself to realize that this was actually the real life there. If you stood up out of the water of course you'd get chilly right away, but if you kept down at shoulder height, you'd be perfectly comfortable in all this frozen [weather].

Beyond Liard Hot Springs the tote road crosses Smith River— flowing south from Toobally Lakes—Coal River, Contact Creek, and Hyland River. At Lower Post it reaches the junction of the Liard and the Dease, an old trading and transportation center. Sixty and seventy years ago prospectors came down the Dease River from Dease Lake, the Stikine River, Telegraph Creek, and the Pacific to hunt fortunes in the gold fields of the Klondike. In 1942 there is a Mountie post here and a Catholic church. Clusters of log houses, each with a cache on log stilts beside it for keeping meat. Casca families. Trappers. Dog sleighs stand beside cabins or hang outside on pegs. Already in late July, native families preserve the winter's fish, and thin strips of red salmon and whitefish hang in the sun to dry. Men think of the fall moose hunt and talk of traplines. Fireweed grows here too. It lines the Liard's edge with pink and dark purple. Fireweed is the flower of the North.

It is only a short jog from Lower Post to Watson Lake over a road built earlier by the Canadian government. Beyond Watson Lake the route to Whitehorse is very uncertain. Available maps suggest that any fairly direct line will have to cross a mountainous plateau at an elevation of about 6,000 feet, high enough to make the road impassable in winter. If so, soldiers will have to build a 500-mile southern loop up the Dease River, west to Telegraph Creek, and north to Atlin. But ground and aerial reconnaissance reveals a heavily forested pass in the area of the plateau, a pass with a quality of forest which at that latitude never grows much above 4,000 feet. "Its discovery," wrote General Sturdevant, "was an important factor in the early completion of the road."

West of Watson Lake and Upper Liard, a Casca village, the line runs up the Rancheria and over the great divide between the Mackenzie and the Yukon River drainages. Then it goes down the Swift and Morley rivers to Morley Bay on Teslin Lake, where the Corps of Engineers builds one of the main base camps. Beyond here it crosses Nisutlin Bay and skirts Teslin Lake, mountain-framed, fingerlike, one of the deep-blue lakes whose waters drain eventually into the Yukon River. From Johnson's Crossing on the Teslin River, the tote road turns southwesterly past Squanga Lake toward Marsh Lake. From Marsh Lake it parallels the Yukon to Whitehorse at mile 918.

J. Pierrepont Moffat

J. Pierrepont Moffat, United States Ambassador to Canada at the time, made a trip over the Alcan in July 1942. He described Whitehorse to his friend, A. A. Berle, Jr.

First, a word about Whitehorse. After lying dormant, a ghost town, for nearly forty years, it is again enjoying a boom. Prices are fantastic. Accommodation is pitifully inadequate. There are twenty males to each female, and beards are coming back into fashion. The hotel is a wooden structure with two beds per room—you are assigned a bed, not a room—with the walls so thin that you hear a symphony of male snores blending together the length of the corridor. All night long the airplanes drone overhead, and when in the morning you go out to breakfast—the dining room is in a separate shack—you pass a couple of rows of men sleeping in the "parlor." These are the unfortunates who arrived too late to be assigned a bed.

Theodore Strauss

A staff writer for The New York Times, *Theodore Strauss traveled the Alcan by truck and by airplane in 1942. His series of four articles about the highway appeared in* The Times, *the following selection from "Alcan Road Booms Vast Untamed Area" on January 1, 1943.*

The dark-paneled lobby of the Whitehorse Inn, adorned with tinted photographs of old gold-rush scenes, totem poles, and the heads of

28

moose and caribou, is now piled high with the luggage of strangers unable to find a room. As in Edmonton, they are the same assortment of military and government officials and commercial travelers.

Grounded by the weather, they stare forlornly at the moose heads, hour after hour, hopefully awaiting the jingle of the eccentric hall telephone telling them their plane will take off within the hour. Sometimes it does jingle. Every one piles pell-mell into the town's single taxi and rushes up to the airport only to find that the flight has again been canceled by the weather. This happens so frequently that it is known as "baggage drill."

From Whitehorse the tote road leaves the Yukon River and follows the Takhini toward Champagne, early trading post on the dog and horse trail to Whitehorse. It reaches the Aishihik—pronounced "A-shak"—and soon skirts the northern slope of the glacial St. Elias Range beyond Haines Junction. Here, past the junction, it edges the southwest shore of ice-blue Kluane, the Yukon's largest lake. Slim's River, named for a pack horse who died crossing it. Destruction Bay. Burwash. Above Kluane Lake the road passes under Mt. Logan, Canada's highest mountain, nearly 20,000 feet. Soldiers see it to the south from mile 1125 all the way to the Donjek, that wildest of rivers to cross. Like the White, 40 miles farther up the road, the Donjek is a crazy, braided, glacial river. Its flood plain is a wide silt flat down which the river pushes in rippling fingers of mucky water. Bridge the fingers if you can. The first flood takes the fill out from around the ends of your spans and isolates them across muddy water on sticky flats.

At mile 1221 the road reaches the Alaska border. It picks up the Tanana Valley and threads Northway Junction, Tetlin Junction, and Tok Junction near Tanacross. On the north of the Tanana River until near Tetlin Junction, the tote road crosses to the south bank where it stays all the way to Delta Junction, the tie with the Richardson Highway. In August the fireweed here is nearly gone. The state flower of Alaska, also called the blooming Sally and the willow weed, fireweed flames muskeg and mountainside with pink in July. By late summer the petals have fallen, and the bare stems turn pastures and meadows to dark purple. There are hard frosts nights. Days shorten. Wolf packs scout the villages. Soldiers will have to hurry.

Cornmeal Cooked
with Tallow

MAPS WERE AVAILABLE early in 1942 for a lot of the country over which the pioneer highway must pass. But they were not accurate enough for building a road. Important terrain features did not show. The maps had rivers out of place; others were not shown at all. Muskegs, lakes, and mountains were not clearly defined. The men would have to make new surveys, therefore, before construction could proceed very far. These surveys occurred in two stages. The first was the pioneer survey, the men traveling in some places in small boats with outboard kickers, in others with horses or dog teams for packing or sledding. Such pioneer surveys as those on the southern sector of the road by PRA men Willesen and Curwen might more accurately be called reconnaissance trips. The location engineers, guided by local mushers, went out to study the lay of the land. Then they wrote descriptive reports of what they had seen and made their recommendations. Other pioneer surveys combined ground and aerial inspection with actual tote-road line location by engineers using transits. The second stage—to come later—was precise aerial mapping with sophisticated camera equipment. This stage would not be completed in many places until well after the engineers had completed the pioneer locations and were cutting tote road. It was the stage which had to precede the construction of the improved roadway.

Trappers, hunters, and packers who knew the country advised the pioneer surveyors about its features, about the best places for a road and for bridges. Many of them hired on to guide and to pack the survey parties. The location engineers followed the old principle—when starting a new job in new territory, ask the advice of the

men who have been over the ground. There were the Callisons—
Dennis, John, Lash, and Pat, the bush flyer. There were Bill Pickell,
Duncan Beaton, George McGarvey, and K. F. McCusker. These
men knew the ways of the North, its weird weather patterns, its
bottomless muskegs, its ground fogs, what its cold could do, how to
get the best out of sleigh dogs and packhorses. They knew how to
work, to fight, and to play. They had a frontier sense of humor, and
they personified an old saying: "We drank together, fought together, worked together. The old northern way."

Often, however, the old knowledge was not enough. The trails
and the winter roads used by trappers, hunters, and native packers
were not suitable for year-round use. Usually they did not follow
the high, dry ground that drains well, the kind of ground a modern
highway requires. Winter trails can cross frozen muskeg and
swamp, but a highway must try to avoid these. Muskegs—pits or
bogs of rotten organic matter and muck, usually overgrown with
bushy ground cover and reindeer moss and scattered with small
spruce and tamarack—are solid enough in winter, but bottomless in
water under the spring rain and the summer sun. The pioneer road
builders must either bypass these or corduroy them with logs cut in
nearby thickets. Since corduroying is slow work and makes only
the most temporary of roadbeds, the best way to deal with the
muskeg is to avoid it wherever possible. This the locators and
construction crews tried to do.

Some of the Public Roads Administration reconnaissance
crews were in the field by late March. They described the essential
features of the land and the problems of traveling across it—the
location of muskegs; high, well-drained ground; shifting river beds
and solid crossing points; box canyons; ridges; and impassable
obstructions. Between March 25 and April 8, 1942, PRA Highway
Engineers W. H. Willesen and Paul E. Warren with Elisha O.
[Lash] Callison, Tud Southwick, and John Harold, guides and
mushers, covered the land from the top of the Minaker River to
Fort Nelson. Engineers J. L. Cheatham and O. D. Van Buskirk
covered it from the top of the Minaker to Fort St. John, going with
guides and mushers K. F. McCusker, Bill Pickell, Duncan Beaton,
and George McGarvey.

Both parties started from the Hudson's Bay Company Post at
Sikanni on the winter pack trail between Fort St. John and Fort
Nelson. They left the low ground and sought the high. West up the

Sikanni Chief River and Trutch Creek to the top of the big divide between Trutch Creek and the Minaker River. Going up was tough work. The steep incline of the ridge required hitching three teams to each sleigh and hauling the sleighs up one at a time over a windblown, bare face.

From the high point at the top, about halfway between Fort St. John and Fort Nelson, the men first looked west into the Rockies, "the rugged snow-covered chain of the Rocky Mountains." It was 10:30 A.M. on March 29. Near this point on the north-south ridgeline, soldiers would build the Alaska Highway. After taking a long look, the men and their dogs dropped over into the valley of the Minaker and made camp for the night.

On the morning of the thirtieth the two parties split, Cheatham's heading south to scout the country toward Fort St. John, Willesen's traveling north down the valley of the Minaker and the Prophet to Fort Nelson. The pattern of the day's work was already set.

W. H. Willesen

The Willesen selections are taken from W. H. Willesen's descriptive report for the Public Roads Administration.

On our trip we would arise about three o'clock in the morning, wash, and then eat our breakfast and next we would roll and tie up our beds; then we would start out walking, leaving the washing of dishes and packing the toboggans to the Mushers. The dog teams could travel [much] faster than we could on foot and they would pass us about one hour out from camp, they would go ahead and when we caught up with them sometime between nine and ten o'clock the Mushers would have lunch ready for us. We would eat our lunch and be on our way again leaving the . . . packing to the Mushers. The dog teams would pass us again and when we would reach camp for the evening the Mushers had the toboggans unloaded, the dogs tied up, and spruce boughs out for our camp beds.

Each afternoon, after making camp, our Head Musher, E. O. Callison, would get out a mixing bowl and the frying pans and he would proceed to make and bake enough bannock to last us until the next afternoon when we made the next camp.

Willesen's crew followed the river because there were no trails on the high ridge. Drifted, melting snow filled the woods along the river, and the mushers had to break trail for the dogs. The party had three teams of four dogs each, with the dogs hauling all the clothing, bedding, camp equipment, and food, as well as the dog feed. Weights upon leaving Sikanni were 400 pounds per sleigh, about 100 pounds for each dog to pull. The dogs got 1-1/4 gallons of boiled yellow corn meal mush and 1/2 pound of beef fat apiece each evening for their work. A good dog is a mighty animal. Each hauls more than his own weight all day long.

On the eighth of April, after a wet trip, the party got into Fort Nelson. The melting snow had stuck to the snowshoes, balled up between the dogs' toes, and prevented the toboggan runners from slipping along easily. Two of the mushers had broken through the ice and gone into the river. The dogs were tired, but on the eighth, headed for a rest, they were high-spirited.

W. H. Willesen

As the toboggans were nearly empty . . . the Mushers could ride on them most of the time. . . . Two trappers that were going in to Fort Nelson after supplies . . . invited Warren and myself to ride in their toboggans, which offer was promptly accepted. The dogs could travel from two to three times faster than we could on foot so the trip on the last day was made in record time. On account of the cold weather we were wrapped in an Eiderdown Sleeping Robe and crouched way down in the toboggan which made it very comfortable. It was very rough to ride in the toboggan as it would jump lots when going over uneven ground. Total distance covered this day about 30 miles.

Farther north, PRA Highway Engineer W. H. Curwen and Senior Engineering Aid F. W. Ambos covered the ground from Fort Nelson west to the summit of the Rockies between March 25 and April 12 with guides John and Dennis Callison. They mushed an old trail the guides said the gold seekers of '98 had used. The trail split just west of Spruce Creek Cabin, and one branch ran northerly to Raspberry Creek above Raspberry Creek Canyon. This was the horse packers' and freighters' trail. The other, the mushers' trail, ran directly west, dropped into the canyon, and followed it downstream 4 miles to the Muskwa River. Then it ran up the Muskwa to Weasel City Cabin near the junction with the Kledo River.

From here Dennis Callison returned to Fort Nelson to replace an injured dog and to pack out supplies which he would cache at

Mill Camp and Burnt Hill Cabin. Waiting for him, the engineers scouted the country for solid, level ground and for good stream crossing points. Curwen spotted the tote-road line well north of the Muskwa, a wide river that overflows its whole flood plain during spring runoff. Since the Raspberry Creek Canyon must be avoided, he spotted the bridge point on the old horse trail, the very place where the Alcan Highway would cross.

Curwen and Ambos shot spruce grouse and got fresh moose meat from local trappers to make their menus more interesting. They ate well. Everyone helped with the cooking, and the Americans probably learned how to make bannock, the camp bread of the whole north. Flour, baking powder, salt, water. Place the dough in the frying pan and set the pan in the coals, or hold it over the open flame until the bottom of the bread has browned. Tip the frying pan to the fire, and prop it up with a stick until the bannock browns on top. The Americans learned to appreciate the traditional Canadian winter-trail hot drink, tea. There was no coffee. They enjoyed their moose meat, which they probably roasted or cut into steaks and broiled. Young moose makes sweet red meat, very much like good beef.

When Dennis Callison returned from Fort Nelson, the party mushed 32 miles up the Muskwa to Tetsa River Cabin on April 2. The next day the dogs broke through brittle snow, and their feet bled. But there was fresh snow, too, and the men traveled on snowshoes much of the day. It was tiring labor, fighting the crust in places and occasionally breaking through, in other places lifting platters of fresh snow with each step. On the third, dogs and men went the 12 miles to Mill Camp. On the fourth, though it snowed nearly all day long, they made the 20 to Burnt Hill Cabin.

In spite of the poor visibility for much of the trip, Curwen saw clearly and described photographically in his PRA report this route the Alaska Highway would follow. "The Tetsa River flows thru a channel 600 to 1,400 feet wide in a shale formation that forms bluffs 50 to 200 feet high." Near "the steep and rugged slope of Steamboat Mountain" the Tetsa "meanders back and forth from one canyon wall to the other and has taken out nearly all of the timber in the bottom of the canyon. Numerous gravel bars block the river channel; by using these gravel bars . . . and at the same time opening the river channel a good road can be constructed thru" this 4-mile section.

The night at Burnt Hill Cabin—the night before the party reached the top of the Rockies—must have been a good one. There was heavy new snow. The temperatures were lower because of the altitude, but the cabin must have been comfortable. No doubt sausages or moose meat sizzled over the fire. Bannock browned in a frying pan. There were dried fruits for dessert, and more hot tea. The dogs, tied outside on short chains so that they could not run off in the night or reach each other and fight, ate their "cornmeal cooked with tallow." They fed quickly and burrowed into the fresh snow to keep warm. The men slept in soft eider-down robes.

The next morning was Easter Sunday, the fifth of April. That afternoon, 12 days out of Fort Nelson, the party made Summit Lake, "crossing the summit of the Canadian Rockies at mile 120 [from Fort Nelson] at an elevation of about 4,320 feet." Curwen's photographic eye was at work all day long, noting distances, heights, depths. Curwen noted too each time that he could only give estimates, rather than exact measurements. A distance in the words of his report is "about" or "approximately." He was obsessed with accuracy as an excellent engineer should be. Always he noticed where the road could best be placed.

W. H. Curwen

The Curwen selections are taken from W. H. Curwen's report for the Public Roads Administration.

The party continued up the Tetsa River about 1-1/2 miles to a fork, took the right hand fork to Summit Lake, the source of this fork of the river. . . . The country between the forks and Summit Lake, a distance of approximately 16 miles, is more mountainous than below, and the rise of the river increases as it approaches Summit Lake. . . . Just below reaching [the Lake] is encountered a limestone canyon about 600 feet long and 50 feet deep; this can be easily negotiated by keeping to the east side of the canyon.

Before starting back to Fort Nelson, the engineers spent a day going down the slopes of McDonald Creek beyond the top of the pass. They camped the night of the sixth at Fly and headed back the next morning. On the last day, going into Fort Nelson, they covered nearly forty miles. "With practically no supplies, but with two members of the party riding on each toboggan, these dogs made 38 miles in 6 hours." It had been a good trip, a useful one. There were no serious mishaps, "due chiefly to the able management of John Callison, the Guide, whose knowledge gained by several years of trapping stood us all in good stead." The survey party had totaled about 330 miles, including the side trips, and had looked at the country for more than 120 miles west from Fort Nelson into the core of the Rocky Mountains.

Curwen's observations were accurate. PRA location engineers and the army Cat skinners would follow the route he had recommended to the Raspberry Creek crossing. From Raspberry Creek, two promising lines branched north and west. Curwen described them both in his report, and the engineers chose one of them—the Tetsa River route. He also recommended reconnaissance of the country from Summit Lake to Lower Post via Gundahoo Pass, country which trappers and guides had told him about. The Alaska Highway would avoid the Gundahoo. It would follow a line as far as Muncho Lake, more than 150 miles from Summit, then would run directly down Trout River to the Liard.

By mid-April parties made up of surveyors with instruments were in the field up and down much of the route of the new highway. The army's bulldozers were also beginning to move by about the same time. Throughout the summer they pushed the location parties, often catching up with and bypassing them. The PRA engineers had had no experience in designing a project the size of this one across such an expanse of wild country, and everyone had to use his imagination and call upon all the technical knowledge and skill he had. Some of the party chiefs did well, while others did poorly. One of the successful parties was led by a chief named Gowan, whose group made the pioneer surveys both east and west from Champagne, Yukon Territory.

Craig Hudson

Craig Hudson was a student at Reed College, Portland, Oregon, in 1942. He and two friends, Marley Brown and Herman Johansen, learned that the government would hire men to help with the surveys of the new Alcan Highway. Craig and one of his friends bought supplies, went to Seattle, and caught a ship to Skagway. From there they rode the White Pass railway over the coastal range to Whitehorse, where they arrived in early April.

We rode up with a train that probably consisted of . . . ten cars. We got stuck in the snow on the way up. . . . Honestly, I thought we weren't gonna make it up because we ran into a snowdrift, and this train faltered and stopped and began to roll back down hill. And we had to roll back down until we came to a place where the engine could stop and get up a little steam and drive ahead again. And it was particularly scary because you'd look out the window and you couldn't see anything below you at all. Looking back [you could see that] the train was fastened out on scaffolding out along the edge of this cliff. . . . It was quite thrilling. . . .

Whitehorse [was] very primitive. The streets were a sea of mud. There were boardwalks from the big buildings. . . . All were frame houses. . . . In the place where we lived, Marley and I shared a bed, I believe it was the Whitehorse Inn. . . .

[On April 13th] I went out with a large number of people to Mile Canyon [west of Whitehorse]. . . . I was told that I was gonna have a job of rear chainman. . . . But when I was sent out on this jaunt, I was stake puncher. . . . And then on the 18th I was assigned to the party that I stayed with. That was Gowan's party. . . . And we went on April 18th to Champagne in a truck. We drove across frozen rivers getting there. . . .

It was while I was at Champagne that I saw the Army bulldozers come in. . . . They were going lickety cut. . . . We had been out doing some surveying. We surveyed both east and west from Champagne. . . . And while we were still within walking distance of Champagne, where we had set up our camp, coming back one evening. . . . I heard some noise and pretty soon I could see trees just plop, plop, plop, like that. And they were just driving the bulldozers right straight through the forest. . . .

There was no survey ahead of us at all. The [army] engineer people that went through when I was at Champagne were following their noses. They just drove out across country. Now, later on I understood that the army got a survey crew going, and they caught up with [the bulldozers] and then went ahead, but they didn't make a very good survey line. They would just put big stakes out and leave much of it up to the choice of the engineers as they came along.

And their roads were terrible. They didn't take time to find gravel. They would just head right off across the swamp, and when the trucks began to settle into the muck, why they would try to buoy it up with trees and brush and stuff like that, make a roadbed out of corduroy. They just made no effort at all to survey to places where they could get gravel, whereas the PRA line was very carefully drawn from gravel borrow to gravel borrow to gravel borrow so there was always enough gravel available. . . .

The chief, Gowan, was always out walking the distance ahead of us. . . . He was apparently one of the best surveyors that they had. . . . Under the chief . . . there were two surveyors . . . one of them would be the chief surveyor and the other would be the assistant. And the chief surveyor did all the line running, and the other one did the topography. . . . And then under the surveyors there were eight experienced surveyor assistants, like chainmen. . . . The rest of us were all college students and Indians. . . . George John was one of them . . . and they were axemen, and they would serve as guides too. . . .

[Gowan] went alone. . . . Nearly every day he'd be out to mark a line. He'd take a compass, and he could do well enough so that he would run ahead. Sometimes . . . because he would make an error in judgment, he'd have to come back, backtrack, and start the line over again, and we had to pause once or twice to go back a mile or so and take another tangent and straighten the line out. . . . He went by himself.

We were never very close friends, but he did talk to me a little bit about the preparation for the party. I had asked him, "How do you know where to go?" . . .

And he said, "Well, we don't have much to go on, but there were some aerial photographs made of the region. . . ." And he said, "We have some drawings, some rough maps, made from those aerial photographs and that's all the information we have." . . .

[We tied in with the next party's survey line near Kluane]. But there was nobody there when we tied in. We just found their stakes and surveyed up to it. . . . And to my knowledge we never saw anyone of that other party, although I'm sure Gowan knew them and was in contact with them. But we didn't have any radio at all, so he must have been in touch with them by visiting, although I don't know how he did that. He was gone for sometimes days at a time. . . .

Herman Johansen

Herman Johansen was another of the college students who worked on the PRA surveys in the summer of 1942. His experience was much less satisfactory than Craig Hudson's largely because of the inexperience of the party chief. The PRA assigned Johansen's party to the country around the Takhini just west of Whitehorse. Later in the summer they were moved to near Lower Post. (From a letter, Johansen to Craig Hudson, 6 March 1975:)

I was a stake puncher. . . . I had to carry a sledge and big chisel . . . to get a hole in the frozen ground to get the stake in. . . . Our first job was to put up a mess tent, then cut a hole in the ice of the river to get water. The ice was 5 feet thick and that was a helluva job. It was exciting to be out in such primitive country, and initially I was thrilled. It soon wore off. . . .

When the thaw came on the Takhini . . . we could no longer use the river ice as a road. . . . We continued to walk the ice just for ease of traveling. This was risky indeed. There were open patches of water and the river was full and fast under the ice. Inevitably it happened: someone went through the ice and disappeared . . . but by luck grasped the downstream edge of the ice with his hands. I'll remember those white fingers desperately clinched on the ice for a good many years more. . . . As luck would have it we were able to get a hold of him, crack the ice and drag him out. . . .

[Later we moved to the Liard, near Lower Post.] B.C. was different country. Instead of rocks and mountains, this was flat, forested, and full of big unnamed rivers. . . . We camped on the banks of the Liard for awhile and I had the best food I had in Canada. I got a coachman fly from the Hudson Bay post at Lower Post and caught myself a pile of grayling trout and fried and ate them! A camp was set up and the survey started; the country was beautiful. Muskeg and lakes everywhere. It was strange to be walking along and see the ground wave in front of you. It was all floating on deep water! In other places on a hot day a few inches down one could find solid, clear ice. The insects were formidable. It was there we really had to use headnets *all* the time. . . .

Working west the line suddenly hit a huge chasm, perhaps of the Liard. . . . We heard a muffled roar, finally a loud roar and the trees behind us collapsed with a crash and here was a huge D8 Cat dozer. The engineers were right on our tail on the survey. A sweaty dirty lieutenant came running up and asked what the hell the matter was. I mutely pointed to the chasm . . . a cul-de-sac. After screaming and raving for awhile, the line of bulldozers switchbacked down the canyon wall and disappeared on their own.

Among the men who worked on the earliest reconnaissance trips and surveys over the vast country from Lower Post and Watson Lake through Whitehorse toward the Alaska border were Norman and Jack Harlin, Canadian trappers. The United States government hired the Harlins in the spring and summer of 1942 to help locate the highway line. The Harlin brothers were quintessential northwestern trappers. They knew as well as anyone at the time the land from Lower Post and Fort Frances west to Kluane and north into the isolated Nahanni River bush and the Northwest Territories. They knew the countless blue lakes and waterways of the Teslin, Atlin, Marsh Lake, and Squanga country. They were personally acquainted with the finest Yukon and north country bush pilots of the day, probably the best ever—Les Cook, Herman Peterson, Stan Emery, Lucien P. "Frank" Barr, Pat Callison, Ernie Kubicek, Sheldon Luck—had flown with most of them, and had spent years living in and looking at the country. The Harlins had worked on the construction of the airstrips at Watson Lake and Teslin. They had flown Northern Airways out of Carcross with Les Cook.

Norman Harlin

Norman describes the use of bush airplanes on the pioneer surveys between Whitehorse and Watson Lake.

We had a packtrain with us all the time, and an airplane. . . . We'd look the country over, and then come back, land, and I'd go out flaggin'. And we had two or three Indians cuttin' brush—cuttin' line of course—and seventeen men on the survey party comin' behind us. . . .

Our grub all come in by plane to the nearest lake. All we used a packhorse for was to move camp every ten days. . . . We tried to run a mile of location line every day. . . . [We] flagged 'em ahead—usually the pilot and I . . . flagged—and they come along behind us with a slashing crew. . . .

But the location mostly was done with the plane. We'd probably fly well over ten miles of it low. The main thing was to make sure we didn't run into bad canyon because they didn't want to bridge that first winter. . . . And we had to be careful that we didn't run into rock or bad canyon, which you can easily pick out from the air. If we had a line in mind that we thought might do, and it run into a deep canyon, we'd have to come back and change it, which we did, several times. Well then the . . . survey party came behind us just followin' our flags. . . .

Not only small bush planes, but also aircraft with photographic equipment were used that first summer. Aerial photographs were then furnished to the parties on the ground as soon as possible. In Alaska, army and PRA locators used boats on rivers and lakes. Between Whitehorse and the border, men also used packhorses for reconnaissance and for moving the survey parties during the late spring and summer.

The summer of 1942 along the Alcan is significant for many reasons. Among other things the summer's work was a cooperative effort between people with strikingly different cultural focuses. The Americans in Canada brought endless equipment, sophisticated engineering knowledge, a strong faith in their machinery and their technological capacity, and a willingness to labor for long hours. The best of the Canadian guides and woodsmen on the other hand—men such as the Harlins and the Callisons—had a nearly infinite experience of the country, bush intuition, tenacity, skepticism of American dreams and plans, and a touch of humor. Such men were expert managers in the woods. They went properly equipped, with the best dogs and horses they could get and with the most able flyers. Their tools and equipment were well organized, their working lives streamlined from long practice. "Mr. Callison who has trapped this territory for several years," W. H. Curwen wrote of John Callison, his guide, "was thoroughly acquainted with the trails and weather conditions on the route reconnoitered. He advised us as to what to wear and what supplies to take. He and other trappers in this territory furnished us with valuable information, as to the possible routes . . . and the materials that could be found from Summit . . . to Watson Lake."

The cooperative effort involved men of very different backgrounds and interests. There were guides, mushers, location engineers, professional soldiers, recruits, freighters, packers, Indians, college men and high school graduates, woodsmen and California boys, easterners and westerners. Theirs was a braided human effort, an accomplishment in woven motion like the glacial rivers of the far north. That accomplishment crystallizes the true substance of the main thrust of the whole North American experience, that motion of humanity westward which Garrett Mattingly called "history in transition from an Atlantic to a Pacific phase." That substance is the joining together of a disparate people whose single overriding interest is the solution of a particular problem, a joining in such a way that their varied interests, backgrounds, and energies form and shape the solution itself.

The Canadian guides and mushers who worked the tote road in 1942, all men who represented the old world of the North—of cabin life and bannock, trapline and snowshoe, dogteam and bobsleigh, steamboat and bush plane—joined university-trained American location engineers to mark out the road that soldiers, construction workers, emigrants, truckers, roughnecks going up to work in the oil and gas fields, hitchhikers, and drivers with every possible motive would beat from the end of World War II down to the very present. For most of those years, this colorful mass of travelers would head all the way west to Alaska. The Alaska Highway is—it has to be—the last of the important westward overland trails, for it runs nearly to America's land's end. Beyond Alaska, where the highway ends, is Siberia, out past the reach of the North American experience.

CHAPTER FIVE

Continuation

NAN AND BARNEY STREEPER have lived in Fort Nelson, British Columbia, since Barney took a job working for the United States government on the Alcan Highway in the 1940s. They are Canadians. They moved to Fort Nelson from a homestead on the Peace River in Alberta where they had lived since 1926. Barney's parents came to the Peace River place as immigrants from Nevada in 1918, and Nan came to Canada from Scotland. After college in Victoria, British Columbia, she moved north to teach school. There she and Barney met and were married. After the war began and the Americans cut the tote road, the Streeper family started a new life. That life since 1942 has been intimately connected with an economy based upon rapid transportation, and with the radically different values caused by the coming of the Alaska Highway and the other recent roads into the North. In that intimate connection with the highway economy and culture, the Streepers are representative of many of the other Canadian families who have lived in the country traversed by the highway since the 1940s.

The Streepers are in many ways a contemporary illustration of the thesis of Frederick Jackson Turner about the meaning of the frontier in North American life. Accustomed to the constant hardship and accident of life in the bush—of clearing land, of sickness far from a doctor's care, of loneliness and silence, of the dangers of storm and snow and of flood and fire—Nan and Barney grew up on the homestead, expecting change and ready for disaster. For them, the problem of living was that of finding new ways of lasting out near-defeat, of knowing how to survive when all the circumstances suddenly took a turn for the worse. So they learned flexibility and lived by it, discovering ways to do things when the natural patterns seemed to go against them. What comforts and conveniences they had, they mostly made for themselves. Conservation of commodities they developed as a habit of mind; there was no nearby store and no ready supply of cash for instantly restocking depleted supplies or for satisfying whim. Consequently, when the highway engineers came, the Streepers and others like them were ready. They moved and took hold again where demand required or opportunity seemed to open. "American social development," Turner wrote, "has been continually beginning over again on the frontier. This perennial rebirth, this fluidity of American life, this expansion westward with its new opportunities . . . furnish the forces dominating American character."

The lure of the West has been strong in the Streepers' lives. The connection between west and human aspiration is as old as the Greeks, probably much older, and it still grasps and often twists men's minds and hearts. Nan herself had moved toward the West from Scotland, and Barney's people had always been on the way west from some place or other—to Utah, then Nevada, and finally to northwestern Canada. The Streepers could not possibly return to the East and settle there or even stay there happily for very long. They are committed westerners. But they sense that the dullness and the comforts, the pettiness and the bureaucratic nature of much that is modern life are fast eroding the western myth—that magic vision of desire to be satisfied somewhere west—and that even men in the West pervert the power of the myth and turn it to the work of destruction and waste. Barney especially feels in his bones the tension between the magic of the myth and his knowledge of its perversion. He sees this perversion all around him and broods upon it—in the ravishment of the Canadian forests, in the way in which the traders and those whom Barney calls "the priests and the do-gooders" have treated the Eskimo, in the fact that every modern kid has a new Mustang car or a fancy Chevrolet and that, if you break down on the highway today, someone is likely to steal the wheels off your rig before you can get back with help.

Nan and Barney believe that hard work is essential, that play in moderation is important, that working together is a necessity. They have a strong family sense. But they understand clearly the price they and others have had to pay for achieving these good things in the North. Hard work has worn Barney out prematurely; the body ages, though the toughness and the humor of the spirit may grow. Daily existence in the West and especially in the North has been a hard set of facts lacking in romance. A young mother dies suddenly, leaving five children. A young woman travels more than 100 miles on the river at night to a hospital because there are complications after the birth of her baby. The towboat business fails because the government builds a new highway to Great Slave Lake, bypassing the old waterway. A man goes from job to job, taking whatever work he can get and doing it the best he can—loading lumber onto railroad cars, working as a farmer, a cattle grower, mechanic, truck driver, power house operator, boatman.

Nan and Barney sense too the spiritual unity between the people of northwestern Canada and the western United States. That spiritual unity was created both by the western myth—that commonly held trust in the goodness and the promise of western life—and by the similarities between every pioneer's experiences of daily living in the bush—fire and washout, cave-in and flood. Both countries have recently seen frontiers. Although the frontier histories of Canada and the United States differ in certain essential ways, the pioneers of both countries hold in common a flexibility, a toughness, a type of humor that helps them all endure, and a reservoir of memories of the hard times and small winnings. The frontierspeople of northwestern Canada—of the country traversed by the Alaska Highway—and those of the United States recognize each other. Theirs is an exclusive fraternity. Its members have a strong sense of the continuity of life. They know that good luck and dreams of wealth end in bad breaks and countless failures, but that there are also good things that last.

Nan and Barney Streeper

Barney: I come to this country in 1918 [from] Nevada. [My parents and my brother Woods and I] settled on the Peace River in Alberta at the mouth of the Pouce Coupé River, or opposite the mouth of the Pouce Coupé River, which is now known as Cherry Point, and we homesteaded there. And [Nan and our two daughters and I] come up [from there to Fort Nelson] in 1943 I think it was. My brother's wife died and my wife come out to take care of his kids, and we come up here. We come up here in '43, on the Alaska Highway workin' for the American army when they was buildin' the highway. . . .

I was a heavy duty mechanic in the garage here from '43 to '45 or '46, I forget just when. And then when the Canadian army took the highway over, I worked for the Canadian army for, well, until they quit. And then . . . my brother and I went into the boat business on the river here. . . . We went to haulin' stuff on the river, with the boats, and I've been doin' that ever since. Well yes, prit near ever since. We were haulin' equipment down to Aklavik and Inuvik and Tuk Tuk [Tuktoyuktuk] to the traders—supplies. . . . I think we made our first trip in '46 down. We was still workin' for the army at that time, and we . . . had built this boat . . . small boat, and we was goin' to the Nahanni Falls, and we never got there. So the next year we said we'd build one that'd get there, so we built a big one. . . . Had two diesel engines in it, and we got up to the falls.

And then we had the boat on hand and we had nothin' for it to do, so we built a scow and hauled seven ton of freight down to Aklavik. And from then on, why the next year we had fifty-five or sixty ton, and the next year we built two scows and from then on up. Well then that stopped when the road come in [the Mackenzie Highway to Great Slave Lake]. We was goin' out of here, could get [to Aklavik and the Arctic] from three to five weeks sooner than what they could [by boat] from the other direction on account of the ice on the Great Slave Lake, comin' in the other way. Well, when they got the road built in, it bypassed the lake, why then that cut that off. They could get out as early as we could, and it was cheaper than what we could get it in this way, so of course that fell through. Well, then there was a year or two we had nothin' much to do. . . . I guess I still worked for the army or some darned thing. I forget what it was. . . .

[At Fort Nelson in the 1940s I repaired for the army] tractors, big trucks, little trucks and cars, and all that kind of stuff. Worked as a mechanic.

Nan: Ran the power house. Alone.

Barney: And I run the power house for three or four years, the army power house.

Nan: He ran the power plant, and later, when he quit, it took four men to run it. . . .

Barney: When the Americans were here, they had American civilians doin' the work, and the Canadians [got] paid . . . a dollar and fifteen cents and a dollar and twenty-five cents an hour . . . and the Americans got two dollars and two dollars and a quarter an hour for the same job. And the Americans was quite willing to pay the price, but Canada said it would ruin their people and they'd want them kinda wages later on. Which made us a little bit hostile. . . .

Nan: We came [to Fort Nelson] as soon as the Canadians took over and they permitted women to come. . . . They didn't allow women [when Barney first came]. They'd had some women at first, but it was an army installation, and if one woman got her porch fixed, everybody else kicked. And finally the lieutenant in charge—good, capable man—he got fed up with it, and all the women had to leave. . . .

It was an awfully decent community [after the families came]. . . . There was young people with children. . . . And it was a little Catholic church up on the top of the hill, up what was Highway Maintenance Hill. Of course it's all moved out now. That's the worst of this country. They always move all the landmarks that people remember, you know. I just don't go for this demolishing things. I went back to Scotland after forty solid years—I was fifty-four when I went back—and I went up the stairs, the very same little stone steps, completely worn out, in the interim department where I'd started school in Scotland. There was my school there. There was the headmistress's room, and I expected to see them walk out you know. And so I hate this demolishing of things. . . .

[Are you Catholic?]

Nan: No. No. No. Oh God no! Presbyterian. I was born in Scotland. I'm Canadian though. I realized it. I went home about, was it ten years ago? Yes, about ten years ago, and I met a chap in Vancouver in the immigration, and he'd been to Scotland, and he says, "Well, what did you think of it?"

I said, "Well, it was wonderful. I wouldn't have missed it for anything." But I said, "I'm Canadian."

He said, "Yes, that's what I said when I [went back]."

He'd made his first trip home. He was Canadian. The horizons are too narrow.

Barney: We was back East last summer.

Nan: You can have it. I'll take the West.

Barney: And we was out of Ottawa there at a little place.

Nan: A place called Cumberland.

Barney: Cumberland. Just out of Ottawa a way. It's a beautiful country. I don't know whether you ever been there or not? Beautiful country. . . . But there's an atmosphere among the people that I detest. They argue over ten cents there, we wouldn't even think of it. . . .

Nan: No, it's a petty atmosphere. It seemed like among all the petty officialdom I noticed it. Bus drivers weren't courteous like they are in this country. You know, a bus driver all you have to do is tell them that you're a stranger, and they'll tell you where to go and how to get there. Those [eastern bus drivers]! They're horrible! . . . You c'n have the East. I wouldn't have it. I think Ottawa's the most beautiful in lots of ways. Nice old polluted stream you couldn't eat fish out of or. . . .

Barney: Well, you take a lot of those people prit near all of them that come from England, they just die to get back, get back to England. They say, "Oh, if I ever get back to England you'll never see me here again." And practically every one that I know that done that is back in about two months. "You'll never see me go back to England again!" I've seen, oh dozens of 'em!

Nan: I think everybody has to go back to their land. I imagine if Barney went back to Nevada he'd want to come back up here awful fast. Although, the cold in the winter here is beginning to get him. He says there should be an easier place to live. I like it. Oh, I like the coast awfully well [too]. I like Victoria and Vancouver Island. My oldest daughter said San Francisco was lovely. She lived there for a long time. She lives in Calgary now. But she lived down just out of Los Angeles, and oh my, it's hotter than the hubs of hell there in summer. . . .

[But] we had a marvelous community over there [at the army base at Fort Nelson in the 1940s]. First of all, they had homes around, you know, just that they built up, scrounged and built up. . . . Everybody was, well, everybody sort of depended on everybody else. For example, there was no store nearer than across the river, so we all sent to Dawson Creek—all our food came on Thursdays from Dawson Creek—and they had big freezers around all over, you know, to keep our things in, and you shared a community freezer sort of. It was really funny. I mean if somebody'd made pie, lemon pie, or something fancy like that, the odd little boy that was sent to get something would stick his finger in it. Oh, I mean it was quite a joke really. You hid it or covered it up if you wanted it to be intact you know. . . .

I guess we were about the third people that came. . . . But we lived all around in places that were given to us. . . . We had a tin hut to start with. They'd bring water around to you and that sort of thing. I don't know where we got the stove . . . and we'd brought some things with us. . . . And later . . . we were finally given quarters down in what they called Lower Slombovia. We didn't have sewers, but, oh, it was much better. . . . There was a wash house where you could take showers and . . . do your washing. . . . For me it was marvelous because I'd been on the farm since I was twenty. I mean, I came to Peace River to teach, and got married you know, and I was on a homestead farm. Well they were pretty tough in those days. I mean that was a *real* experience. It always makes me mad when I hear teachers around here yelling about the poor quarters they have. My God, they don't know how lucky they [are]! . . . When my baby was born, my first baby, I was taken in a boat to Peace River Crossing. How many miles would it be, Dad?

Barney: A hundred and twenty miles down the river.

Nan: A hundred and twenty miles down the river to the . . . hospital there. The doctor couldn't get in from Pouce. He was tied up with, you know, sickness, and I mean I've been through that sort of thing. . . . People just learn to cope. . . . The baby was born at home, and there was sort of complications, and I had to go to the hospital. And the baby was bounding at my side. And we made this trip, and we went to the hospital.

Barney: We were on the river at night.

Nan: Uh huh, we ran the river at night.

Barney: Peace River. . . .

Nan: Aw phooey. To heck with some of those Johnnies-come-lately that think they know it all, Dad. . . . It's just that I think a little hardship is good for people. I think learning to face things is good for people. I think that's what's the matter with our young people today. That's why they're bored. They just didn't have enough real hard work to do. And then they get in trouble. . . . We never thought of those things. We didn't have time. Oh sure, we'd drink a little moonshine once in a while I guess. But—

Barney: You made a mistake. It wasn't a little, Honey.

[How did you happen to leave the homestead?]

Nan: My brother-in-law, Woods, had a young family of five children, and Barney and I were left to the farm—his mother had been there, but she was getting old and she went to Kansas City—and we were on the farm and [Woods's] wife died suddenly. She was just thirty-two. She died of diphtheria, and there was five children. The youngest was two and the oldest was twelve. Well, I went out and took over. I mean, we left the farm, we rented it. . . . And Barney went out, and Woods was running the sawmill—they went in together on it—and I looked after the children for two years until he married again. . . . We never split them up. We [kept] them together. From two quiet little girls [of my own], I had seven noisy kids you know. . . . That was how we came to leave the farm. We'd never have left the farm I don't suppose because it was quite a good farm. . . . [The Streepers had] been the first settlers there. . . . They cut all the trails and everything else. They squatted.

49

Barney: There was nobody there but a rabbit when we went there.

Nan: When I [married Barney] they were still squatting. I mean we all filed afterwards. But they'd been there alone. . . . They'd just moved in on this [land]. We were married, and I went there to live. There was only my mother-in-law with two children, two younger children, and then the two older boys. There was sort of two families. . . . I taught the children. . . . We homesteaded the hard way. Horses.

Barney: We tanned our own hides and made our own moccasins and everything like that, and made our moonshine. . . .

Nan: We were almost completely self-supporting. There was twice or three times a year they'd go out—flour, sugar, coffee, tea, baking powder, and so on. We grew everything. We had a marvelous river flat, just, it was off the river about three quarters of a mile. . . . We had the most marvelous garden. It was famous throughout the Peace River Country, the Streeper gardens. . . .

The Streepers were go-aheads. They built all the trails. . . . They cut the trails. They needed the hay. . . . They got cattle. They really did. They were going hounds. . . .

Barney: We sold pigs, 200-pound pigs, for a dollar and a half apiece.

Nan: That was in the hungry thirties you know.

Barney: In fact, we sold them and haven't got the money for 'em yet!

[How has the Alaska Highway changed the North?]

Nan: It put this country 200 years ahead. Oh, I'm sure it did. . . . I remember riding up in the bus one time, and there was a bunch of old-timers on, and they said that they used to use four-ups, four-up horses, and it would take two days to pull that Peace River Hill, a load, with loads of wheat, taking it out to. . . . Where would they be taking it to, Dad?

Barney: Spirit River.

Nan: Spirit River. And here we were whizzing on this! I mean it really put the country on the map. Have you been to Dawson Creek? Huge schools and everything else. When I came to teach, I taught at North Swan Lake. There was one school with three teachers. And look at it now. It's been marvelous to see this thing grow. Every time I think about it, I think just how much of history I've seen. That wee little place there. [I] remember a hotel there, and everybody walked in. Everything was put on the table, and you helped yourself. . . .

Pouce Coupé. Dawson Creek. Those little places sparked off the Alaska Highway. All the trail bearers, you know, all the people that pointed out [the highway line] were trappers that'd been around and knew their way in, and, you know, guided the engineers. Must have been an awful drunken trapper in some cases. . . .

Barney: [There's stories about that. The Cat skinner] he asked the boss where to go. "Well," he said, "You see that black object?" He said, "Stick to that."

And it was a moose, and he just followed the moose wherever it went, see?

Nan: [Before the highway] there was nothing here. There was nothing for us. There was nothing for people but hardship. . . .

Barney: We sawed our own lumber and all of it. We never went short of food. We went short of money lotsa times. We always had cattle and pigs and a few sheep and that kinda stuff. Sometimes we put patches on our patches on our overalls though. But we were never without.

Nan: No, we were never without things. There was always heaps of reading material. I mean everybody sent us reading material from home.

Barney: I trapped some and kept things up that way. . . .

Nan: Now this is opened up to civilization. This is sort of the last frontier. This is a chance for the children that never had a chance before. There are young men today, children of pioneers, that are sitting very pretty. I mean their wealth. They've got more money in ten minutes than their parents ever had. Of course, I can see flaws in them.

Barney: Well it don't make any difference [about] their flaws. You take, if you're going to advance in what we call civilization, if you're going to advance, why you've got to put up with some things. There's been all kinds of mistakes made, we'll admit that, but then we'll say if the road hadn't went through here—it may have went through later—but as it went through when it did go through, it paid up a whole lot of grocery bills, now I'm here to tell you! Thousands and thousands of dollars. People just couldn't pay. . . . I bought wheat on the market for thirty-five cents a bushel. I figured it *couldn't* go any lower! But it did. It went to nineteen cents a bushel. But we lived. Well, we existed, we'll put it that way. And as far as—"Oh, the good old days"—but who in hell wants 'em? The good old days! Went out in sixty below to a can outside. Heh! You could buy a Ford car for—new Ford car—for eight hundred dollars, but you didn't have eight cents to buy it with, and now they cost you three thousand but every kid's got one. . . .

I would admit that there's been things that shouldn't have been done. I would admit that the white man has destroyed as much or more than what he has accomplished. There always has been somethin' that comes in and takes the place. The buffalo disappeared, but there's millions a head a cattle took their place. Which is a damn sight better eatin' than buffalo was. . . . These big tales of what wonderful meat buffalo was. It was all right when you was hungry. And you take, instead a takin' six months to come across the plains in a covered wagon behind a buncha wringtails, why it takes about—what is it?—three hours now to cross, well, four hours and a half to go from New York to San Francisco.

So I don't know. But we've denuded some of the forest lands all right, which, if they had done then what they're tryin' to do now on the reforestation . . . but it was so immense! . . . You can take today and you can go up on the mountain here—onto the coast—and take a look. There's *miles* a timber! Well what! [Some say]: "We never can git to that!" But then you turn it around and put your picture the other way and they's just *acres* of people, just *acres* of 'em! [And we've wasted so much]. You take, now then my mother, she got one row of pins, maybe just one a year, and she still had nine-tenths of that row left at the end of the year. Now you get a boxa pins, and in two weeks you go git another boxa pins. And you take, one boxa matches in Utah done for two or three years. You took your paper and you rolled it up into—what the hell they call twills or some darned thing—and you lit the darned thing in the fireplace and lit your pipe or lit the fire and put it out. And one a them done you for a week! You'd use it up. . . .

You take the Eskimos and the Indians up north here. The northland—which I've been in and heard a lot of—has its own law. What I mean, it'll take so much and when you go over that so much, why then you get starvation and that. It only can carry so many people. Well the Eskimos and the Indians up there . . . they had their own laws and that, and they'd multiplied up to the point where that the land could carry them. Well, when game would come short and one thing and another like that, they let the young ones and the old ones die. They had to. The old ones couldn't carry on the tribe, and the young ones couldn't carry on the tribe. It was the middle ones that could carry the tribe along. Well, then the religion come in, the priests and the do-gooders . . . and they told them that—well, they eat *all* the fish, they eat *all* the caribou—[but they told them]: "Oh, you don't eat that, that's nasty. Intestine. That's nasty. . . . "

So they got them that they didn't eat the plunkin and the bum gut and all that stuff, the stomach. But then they had to start losin' their teeth and their hair. So they had to get something to take that up. So they bring oranges in. . . . So we said, "We'll bring the oranges in to catch fur. Twenty-six dollars for a case of oranges, and we'll give you three dollars for a beaver skin." We set our own prices, we set our own deal and everything else on it. And I maintain if we'd a kept our damn nose outta there they'd been better off! They'd been better off, and we'd been better off!

[How did the Streeper family come to be in Nevada?]

Barney: Well sir, my granddad was a Mormon, and he come into Utah with Brigham Young. Over the plains from the East. And my grandparents apostatized from the Mormon church. . . .

Nan: Had a row with the bishop in other words. . . .

Barney: Well, they was a gold rush, open land in Nevada. . . . Rawhide was boomin', and the goldfield in Tonopah, and of course the lure of gold, why people go crazy over it. . . . And we went to Nevada and we took up, my dad had a lease, and they made some money, but they put it back in the ground. Well, then they took up a homestead, and it was irrigation and it was just like things happen here. We was gettin' six dollars a ton for hay and eight dollars a ton for alfalfa hay. . . . Well, it went down to two and a half or three dollars a ton. Well you couldn't make a living. . . . And the alkali come up, and they couldn't raise nothing but a dust. It practically all went alkali.

Well at that time what a wonderful country Canada was! Well you know what a brochure is. They can point out all the good places, but they leave out the bad spots on it. So, well then, we've always been [the kind that] when it got a little too thick, we moved on. So we moved up. . . . And we just kept comin' a little bit farther and a little bit farther, and we heard about this place, and went down, and a nice little lake there, and looked like quite a lot of open land. . . . And all that grass. Where we was from it was desert.

But we brought our ideas, which didn't work up here too good. Well, we got cattle, and the cattle outgrew the feed. The grass . . . when we cut it twice, it didn't come again, and we had to break up land . . . and things got down to, as I say, that we was loggin' for eleven dollars—puttin' lumber on the car for eleven dollars a thousand. Well, we wasn't makin' no fortune at it; we was makin' a livin'.

And the highway come in. On the highway, as I say, we got a dollar and a quarter . . . an hour, which, before, we was gettin' three dollars, and two and a half . . . a day. And that was a day! Not eight hours. That was a day. Well, of course, that was big money. It looked like big money . . . but now then it's no money at all.

Nan: It's taken an awful toll on human health and that sort of thing. I mean, Barney's sixty-nine, and he looks way older than that. And is. I mean, he's worn out in lots of ways. . . . He's done probably three times more work than any of the young people growing up today. I think it's been worth it. I think we built the country. . . . But I have noticed that the women that went through all that, all of them show age and that sort of thing, but they've got something that an awful lot of them don't have. They're pioneers. It takes a certain—there's only certain people can be pioneers. I think it takes a particularly tough [spirit].

[I think of Canada and the United States as just one large country. North America. People's families have lived down there and moved up here, and the other way around.] Yes, I do. . . . A continuation. I do.

The Quiet of My Little Station Was Shattered

AMERICAN ENGINEER soldiers were already headed for Dawson Creek early in March 1942. They moved their heavy equipment quickly into the northern field. In March the days rapidly lengthen. Blood-red sunrises of skies clotted with purple and pink cloud layers spread open across the North. Snow melts. Rivers run bank full with muddy water. Daylight begins to come at 3 or 4 a.m. Aspen and buckbrush awaken and move in their roots. Nothing yet is green. Color is the red of the sky playing over the deep blue of late winter and early spring. Nights whisper with the changing roots, with the crack of ice warming, and with the clogged and pushing flow of water. Often it rains.

There was an alien sound now. Diesel Cat engines growled for miles across the million-year quiet spaces of the old north. The moving roots may have heard it, the torn earth felt it. All the North's people noticed it, and many of them clearly remember the time when that sound first entered their consciousness. It is an alternating rumble and roar, rumble and roar. Roar as the D8 Cat bears down hard on its job, leaning its steel blade into tangles of the spongy bottom of the boreal forest, the taiga, forcing it loose and pushing it away, ridging it up to make a place for the road. Rumble as the D8 backs away, angles slightly off to the side and waddles forward for the next bite of taiga bottom. Get seven or eight of these 23-ton D8s working on the same stretch, and the sound never ceases, though it alternates and makes chords of weird metallic music. You can steer by it if you are lost in the muskeg and forest. Wait the night out where you are. As the daylight begins, go to that

55

sound, as for years before you would have followed ridgelines and river bottoms to camp. Not far from where you find the D8s, you will find shelter, eiderdown robes, hot coffee, breakfast, talk. The barrel stove in the cookshack will be popping and cracking with fire and heat, the men mumbling of bolts and tracks and steel gears, valves and pins and generators.

Old northerners reminisce about the first time they heard that sound, saw a bulldozer and talked with a Cat skinner. With his big Cat the skinner could do a colossal day's work. For people whose labor had forever been accomplished with hand and horse and dog team, who, if they knew about powerful engines at all, had probably seen and heard them only in the occasionally passing small aircraft—the old Fokker or the Waco or the newer Norseman packing the mail—these tons-weight machines were astounding things. Bigger, heavier, louder, capable of more work than anything you could ever imagine! Seeing and hearing a Cat bite bush was an experience matched only in wonder and admiration by that of a seventeenth-century American Indian's watching a white man shoot a gun or study a compass, as its tiny needle always mysteriously swung around and pointed toward the North.

Original impressions of the first meeting of these alien civilizations—technological with northern—are significant. The impressions are focal points—crystals—in the constant movement and change of the Pacific transition. They are important because they are remembered and because the northerner used them to measure time and experience by as he came out of the old world, the natural world of the North where he had moved by seasons and shadow, ice and sunlight and snowmelt, runoff and salmon spawn. No doubt, too, the American soldier—the Cat skinner—remembers these moments. As the unofficial representative, the point man of his highly mechanized civilization, he first met and shook hands with the northerner at these moments.

The memories rumble of many things. Sound itself. Alien. Loud. They rumble of a generosity that Canadian and American officials would later call waste, and sometimes even corruption, because in the early days of building the highway that generosity was unlimited. Of humor. Of men whose power seemed epic because of the size and the strength of the D8s they held in hand, machines whose power sometimes mastered their own skinners' imaginations. Of disbelief. If a Cat could move so much earth in a day, what else might it yet be able to move, and what else might technological man yet be able to do?

Jack Baker

Jack Baker was stationed at Watson Lake for Yukon Southern Air Transport, Ltd., when he saw his first Cat. Just before the Alcan Highway was built, the Dominion built the Northwest Staging Route air bases at Fort Nelson and Watson Lake. The contractors brought in supplies on the Dease River to Lower Post and pushed a tote road through to Watson Lake from there.

I was at my station there at Watson. You know, it was quite a remote spot was Watson. [I was with] the old Yukon Southern, before it became C. P. Airlines. And this one day—it was in the middle of the afternoon—and I heard this crashing in the bush, and I wondered what in the hell! First I thought it was a moose, you know, in the distance, and I could hear it, and I thought, well, that's too loud for any moose to be crashin' around there you know. And I kept listenin', and it'd get louder and then the rumble of a motor, an engine, big engine. So it wasn't more than maybe an hour, and here the damn thing started pushin' trees right out, right close to my station. . . . So that's the first time I ever saw a bulldozer. Broke through the bush. And I forget the name of the operator on it. I had quite a talk to him. It was so astounding you know! The quiet of my little station was shattered.

Bill Blair

William Arthur Blair moved to Alaska from the States in the early part of the century. He prospected and trapped. In later years he moved to Beaver Creek, in the Yukon Territory, where until recently he trapped, placered for gold, and worked as a laborer. This is the way he first learned of the building of the Alcan. His account is representative of the first meetings of the Cat skinners and construction workers with the Canadian prospectors and trappers, whose lives were lived almost entirely in the bush and who had little news of the outside world.

We was prospectin' when the first Cat come through there. [When] the first Cat come through, I was goin' down to Snag to git some grub, and here I run acrost a guy and I says, "Where *you* goin'?"

"Wher'm *I* goin'," he says. "Wher *you* goin'?"

I says, "Prospectin' out here with Pete Eikland, and we bin here many years. What the hell you goin' to cut here now?"

He says, "This is the *highway!*"

"Well," I says, "That's good. Wher's it comin' from?"

And he says, "We're on our way now to Burwash."

"Well," I says, "I've come fer some grub."

He says, "Ther's camps along there. Go and see them."

Well, I went out and asked the fellas fer a little bit o' grub, and I wouldn't have to go any further.

The cook says, "Whadda yuh want?"

I says, "I want a pound o' tea anyway."

He says, "Take a hunderd pound! We don't need tea. We're coffee people."

I says, "That's all right."

He says, "There's the tent that's full o' grub, and the door's open. Hep yerself."

Well, I had three dogs, and I says, "Now, I won't git in trouble goin' back home. Do you wanta git paid?"

"No. No. No. No pay! Jist hep yerself! Sugar and rice." And he says, "What you need! And don't fergit, take a hunderd pounds o' tea."

Well, fer Chris sake! I thought he was kinda *nuts*, and I as much as told 'im. I says, "I don't want to git in trouble. I got the money in my pocket."

He says, "No money!" He says, "That door's open. Hep yerself."

And he says, "Wher you workin'?"

I says, "Twenty miles up here, on a placer prospect."

"Well," he says, "I'll git this Cat to run you up there. . . ."

Yes, sir. And he put in everything, that fella. He was the head Cat man, and he just throwed stuff in there, and he says, "You'll need this, you'll need that." And he says, "Later on we'll bulldoze a trail up [there], and you won't have no hard time gittin' grub." And they did!

Oh Yow. . . . I got an awful kick outta them fellas. . . . And we loved this road comin' through. But we thought, Hell, they'll never git through, yuh know. But Goddammit to hell in three years!

George Nelms

The incident George Nelms describes happened at mile 8 as it was known in 1942 and 1943, eight miles west of Fort Nelson at the big army camp. The site is present mile 308 on the Alaska Highway.

There was a Finlander, he was a Cat skinner, I can't remember his name offhand, but the Canadian Bank of Commerce had a bank branch there, you know, and it was one of these Quonset huts, one of these curved Quonset huts. And it was the only bank north of Fort St. John, from between there and Whitehorse I think. But the fellows used to, you know, get their paychecks every, I forget how often we got paid then. I think it was every two weeks. But on this particular time, the pay come in, and this fellow got his check, and he wanted to get it cashed. . . . Well, for some reason or other the bank was gonna be closed in the afternoon on this particular day, you know, and he didn't get his check cashed. Well . . . it was right after a weekend, and I guess he'd bin doin' a little celebrating at night over the weekend, so he said he got really mad.

"If I don't get my check cashed," he says, "I'm gonna run my bulldozer over there and go right through the front of that bank!"

Of course everbody was primed for this, and they were just wonderin' how far he'd go with this thing you know. And so, anyway, he did. He got his Cat and he run it right over to the front of the bank, you know, and he said to the banker, he says,

"Look, if you don't open up that so and so bank," he says, "I'm gonna run right through the front of youse. I'm gonna get my check cashed."

But the thing of it was, they didn't open the bank for 'im, but they did give him some money for his check. So I guess, as a matter of fact, they both saved face. . . . He got some money for his check, so he didn't have to run through the front of it.

Norman Harlin

There are endless stories told along the Alaska Highway about the amount of heavy equipment lost in 1942 and 1943, about Cats and trucks and power shovels dropped through the ice into rivers and lakes or left behind under the tote road grade. It is difficult to document these accounts. Some are no doubt accurate; many are certainly not. Norman Harlin's account is typical, and it is probably accurate. He was there at the time. Perhaps the most important thing about such accounts, however, is not their accuracy, but the contrasting attitudes they reveal on the part of the Americans and the Canadians. Used to endless equipment, the Americans took the Cat for granted. The Canadians, on the other hand, because they admired a machine which was new to them, incredibly powerful and expensive to acquire in the bush, wondered at how the Americans could treat it with so little regard.

But they cared *nothing* for equipment! I mean, they tried to look after it, but a Cat broke down, they'd shove it aside. Build the road!

We had a case up here where [mile] 721 is now. Being a Canadian with a little Scotch in me, we had a Cat there with a track off, and the Captain wanted to leave it, and I said, "No! We can pull it back down off the grade, and we can fix that thing up."

And it finally ended up that it was holdin' up seven other bulldozers, and he says, "Push 'er over the side."

And that's where the Cat is today, under the grade. . . .

I was camping with him, and that night in the tent I said, "Isn't there some way you can hold things up long enough for us to get that thing out of there?"

"No," he says. "There's three or four thousand men comin' behind. We're not gonna hold 'em up for one D8."

And that was it!

Long Ways from Home

AUGUST 28, 1973, Sunday evening. At Atlin people are burning coal tonight. Wind whips in off the dark gray lake. Wave caps break on the beach and lift stern ends of boats whose bow ends rest in willows. A tern rises with an updraft, holds steady in the wind, drops straight down to touch and ride the water. An old 180 bobs at the edge of the lake. Waves lap and slop its metal pontoons.

I camp on the beach beyond the end of the town in front of the Catholic church and the native village. Two Indian men walk up. They carry buckets for water.

"How you like Atlin?"

"Fine."

"Where you from?"

"New Mexico."

"New Mexico! Holy Kee-rist, you're a long ways from home.

"Hey Charlie!" Charlie has been down to the lake's edge dipping his bucket full of water.

"You know where this guy's from?"

"No. Where?"

"New Mexico."

"New Mexico! Holy Kee-rist, he's a long ways from home!"

At daylight the 180 leaves for somewhere back in the bush. They crank her up, and the pilot warms the engine carefully, building oil pressure. She's tied to the pier. He speeds the engine now, racing her to high rpm's, listening, checking her out to see if she's running right. Satisfied, they untie her pontoons, let her go. She taxis downwind—stiff gale of a wind—her tail lifted, her nose and prop pointing slightly downward toward the water. A few

61

hundred feet out, the pilot stops her, turns her about into the gale. She trembles for seconds, rising and dropping with the choppy wave tops. Then he firmly shoves throttle toward firewall.

Slicing circle of the prop bites a pillar of spray, blows it straight back toward the far shore, soaks the windshield and fuselage. Floats shove water up, nose tips upward. She plows ahead, then quickly planes off level with the top of the water. Bold rush forward now and instantly off she lifts with the wind, like the tern riding the updraft into the sky. Two men watch from the beach below. Their heads circle as they follow the plane, banking toward dark mountains across the lake, fighting for the right air currents, buffeted by updrafts, downdrafts, crosswinds.

"Jesus, I'd hate to be up there with her!"

"By God, I'd hate to be up there without her!"

A native opens his cabin door to wait and watch. Two goggled husky pups stop their play beside a broken old lapstrake on the beach. They stand four-footed on the earth to study this great sky event.

In the summer and fall of 1942, men labored at a great earth event: they opened the Alcan Highway across the rounded space of northwestern Canada hundreds of miles into eastern and central Alaska. General Sturdevant had assigned the 18th, the 35th, the 340th, and the 341st Engineer Regiments to cut the pioneer road. He had made these assignments in his original plan. Because of the size of the job, the army later added the 93rd, the 95th, and the 97th, all black regiments. The total military force, including support and service detachments, reached 394 officers and 10,765 enlisted men.

On the Southern Sector of the highway, the 35th moved from Fort St. John to Fort Nelson in March and early April. To reach Fort St. John, they used a dirt and gravel highway the provincial government had already completed from Dawson Creek. Though Sturdevant reported this provincial road "passable in winter and dry weather," his report was irrelevant to its condition at the time. For this was the season of the northern spring. Sun warmed the atmosphere, rain melted the crusted snow, roads washed out, winter trails sank down into their own muck. Truck wheels churned the mud.

A winter trail already cut by the Dominion government ran west of Fort St. John to Fort Nelson. But this trail would become useless after about April 1, and the 35th would therefore have to make their long haul with ground conditions becoming steadily worse. Their problem would be complicated by their supplies. They would have to pack enough for four months' subsistence since the winter trail back would be cut off by spring thaw.

The crossing of the Peace River near Taylor and Fort St. John was the most dangerous part of the haul. Alexander Mackenzie had passed here in the spring of 1793 bound west for the Pacific. He had found the river very bad when he broke camp on May 9, "the waters being then very high and strong, owing to the melting of the snow." The river had not yet broken up at Taylor when the 35th crossed it nearly 150 years later. Here this northern river is 1,800 feet wide. There was no bridge, and the ferry could not operate before breakup. Freighters and travelers had simply crossed on the ice in the wintertime since the very beginning of travel in the North, but now that the days lengthened and the sun warmed, the ice had become rotten and ready to go out. The soldiers planked the river and spread sawdust over the spongy surface of the ice. Then they drove their equipment and supplies across without an accident.

They pushed immediately ahead toward Fort Nelson, still 265 miles away across muskegs which were mucky in the daytime, though the freezing nights hardened them again. Men suffered from the wind and from the extremes of temperature. No one rested. The heavy equipment operators had a bad time of it. Tractors, shovels, D8s had to be ridden through, and the skinners sometimes went for 40-, even 80-mile stretches without relief. Determination. Fear of failure. The pressures of war and the northern weather. One week into April—on the fifth—they pulled into Fort Nelson with 900 tons of supplies. They had sweated by day and frozen at night. Temperatures in March had ranged from 50 degrees above zero to 35 degrees below. The regiment had come all the way from end of steel at Dawson Creek, 300 miles back, in five days less than one month's time. "A remarkable performance," General Sturdevant called the long march of the 35th.

To build and improve the southern end of the Alcan so that fresh supplies and equipment could be gotten to the 35th as soon as possible, two regiments went to work between Fort St. John and

Fort Nelson when the bush began to dry out. The 341st Engineer Regiment arrived first, and, in May, suffered a bad accident, probably the worst to occur on the highway in the early days. On May 14 at about noon, one officer and ten enlisted men drowned when a jerry-built raft sank in the cold water of Charlie Lake a few miles west of Fort St. John. The men had built the raft of three pontoons dogged together and had powered it with two outboard engines. Since the Alcan road was to parallel the lake, the soldiers had loaded a small tractor and other equipment onto the raft and were trying to move these things up the lake from the southern end. When they rounded a protecting point, a squall caught and swamped them. The water temperature was only slightly above freezing. Eleven of the sixteen men aboard disappeared within minutes. Gus Hedin, a local trapper who had watched the raft from his cabin on the near shore, looked away for a few minutes, then looked again. He saw that the raft was gone, but that small objects and men floated in the water. Hedin made several trips in a small skiff to save those still afloat, only five in all. He took the fortunate ones to his cabin, warmed them and rubbed them down.

In spite of the accident, the morale of the 341st held. By August 26 they made contact with a detachment of pontoon soldiers and a group from the 35th completing a bridge over the Muskwa River near Fort Nelson. Before fall, the 341st and the 95th Engineer Regiment, which had graded, ditched, and built culverts behind the 341st, opened a road passable for military traffic from Fort St. John over Pink Mountain and Trutch down the Prophet River valley into Fort Nelson.

Soldiers were on the move everywhere on the Alcan in the summer of 1942, working toward the west and toward the east, trying to open the highway by early winter. On the northern end of the road, the 18th and the 97th Engineer Regiments cut tote. Their section, between Whitehorse and Tok, Alaska, was perhaps the most difficult of all. Permafrost was everywhere. The glacial rivers of the North were the hardest of all to bridge. The Duke, 1,700 feet wide; the Donjek, 1,200 feet; the crazy White, 600 feet. The country itself was all bad. North of the vast ranges of the St. Elias, the Nutzotin, and the Mentasta mountains, low ridges and wide muskegs covered with bog blueberries spread forever. It was this low country north of the mountains the soldiers had to cross. Maps and surveys were inadequate. PRA and army location men had to make several ground and aerial inspections to discover the best route over this difficult land.

To make ground inspections, PRA engineer John McGillivray and U.S. Army Major Hodge led a party west by jeep and truck from Whitehorse in early May. They traveled the old wagon road toward Kluane Lake. At Jarvis Creek just east of Kluane the party mounted a string of horses and packed from there 300 miles to Northway, Alaska. They carefully observed the land and took notes all the way. McGillivray was optimistic. Optimism was a necessary virtue in the north in the summer of 1942. "Over practically the entire section of the route reconnoitered . . . ," he noted down, "swampy terrain is much in evidence, but on detailed investigation, suitable material for road construction was found beneath the matted growth of moss and grass. This mat ranged in depth from six inches to three feet and averaged about 1 foot in depth." McGillivray seemed not fully aware of the trouble road builders would have when they skinned this matted cover of insulation off the permafrost. "With adequate drainage and the removal of the Muskeg coverage . . . ," he wrote, "very good results, I believe, can be obtained."

Permafrost, permanently frozen ground, underlies much of the northern muskeg. Once men strip the cover away so that the sun's warming rays can get to ground frozen since early Pleistocene times, perhaps a million years ago, the ground begins to thaw. The thaw spreads as warmth and water melt still more frosted subsoil. There is no quick natural end to this process. Drainage is nearly impossible because water only stands in ditches and thaws more chunk ice and frozen ground. By late spring and summer in such country nothing remains but a fathomless mess where Cat skinners have gouged away covering mosses and bush. Only thousands of tons of rock and gravel fill or actual relocations to dry ridges can make the base suitable for a road. What is more, engineers must learn not to skin off the muskeg, but to dump fill over the top of the natural cover so as not to disturb the insulating layers of plant life and rotten organic matter. No one at the time knew very much about what permafrost would do except that it would be very tricky. Many people seemed to assume that thawing water could be drained off by a system of ditches. The army and the PRA engineers learned lessons from trying to build road on permafrost, but they learned the hard way, and the land did not recover quickly.

Walter Williscroft

A "million miler" on the Alaska Highway, Walter Williscroft, a Canadian, first worked for the army engineers in May 1943. For five years, 1945 to 1950, he was Superintendent of the highway section headquartered at Destruction Bay on Kluane Lake. He was in charge of maintenance from Whitehorse to the Alaska border and of the Haines Road. A stream is named for him at mile 1066—"Williscroft Creek."

We all learned a lot of lessons from the permafrost. . . .

Just as a little example, there was quite a bunch of Congressmen comin' up, and . . . the colonel [said], "I want you to ditch up there."

Well, I said, "Now look," I said, "I don't mind doin' the ditch, but I don't think we should ditch there."

He said, "Why not?"

"Well," I said, "I've been talkin' with Mr. Pringle from Alaska. . . . And he said, 'Whatever you do, don't make the same mistake as we did in Alaska. Don't put ditches along there. . . . You go across the border and take a look in Alaska and see what we done over there.' He said, 'You take that machine and dump it in the river.'"

Well, we just had to have [that machine] working, and we had done maybe a couple miles by the time this Congress party came through, and by the next year we had to go and put it all back. It eroded so fast. . . . There was that much water movin' over that permafrost, and it just eroded something terrific. Well, I suspicioned what would happen, but I wasn't an authority on it at that time, but I was a better authority on it the next year. . . .

[You see, if you put in ditches, then the permafrost melts and the water stands in the ditches and flows under the road.] The water just kept getting deeper in the ditch and the road kept goin' down. . . .

In 1946 . . . we filled 'em all up again and eliminated the ditches.

The Army theoretically equipped the seven regiments which cut the tote road in 1942 with twenty D8s each, twenty-four D4 and R4 tractors, fifty to ninety dump trucks, two half-yard gasoline-powered shovels, six tractor-drawn graders, a truck crane, a portable sawmill, two pile drivers, and an assortment of jeeps, cargo trucks, pickups, and carryalls. In operation, a regiment cutting road either followed one of its own locating parties, one of those supplied by the PRA, or one of the military topographic units. The locating party marked the centerline of the highway with stakes or blazes, and a clearing crew with two or three shifts of Cat skinners came behind. In midsummer, when the days were longest and midnight was no darker than a soft red sunset-sunrise, the clearing skinners worked around the clock. One D8 plowed along the blazed centerline opening a narrow swath. Other tractors then pushed the trees to both sides, widening the trail. Another crew, usually a whole company, building log culverts and small bridges, followed up the clearing crew. Still another crew followed to ditch, rough-grade, corduroy, and improve the pioneer road enough so that trucks could drive through in dry weather. The remainder of the regiment labored along the road thirty to forty miles to the rear to widen the narrow places, improve grades, and spread a thin surface of gravel or crushed rock.

In the meantime, the light ponton companies placed floating bridges over streams and rivers that could not be forded or bridged quickly with piles and trestles, or they operated ferries where even pontoon bridges were not practicable. In places, all hands, including the cooks and the clerk-typists, turned out to lay corduroy when a company got bogged down in a muskeg. The 18th Engineers, for instance, ran into a 50-mile stretch of highly unstable country between the Donjek and the White where permafrost lay only inches below the surface. Leaving all their heavy equipment behind, the regiment cut whole trees and laid them side by side, branches and all. Then they spread a layer of gravel over this springy corduroy to help insulate the melting ground ice from the sun. In some places along the highway, soldiers were said to have used as many as five layers of corduroy and gravel.

Often this plan of assigning specific tasks and sections of the road to different companies from a given regiment did not work well, for weather, geography, and supply problems varied. Officers and men had to be ingenious. They had to create new ways of doing the job where this so-called train system was inadequate. West of Whitehorse the 18th Engineers used the "leapfrog" system. Officers gave a section of the road 5 to 10 miles long to each company. When a company completed its section, it leapfrogged ahead to a new section in the front. Leapfrogging was possible here because of the old wagon trail between Whitehorse and Kluane Lake. The soldiers who had completed their work could simply pack up and move ahead over the old trail.

Beyond Kluane Lake, however, there were no trails suitable for the pioneer road or for moving troops and supplies out in front. Having reached Kluane, some companies from the 18th were ferried up the lake to Burwash Landing. From there they returned to modifications of the train system: a pioneer party or point drove the head of the swath as rapidly as possible toward the Donjek and the White while the other soldiers followed up, completing the tasks necessary for making the road passable. The other companies of the 18th remained behind to build the new road around Kluane Lake, construct the pile bridge across Slim's River, and complete the rock cuts past Soldiers Summit.

The problems of bridging the glacial rivers in the country beyond Kluane Lake were something new to the army engineers, for these rivers not only changed their channels often, but they were actually ice bottomed. Spring runoff made them especially dangerous. Soldiers had to guard a temporary bridge over the White twenty-four hours a day when the country was freezing and thawing. Ice jams tumbling downstream rammed into the bridge again and again and had to be dynamited as soon as they began to form. Otherwise they would take the bridge out with a rush. There were times when soldiers had to dynamite eight or ten times a night. They could not drive piles in bridging the White. The ice and icy gravel of the river's bed simply shattered the piles if the soldiers attempted to drive them into place. If men used air hammers to pound holes in the frozen gravel, they had to stop and warm them every few minutes over fires kept going in oil drums.

Winter temperatures seemed incredible to the Americans in the ice-blue land of the Donjek and the White. Thermometers registered 56 degrees below zero here on the night of December 1, 1942. Not only the air hammers, but all metal tools and equipment tended to freeze and tire quickly in such temperatures. Metal parts cracked or broke at the most inopportune times, and men usually deadlined "frozen" equipment until the weather warmed up, because attempting to heat cold engines with a torch normally shattered the steel. The only way to prevent the steel from freezing and shattering was to keep it warm around the clock. Machines left outside idled all night long and worked all day. Men repaired tractors and trucks under tarps stretched over quickly-made wooden frames, or inside tar paper shacks where fires could be kept going night and day. Bridging the Duke, the Donjek, and the White required such twenty-four-hour-a-day warming operations.

Engineers soon learned that the most effective way, indeed the only effective way, of setting piles in permafrost country and in ice-bottomed rivers was to use steam jets.

Walter Williscroft

Up there in the North you could dig down, oh, a foot and hit nice blue ice. . . .

We found out by driving piling up there we had to jet the piles. A couple of bridges up there's jetted into twenty-two feet of clear ice. . . .

They don't drive [the piles] at all. You just jet the hole with steam. . . . Take two steamers and start the hole. . . . Then you grease the pile and wrap tar paper around it and then [set it in the hole and] fill [the hole] back with water and let it freeze, and [the pile] don't even move because the grease on the tar paper acts as a slick on the pile, and there's no friction to [push] the pile out.

You see what I mean. It's just like a sleeve to slide up and down the pile, and the pile sits still and the country can heave up and down, and the pile stays there.

One of the unique bridging problems on the Alcan was the construction of the Nisutlin Bay bridge at Teslin Lake. Nisutlin Bay is practically bottomless. The piles of the modern steel structure go down 247 feet into the muck, but the original builders, using local timber instead of steel, could not go that deep. That the old wooden structure did not have to be replaced for several years speaks well for the designers and the men who put it together.

James Quong

An engineering student at the University of Saskatchewan when the war began, James Quong was recruited to work for the Public Roads Administration out of Dawson Creek and Fort St. John. He now lives in Whitehorse where he is Manager of Technical Services, Canadian Department of Public Works, Yukon District.

Talk about bridging, the bridge on Nisutlin Bay, the original trestle was twenty-three odd hundred feet long. It was the longest trestle on the whole Alaska Highway. . . . The original trestle, not only was it long, but . . . there was no foundation except for thin layers of sand . . . and it's on these thin layers of sand that the new bridge is founded. . . .

But the original trestles, the longest piles were 180 feet long or something like that, three piles put together. And the foundation was mud, you see, so loose that I still say that except for the stringers . . . that were pinned together on the ends . . . , the whole length of it was so pinned together that it was like a string of beads so that the bridge was really a string from one side to another. You'd look along the centerline, you'd see it wow to one side and then back again. . . .

We used to have tremendous blocks of ice. . . . There was one block of ice that I saw drifting down . . . just moving like a great big battleship, and when it hits that bridge, you know, she really leans over to one side. And we used to spend many, many winters just repairing the piles that [were] bashed up by the ice. . . .

The 18th Engineers arrived in Whitehorse on April 29 over the White Pass and Yukon Railway from the port at Skagway. Aspen leaves had fallen when on October 25, working west 280 miles from Whitehorse, they met the troops of the 97th Engineers near Beaver Creek not far from the Alaska border in the Yukon. The 97th had moved from port at Valdez, Alaska, up the Richardson Highway and the Copper River to Slana. From there they had cut tote road over Mentasta Pass—this stretch later became part of the Glenn Highway from Tok to Anchorage—to the Tok River Junction. At Tok the 97th had angled southeastward past Northway toward the border and Beaver Creek. The 97th's road from Tok to Beaver Creek, 118 miles, was a part of the Alcan. From Tok to Delta Junction on the Richardson Highway, the Public Roads Administration contractors built the pioneer road. Men of the Alaska Road Commission also worked hard on these stretches in Alaska.

While all this work was going forward on both ends of the road, PRA contractors and the soldiers of the 35th, the 93rd, and the 340th Regiments struggled to close the large gap in the center from Fort Nelson to Whitehorse, 618 modern highway miles. The PRA men opened about fifty miles of the tote road between Whitehorse, modern mile 918, and the point called Jake's Corner, modern mile 866. The 93rd had arrived in Skagway in April but were held up until June, awaiting the arrival of their heavy equipment. As soon as they were equipped, they began cutting a road from Carcross, a stop on the White Pass and Yukon line, toward Teslin Lake. In August, they met the soldiers of the 340th at Nisutlin Bay near Teslin, the Tlingit village, modern mile 803. The 93rd had cut about one hundred miles of road since June. Sixty-three miles of this road were a part of the Alcan.

Living conditions for the 93rd and the other construction regiments in the field were rough at first. The men lived in tents heated by wood stoves. They slept in down sleeping bags. Since they were often on the move, they were always packing up their tents and simple belongings and throwing them on a truck or carryall. Sometimes they carried things on their backs or used packhorses. As time went on, especially after the civilian contractors got into the field, living conditions and food improved. Men built barracks at permanent road camps, or they constructed prefabricated, movable living units which they transported on sleds, trucks, or railroad cars. Others assembled completely furnished living units, which included a bunkhouse, a storeroom with tools, and a mess hall. They loaded these onto flatcars at Edmonton, shipped them to railhead at Dawson Creek, and hauled them from there by sled or truck to wherever workers needed them.

With all the problems of permafrost and icing, the cold weather, when the fall and winter began to come on, did have its advantages. In the summer of 1942 the soldiers had lived mainly on canned Vienna sausage and chile con carne. In the winter, however, they could shoot and then preserve fresh meat, for the low temperatures were a natural deep freeze. Men could begin now to feast regularly off the land. By November, frozen whole sides of moose dangled from birch or spruce trees behind the mess halls. The cooks went out in the morning with handsaws and sawed off roasts or ribs, or they cut steaks for the day's meals. In the coldest weather of December and January, however, everything froze stiff. The cook sometimes had to thaw potatoes out before he could bake them, or he had to melt ice to brew the morning coffee. Occasionally his fresh-stirred flapjack batter froze in the bowl while his pancakes browned in the frying pan. Drivers trucked clothing back from the nearest laundry in chunks which men had to warm beside oil drum stoves before they pried their socks and T-shirts loose and dared to put them on.

Roman Catholic Bishop Coudert met a black soldier from the

93rd guarding a bridge at Carcross. The soldier had wrapped himself up in a parka to try to keep warm.

"You look like you're well dressed," the Bishop said. "Are you cold?"

"Man, I sure *am* cold!"

"Well, what do you think of the Yukon?"

"Yukon? Yukon *have* it!"

The soldiers from the American South tried to keep warm, though few succeeded. To cope with the cold they overdressed, sweated, then grumbled and laughed about it. They sang, they swore, once in a long while they bathed: there were too many mosquitos in the summer, and it was too cold in the winter. The northerners, totally acclimated to such problems, were endlessly amused by these greenhorns.

Pen Powell

Pen Powell lived at Charlie Lake, British Columbia. He became well acquainted with several of the soldiers from the 341st and the 95th Regiments. He had many hours of fun over their predicaments because of the extremes of the northern climate to which they were unaccustomed.

When they were here [camped at the south end of Charlie Lake] they were all in tents. It was just unbelievable. I just give anything to had some films, some pictures, some of those guys the way they were dressed. You know, no Eskimo could touch 'em . . . for clothes. There was no end to what they could pile on, and of course I guess the cantina or wherever they was gettin' these damn things, there was no end, they'd just give 'em everythin'. Christ, their feet'd be that long, great big fat boots, one end tied to the other. And they wouldn't get out of 'em for two or three weeks at a time 'til a Chinook would come, you know, and warm it up a little bit. Then they'd take some off and have a half-ass wash of some kind, you know.

The cold weather caused human tragedies, too, for people who hadn't the experience to know what to do about it. At times, even though there was adequate equipment on hand, men simply died, apparently from the lack of experience and no doubt from the fear of the cold itself. Northerners were struck by such accidents in much the way that a Death Valley desert prospector might be struck by a greenhorn's death from thirst. There are ways to stay alive if a man knows the country and how to use its resources, if he doesn't lose his head.

Norman Harlin

The colonel told me that one night in Whitehorse—that was a hell of a cold winter, seventy-two below—they lost twenty-seven men froze to death in one battalion. Not properly dressed. Didn't realize what that cold can do. For instance, there was three of them just a few miles out of Whitehorse comin' in with a load of used tires, on a six-by-six, and the truck froze up—gas line—and when they found them in the morning, they were huddled together, froze stiff of course, and a buncha burnt matches, and they'd been trying to start a fire with green, frozen spruce needles, and that truck sittin' there fulla gas and an axe hangin' on the side. Any of us woulda tried to get a fire goin'. If we couldn't, we'da taken that axe and chopped open [the gas tank]. Sure. That loada tires woulda burnt for three days. Beautiful fire!

By the time the men of the 93rd reached Nisutlin Bay and met the soldiers of the 340th, the men of the 340th had built a lot of road. While one battalion had marched overland from Carcross to Teslin, the main body had moved from Whitehorse by steamboat early in the summer up the Teslin River and down Teslin Lake to Morley Bay where they had built a base camp. From there some of them had worked northwestward the few miles to Nisutlin Bay and the meeting with the 93rd.

In the meantime, the main body of the 340th had cut tote road southeastward toward Contact Creek, close to 200 miles away. In about three months' time, to close the gap between the Northern and the Southern Sectors of the Alcan Highway, they went up the Swift River and crossed the Arctic-Pacific divide between the Swift and the Rancheria. Then the 340th followed the Rancheria toward the Liard River—Alexander Mackenzie had called it the "River of the Mountains" when he passed its mouth on Wednesday, July 1, 1789, canoeing down a big river (later named the Mackenzie) which he hoped would flow into the *Mer d'Ouest*, the Pacific. Both Mackenzie and the soldiers of the 340th saw the fireweed, the pink flower that covers that country in midsummer. Both knew what it meant, that winter could not be far away. Mackenzie was wrong about his destination that year. His river flowed into the frozen sea, the Arctic Ocean, which he reached—"the limit of our Travels in this Direction"—on Sunday, July 12, 1789. But the soldiers of the 340th were on course. Down the Rancheria to the Liard, past Watson Lake and Lower Post, across the Hyland River and Iron Creek to Contact Creek, mile 588.1, modern highway mileage. The 340th made Contact Creek, the end of the Northern Sector of construction on the Alcan, by September 24, 1942. Here they met the soldiers of the 35th Combat Engineer Regiment, just arrived from Fort Nelson, nearly 300 miles to the southeast on the eastern slope of the Canadian Rockies.

Heavy rains and the spring runoff west of Fort Nelson had held the 35th up until late June. By July the country had dried out enough for the steady, grinding labor of building road over the Rocky Mountains to Contact Creek. Up Curwen's trail the soldiers went—the route pointed by the Callisons and used years back by numberless trappers, gold seekers, and travelers—to the Raspberry Creek crossing. The fireweed was in full bloom now. Vetch, wintergreen, kinnikinnick, wild grasses grew green in the aspen forests along the rivers and on the lower ridges. D8s rumbled along. Soldiers drank gallons of coffee and labored on. They crossed the Kledo, rounded "the steep and rugged slope of Steamboat Mountain," waded Mill Creek, reached the Tetsa. They pushed upward then into the heavy spruce forest of the Rockies. Up the shale and limestone box of Tetsa River to Summit Lake—"the summit of the Canadian Rockies . . . at an elevation of about 4,320 feet"—following the route recommended by PRA engineer W. H. Curwen and the Callison brothers, his guides and mushers. Then the 35th angled downward from the top to Muncho Lake and the Liard, named by a Frenchman for the aspens that grow along its bottoms. There they turned west and followed the banks of the Liard to Coal River and Contact Creek.

On September 24 the Cat skinners of the 35th and those of the 340th closed the gap between North and South in the waters of Contact Creek. There is a handful of black-and-white snapshots of the meeting. For a moment the men stopped their work, perhaps felt free. D8s were badly battered, tracks caked now with northern mud. Diesels idled. Soldiers, PRA men, and steel machines had cut the Alcan road more than a thousand miles over timber, mountain, and swamp in one summer's season—rain, slanting sunlight, midnight shadow. In one of the photographs a camera hangs from the neck of a man who stands on the hillside above the creek. The water is low, the stream runs clear. Officers and men wear soft caps, dress in light jackets and workshirts, unbuttoned and messy. All are smiling. One balances on a big blade as if he were trying to walk a rail. Some pose for the camera's eye, while others simply stand and talk. Dark spruce trees frame the scene behind.

Elliott's Fleet and Parker's Navy

SUPPLY PROBLEMS in the summer of 1942 seemed nearly insurmountable. The North was unlimited distance of mountains and muskegs woven with crazy rivers. It lacked adequate roads, trails, airways, railroads, or boats and barges for transporting rapidly the millions of tons of equipment and supplies which had to be there on the ground when the troops and the civilian contractors were ready to go to work. The task of supply required a few special men with much experience in organizing and pushing the thousands of ordinary men who would locate, assemble, service, inventory, pack, load, ship, and unload the tons of highly varied matériel. General Hoge, who had recently been promoted from colonel, General O'Connor, J. S. Bright of the Public Roads Administration, and E. W. Elliott of Seattle were such special men. There were probably a double-handful of others. Even with such leaders organizing the flow of supplies, machines, and tools, delivery was slow. Often it halted altogether, and there were countless foul-ups. A quartermaster truck company docked in Skagway without Arctic clothing, trucks, mess equipment, or bedding for the men. Someone had told their company commander in Seattle that he could draw these things from supply in Skagway. But the supply people there were empty-handed. What the competent leaders and officers had to do battle with were distance, geography, dangerous sealanes, competition from other military units for the same supplies and equipment, human foibles, bad luck, bad weather, and time itself.

The operation of the whole Alcan project in the summer of

1942 required a great deal of determination and flexibility on the part of the top officers whose area of responsibility began with the main delivery points and ports of supply—Edmonton and Dawson Creek on the east, and Seattle and Prince Rupert on the west. It included the problems of getting the matériel from those points into the back country where the troops were to cut tote road and of organizing the construction operation itself.

Soon after Hoge took command of construction in the spring of the year, he divided the Alcan into two large sectors, the Southern Sector headquartered at Fort St. John and the Northern Sector at Whitehorse. At first an executive officer ran each sector while Hoge raced up and down the road by airplane and car, staying in touch with the two commands by radio. Because of the size of the project, this arrangement quickly became impracticable, and on June 6 Hoge took command of the Northern Sector while Col. James A. O'Connor took command of the Southern. Both officers reported directly to the chief of engineers in Washington.

By late summer it was clear that this arrangement was in trouble. Wider command, completer control of the whole operation, including not only the construction but the supply too, needed to be centered in the field itself where the work was going on, rather than in the distant offices of Washington. Hence, the engineers tried still another plan. On September 4 they established the Northwest Service Command with headquarters at Whitehorse in the center of the operation, and named James A. O'Connor commanding general. The mission of the Northwest Service Command (NSC) was to manage all "construction, maintenance, and supply activities" of the United States Army, not only for the Alcan but for all the army's other activities in northwestern Canada. Since supply had been one of the most urgent problems, the commanding general specifically took charge of "movements by sea to Skagway and to other destinations" covered by the NSC. This arrangement gave the field commander a stronger lever on the big ports of supply at Seattle and Prince Rupert. On the Alcan Highway itself, the two-sector plan remained in force. Each sector—the two of which joined in the meeting of the Cats at Contact Creek—still had its own commanding officer, but each of these officers reported directly to NSC headquarters at Whitehorse, rather than to the chief of engineers in Washington.

Soon the army tried other reorganizations for the purpose of greater efficiency. In October it temporarily established the Northwest Division of the NSC in Whitehorse. Later, the Northwest Division Engineer's office moved to Edmonton. The division operated six district offices at various points along the highway and elsewhere in the Canadian northwest and Alaska. The purpose of the Northwest Division was to manage all construction, maintenance, and repair along the Alcan Highway and throughout the territory covered by the Northwest Service Command. The NSC itself remained in control of all supply activities in its area—British Columbia, Alberta, the Yukon Territory, the Northwest Territories, and Alaska (excluding the specific duties and areas covered by the Alaska Defense Command). The NSC also theoretically remained in charge of the Northwest Division. But command problems between the two distant offices were troublesome, and as the war wound down there was less need for both of them. Consequently, the two merged under the Northwest Service Command at Whitehorse in March 1944.

Besides being headquarters for the Alcan, Whitehorse acted as one of the main supply points on the highway. After the ships unloaded at the port of Skagway, the narrow-gauge White Pass railway packed their matériel over the high mountains to Whitehorse. The two other main supply points were end of steel at Dawson Creek and Alaska herself, where the Territory's railroad hauled supplies, while trucks packed tons of stuff up the Richardson Highway from the port at Valdez. By late summer, the trucks could also tote supplies on the new road built by the 97th Engineers over Mentasta Pass to Tok. Teslin Lake in Canada was another access point. White Pass and Yukon steamboats carried supplies from Whitehorse up the Teslin River past Johnson's Crossing and the Tlingit village on Teslin Lake to Morley Bay for the 340th Engineers, who operated from there southeastward to Contact Creek. The army also considered the old access point at Lower Post, but decided not to use it. Men could reach Lower Post from the Pacific by going up the Stikine River, then over to Dease Lake and down the Dease River. Klondike gold seekers had followed the route around the turn of the century, and the Dominion government had used it for supplying the construction of the Northwest Staging Route airbase at Watson Lake. To the Corps of Engineers, the

Dease Lake route to Lower Post looked as if it would be more trouble than it was worth. Aircraft provided another important means of supply; they flew emergency and top priority equipment over the air route from Edmonton.

The other supply route for the Northwest Service Command was the Mackenzie River waterway from end of steel at Waterways, north of Edmonton. This route served the CANOL oil field project at Norman Wells on the Mackenzie River rather than the Alcan Highway. The army designed the CANOL oil field and the CANOL Road from Norman Wells to the Alcan Highway at Johnson's Crossing for the purpose of serving the installations and air bases along the highway and in Alaska in case the Japanese should succeed in cutting off the Pacific sea lanes. Hence, the Mackenzie River waterway to the CANOL field was another means of support for the whole Alcan project.

The White Pass and Yukon Railway itself was the only link from the port at Skagway to Whitehorse. This ancient narrow-gauge line had had her beginnings with the Klondike gold rush around the turn of the century, and men had used her since as the main supply route from the sea into the center of the Yukon. As the mountains of American matériel began arriving in Skagway in May and June, 1942, the Army pressed the line with its twelve little steam locomotives into service around the clock. But the railroad had trouble keeping up with the work she had to do, and in October the U.S. Army Military Railway Service took over management and operation through an arrangement for leasing the line from her Canadian owners. An exchange of diplomatic notes by the two governments formalized the arrangement early in 1943.

The Americans, besides operating the line, rebuilt some twenty miles of the 111 miles of track and maintained the rest of it. They added new equipment, including several steam engines purchased from the Denver and Rio Grande Western and shipped up from Colorado. The White Pass became so efficient, her chuffing engines pulling miles of small flatcars over the high mountain pass, that in 1943 alone she packed 22,000 passengers and 284,532 tons of freight. The railroad averaged 40,000 tons a month that year. She even packed in a whole refinery from Texas for the CANOL project in Whitehorse so that crude oil piped down from the CANOL oil field at Norman Wells might be processed on the spot.

Her heavy workload seems the more remarkable when one realizes that the railway climbs from sea level at Skagway to 2,900 feet only 20 miles away, that the grade is 4 percent, the curves going into Carcross 22 degrees.

Ships and boats for carrying supplies and equipment to the ports at Valdez and Skagway were often unavailable, and Generals Hoge and O'Connor got headaches from trying to keep the matériel flowing. At times the lack of available ship bottoms held up the construction regiments altogether, and the commanding officers had to fly to Seattle to straighten the troubles out. Communications between Whitehorse and Seattle seemed sometimes to break down altogether. When the first QMC truck company arrived at Skagway without any equipment, signal operators sent messages frantically to Seattle saying that no equipment was stored at Skagway and that no other truck company was to be sent without subsistence supplies or heavy equipment. Shortly, however, the second truck company arrived unequipped. More radio messages hummed toward Seattle threatening consequences calculated to whiten the liver of any soldier, captain, or stevedore if a truck company, scheduled to sail in two weeks, should arrive without supplies. Three weeks later the truck company steamed into Skagway without wheels, bedding, food, or mess equipment. Officers simply assigned the men to an old airplane hangar for shelter until their equipment at last arrived. One anonymous soldier with a typewriter and a sense of humor wrote of Skagway in the spring of 1942:

> Another example of the unthinking way in which this Sector was supplied occurred in May, at a time when practically no construction equipment had as yet been received. Numerous requests had been made for this equipment to be expedited, because each day's delay in the receipt of a bull-dozer, or a grader, reduced the chances of completing the construction during the season. At this time, a boat arrived at Skagway carrying 45 tons of Coca-Cola, 45 tons of beer, several hundred tons of coal, and several hundred cords of slab wood. Since the coal was not needed, it was left in Skagway, and later turned over to the White Pass Railway, and to Chilkoot Barracks. The slab wood, undoubtedly, is still in Skagway.

The 18th Engineers had to build tote road 300 miles from Whitehorse to the Alaska border during the summer. Since the country they were to cross was the worst the North could offer, the troops had to have their machines and tools at the earliest possible moment. Every hour counted. The regiment had arrived in Skagway early in April. They moved to Whitehorse and bivouacked on the bluff west of town. Weeks passed. They did some preliminary locating and clearing west of Whitehorse, but full operation stood still. In mid-May General Hoge himself flew to Seattle. There he discovered that the bulldozers, graders, cranes, carryalls, and trucks lined the docks and harborside storage yards because ships and other equipment for moving them could not be found.

Hoge went to E. W. Elliott, a construction expert and an Annapolis graduate, who knew all about boats. "If there is no commercial transportation available," Elliott is supposed to have said earlier, "then there is only one thing to do and that is to make it ourselves. If there are no large boats obtainable, then we will have to use small boats." Elliott and his company agreed to move immediately as much equipment as they could. They had in fact already thought of the possibilities, for Elliott had proposed to the Public Roads Administration in March to transport construction supplies to Skagway and Valdez. His operations had begun in April with a tiny fleet of three tugs and a few barges which moved up the Inland Passage—inside the islands of the British Columbian coast—from Prince Rupert, where port facilities were not as jammed as they were in Puget Sound, and where loads could arrive overland on the Canadian National Railway. Shortly, however, Elliott established new southern terminals at Tacoma and Lake Union. The Tacoma docks were to be used for the tug- and barge-towing equipment, and the Lake Union facilities for another project Elliott had created—transporting civilian workmen to the North for the Public Roads Administration. Immediately, Elliott began increasing the size of his fleet by purchasing whatever tugs, barges, yachts, and small boats he could locate. General Hoge in the meantime placed an army major in charge of balancing the shipments of equipment from Seattle. Hoge gave the major a staff and office space and ordered him to check all shipments, to expedite especially the moving of heavy construction equipment, to work closely with Captain Terry, Hoge's supply officer at Skagway, and to see to it that all shipments were appropriately balanced. "For example," the major was ordered, "if there are 15 air compressors and 15 gas shovels awaiting shipment and it is only possible to ship one half of the total, an equal amount of both air compressors and shovels should be shipped." Hoge wanted no more jams, unbalanced shipments, or loads of coal and slab wood.

Elliott rapidly increased the size of his fleet. He bought up several elegant pleasure yachts and converted them for transporting workmen. The yachts included such classics as *Sueja III*, flagship of the Pacific All-Coast Regatta held at San Francisco in 1925; *Holiday*, a former Los Angeles yacht; *Alician*; *Westward*; and *Caroline*. He outfitted four tugs from Puget Sound—*Iroquois*, *Highway*, *Redondo*, and *S. H. Finch*—and six Canadian tugs—*Sea King*, *Sea Wave*, *Cheerful*, *Daly*, *Pachena*, and *Snohomish*. He added three freighters: *Eastern Prince*, *Donna Lane*, *Superior*; a schooner, *Daylight*; a barge, *Scottish Lady*; and several other barges and scows. Carpenters thought of everything possible to increase the carrying capacity of the fleet. They stripped away all the conveniences and most of the trim from the yachts. Mahogany and teak woodwork had to go. Workmen boarded-in deck space once used for guests, who had lounged, cocktails in hand, and watched the blue seas roll by. Elliott's men used the space for more bunks and added cooking and washing facilities. Pleasure yachts once used for parties of six or eight could now carry thirty to forty people. While Elliott used his heavier craft for the route outside the shoreline islands to Valdez, the lighter ones ran to Skagway and Haines inside the islands. Elliott's little fleet got most of the needed equipment to the 18th Engineers before the end of May so that they were able to begin their push toward Kluane Lake, Burwash, and the border by early summer. He continued to carry for the Public Roads Administration as the war went on.

For protection, Elliott's fleet and the other ships and boats bound for Alaska and the Yukon had "Parker's Navy." In 1940 after military leaders activated the Alaskan Defense Command, the United States Navy created an Alaskan sector headquartered at Seattle and commanded by Capt. Ralph C. Parker. At first Captain Parker commanded little but paper and a few sailors. He did get a gunboat, the *Charleston*, as headquarters "flagship." Soon he purchased three small fishing boats which he converted to patrol craft. By May 1942, six months after the Japanese had grabbed the power in the Pacific, "Parker's Navy" consisted of two destroyers, three Coast Guard cutters, ten Catalinas, and an assortment of doctored fishing boats. The *Charleston* was the only one of the vessels with sonar and with guns larger than 3-inch. She and the other boats ran day and night escorting freighters, tugs, barges, and yachts packing construction workers and equipment for the work in the North. Never was there a more dedicated, harder working, or more fortunate "navy." Parker's command did not have to tangle with the Japanese. "The set-up offered unusual opportunities for enemy submarines," wrote Samuel Eliot Morison, "but, as if in answer to prayer, the big Japanese I-boats confined themselves to reconnaissance."

With all these supply problems and with the extremes of weather and distance under which the engineers had to labor in the summer of 1942, it is clearly a wonder that they were able to open the road by early winter at all. When they did open the pioneer highway, it was not a good road. It was certainly a crooked one. Still, the Alcan was passable for military traffic: that was the objective the Corps had intended to achieve. The fact that the highway was passable amazed the Canadians. The fact that it was a crooked road built with so much hard work across such a large wilderness produced a characteristic humor and certain myths about the plan of construction which still persist. More than anything else the pressure of time made the road what it was.

Earl Bartlett

They were great for humor; in an isolated place you have to be. The Americans took signs and put them up in all sorts of places they shouldn't be. They pulled one off a beverage bottle and pasted it on the toilet door, and it says, "NO DEPOSIT, NO RETURN." A water truck had a big sign on it, "NO SMOKING WITHIN FIFTY FEET." There was a grader screeching along in the dust with a sign on it, "HOSPITAL ZONE, QUIET PLEASE." A Caterpillar lumbering along the road says, "ALL VISITORS MUST REGISTER HERE." The one I think I enjoyed the most was the one they got off a mess hall, had it hung on a garbage truck. It says, "POSITIVELY NO MEALS SERVED TO TRANSIENTS."

George Nelms

[The road is crooked.] There are places where you'll drive along now and you'll say: "Now what in the world did they ever make this road so blamed crooked for?" . . .

[Of course there are theories about that. One is that they had to make it crooked] so if the Japs came over they couldn't strafe it. . . . Another story is [that] they had engineers . . . just learning then . . . and why anybody, you know, can look through a survey instrument and [go straight. But] they had to put their curves in, get experience and all this kind of stuff. But in actual fact the reason that it is like that . . . was on account of drainage. They were . . . starting out in virgin timber and bush, and they didn't have any drainage. . . . They were dodging potholes and . . . creeks . . . as best they could. So, say, to go from A to B, which would normally be one mile, maybe they had to go a mile and a half, but it was quicker to do that mile and a half than it would have been to have done the straight mile through. And the same way with a lot of their grades. . . . They didn't have the time or the equipment [to get proper gradients]. . . .

CHAPTER NINE

Ruffles and Flourishes

THE OFFICIAL opening ceremony of the pioneer highway took place at Soldiers Summit above Kluane Lake on November 20, 1942. There would be other ceremonies—for the "completion" of the highway a year later by PRA and Canadian contractors, for the change of hands from the American to the Dominion government after the end of the war, and for the changeover from the command of the Royal Canadian Army to Canadian civilians still later—but this was clearly the most striking of all. It was a cold winter day. Snow lay everywhere in the spruce forest. Kluane Lake below in the distance seemed to steam and smoke, its deep waters unfrozen. The great peaks of the St. Elias Range bordered the country in ice to the south and west. Glacial Slim's River flowed immediately to the south, the pioneer road winding up the ridge to Soldiers Summit from the river crossing. Northward up the lake were Destruction Bay and Burwash Landing. Just below the ceremony site was a trapper's log cabin, already old (still standing and covered with the dust of the new road in 1973). A snow-covered island lay out in the lake directly in front of the speakers' stand.

A handful of the soldiers and PRA men who had built the road, an army band, a detachment of Mounties, and several military and civilian dignitaries were there. Col. K. B. Bush was the master of ceremonies. Gen. James A. O'Connor, Commanding Officer of the Northwest Service Command, spoke for the United States Army Corps of Engineers. Minister Ian Mackenzie represented Prime Minister Mackenzie King. E. L. Bartlett, Secretary of State for Alaska, read a message for the Governor and the citizens of the Territory, and District Engineer J. S. Bright spoke for the Public Roads Administration and its civilian contractors. The celebration had begun the night before with a dinner in the best army style. The cooks provided all the delicacies they could find, and they gave them appropriate names, the names of places familiar to the soldiers and civilian workers who had opened the pioneer road. The menu for the dinner on the nineteenth and the breakfast on the twentieth lists such things as St. Elias Mountain Sheep, Takhini Corn, Nabesna Peas, Tanana Potatoes, Slim's River Salad, Chisana Apple Sauce, Aishihik Sausage, Dezadeash Eggs, Champagne Soup, Pickhandle Beans, and Horse Camp Pudding.

On the morning of the twentieth, the celebrants moved outside to Soldiers Summit, named for the troops who had labored on the tote road. The army band waited in the cold, the musicians trying to keep their instruments warm. Two or three dogs wandered here and there. Journalists were not permitted to quote temperatures, and the speakers' voices shook, often very noticeably. Most of the speeches were patriotic; they were too long for those who had to wait in the freezing weather. But men opening an international highway in the names of their countries, especially if they themselves have worked on it, must be forgiven long-windedness. Occasionally an original thought or impression came through. These were practical men who had been consumed with the building of the road and with other wartime affairs, men who had had little time for contemplation. Yet the speeches reflected the sentiments of diverse peoples and nations who had labored together very hard under the pressures of war. And they reflected some knowledge of all the efforts—both the failures and the triumphs—which had preceded the work of the American and Canadian builders of the Alcan Highway across this land, a knowledge of the early explorers and the trappers who had pioneered this wilderness, the last on the North American continent. Some of the speakers seemed both sad and happy about that fact—glad that they had had a part in building the road, sorry that the real pioneering had ended for America and Canada, that engineers had spanned the last wilderness. The official opening ceremony, then, was both a monument to the humanity which had for so many years tried, failed, tried again, and finally won in the complex effort to build permanent trails across the North, and a memorial to the dying wilderness itself.

Canadian Broadcasting Corporation men J. Frank Willis and

Peter Stersberg broadcast the opening ceremonies from Soldiers Summit on the twentieth. Following is a selection from a recording of the actual broadcast:

Frank Willis: Ladies and gentlemen, I am speaking to you from an improvised control room in the rear of an American army truck parked away up here on the Soldiers Summit, the high pass on the Canada-Alaska Highway, and where at this moment some hundred yards from my vantage point, the official opening of this great road is taking place. In the belief that this occasion is making history, we have traveled over three thousand miles in order to bring you the official remarks in connection with the opening. Others too have made the long trek to Soldiers Summit. I would say that there are about three hundred persons in all gathered around the speaker's stand. They are, for the most part, soldiers and civilian road workers from nearby camps, but, too, there are a good many civic and military dignitaries. As Colonel K. B. Bush of the United States Army Corps of Engineers . . . said in his opening remarks, "We who are gathered here in this imposing wilderness today are but the symbols of the countless thousands who have made this undertaking possible." And what an undertaking it has been! Surely this road will rank for all time among the greatest engineering feats the world has ever seen. From Dawson Creek to Fairbanks in Alaska, a distance of 1,650 miles, American Army Engineers have punched through this highway at the blitzkrieg speed of eight miles a day.

The scenery along the highway is unsurpassed in grandeur. The towering Rocky Mountains are on all sides. The mighty rivers of the northland wind their way along the route—the Liard . . . and the fabled Yukon. But of all the beauty spots to be found, this opening ceremony is taking place in quite the most arresting. From the Soldiers Summit we are looking down on the blue-green waters of Lake Kluane, surrounded by the white ramparts of peaks that tower ten thousand feet above us. Kluane waters are too deep to freeze, but they're steaming and smoking in the cold, and the lake glows like an emerald in a setting of gigantic diamonds. It's bitter cold here today. . . . I can tell you that all of us up here envy all of you by your firesides out there.

It's a very colorful scene. . . . On either side of the dividing tape that is symbolic of the Yukon-Alaska border fly the Stars and the Stripes and the Union Jack. On the Canadian side of the line, we have a detachment of the Royal Canadian Mounted Police—the real soldiers of this frontier land—and on the Alaska side are the American troops standing smartly to attention with their parka hoods done up and their skis at the present. . . .

[Colonel Bush introduces E. L. Bartlett who speaks, then presents an Alaskan flag to the Corps. The colonel introduces General O'Connor.]

James A. O'Connor: We are witnessing the breakthrough of the road joining the United States, Canada, and Alaska. . . . It is also the end of the pioneering, the romance of the pioneering of the road. . . .

This highway, stretching from Dawson Creek on the British Columbia–Alberta line to Fairbanks in the core of Alaska, is a real and unique tie between our countries. . . . For those who have become acquainted with the land through which the highway passes, with its forests, rivers, mountains, plateaus, words alone are not impressive. . . .

The history of this section of the Dominion is new to me, new and entrancing. . . . There were gold seekers who crossed the icy passes of the Yukon . . . , the bold farmers who first plowed the northwestern Canadian plains, the trappers who explored the magnificent Caribou Region, and back a little further Alexander Mackenzie and Fraser and others whose feats of exploration in Canada match . . . the deeds of our . . . main American explorers. Knowledge of this . . . past makes us of the . . . American army more proud than ever that we have been privileged to build the Alcan Highway on Canadian ground. . . . For those who have had a share in its construction, the Alcan Highway will be an indelible memory. . . .

Colonel Bush: I have in my hands a pair of scissors specially engraved for this historic occasion. On each blade, in plates of genuine Alaskan gold, has been inscribed: "Dedication, Alcan International Highway, November 20, 1942." After the conclusion of this ceremony, the blades of the scissors will be parted. One blade will be sent to President Franklin D. Roosevelt for the National Archives of the United States, the other to Prime Minister King for the National Archives of Canada. Mr. Mackenzie and Mr. Bartlett, as representatives of the two vast lands linked permanently together by this road, will now cut the ribbon which symbolizes the opening of the Alcan Highway.

Peter Stersberg: Mr. Mackenzie and Mr. Bartlett are stepping over to the red, white, and blue ribbon which is stretched across the highway just in front of the speakers' stand. The ends of the ribbon are held by four of the American soldiers who built the highway. They are Sergeant Major Sharp, a Negro soldier, and Private Alfred [Alfunce] Jalufka of Kenedy, Texas, who are from the Northern Sector of the road, and Master Sergeant Andrew E. Doyle of Philadelphia and Corporal John T. Riley of Detroit . . . representing the southern end of the road.

[Here handclaps and cheers break in, a dog barks several times, and the band plays "God Save the King" and "Stars and Stripes Forever."]

Peter Stersberg: They've cut the ribbon. The Alaska-Canada Highway
is now officially open.

In their talk of the harmony, the "tie," between the two national
governments, O'Connor and the other speakers left much unsaid.
There had been throughout the 1930s a great deal of disharmony
between the United States and the Dominion over the proposed
road to Alaska. Since the late 1920s various Canadian and American figures had tried vigorously to achieve the authorization,
funding, and construction of the international highway, but without
success. The story of these political efforts and failures is an
important part of the history of the Alaska Highway. Some of the
men who had long wanted to build the road saw their dreams
fulfilled; and others saw their dreams frustrated on November 20.
The harmony, such as it was, had been finally hammered together
under the circumstances of the war. In the background, too, as
General O'Connor suggested, were the earlier trail builders. There
were men who had traveled by dog team, steamboat, packhorse,
and bush plane, men who had done much to open the wilderness, to
map it, so that the engineers in 1942 could work with some sense of
the lay of the land. The history of these other pioneers is important.
There remains, also, the story of the actual completion of the
modern Alaska Highway during and after World War II and of its
peacetime uses.

PART 2

I divide the Yukon into two eras, as far as people, and communications, and roads are concerned. The first era was the time from about 1887 to the building of the highway, and this was the time when there were no roads. There was a winter stagecoach road . . . but that was all. The *River* was the highway, and everybody lived on that highway. The woodcutters, the trappers, the prospectors, the traders, little trading posts. That's where everybody lived. And then when the highway was built, very soon thereafter, this ended. When the war ended, the ships [Yukon River steamboats] were all tied up. That was the end. It was dead. It was an era that I must say I liked much better than the present one. *You never worried about time then, you know. You went down the River, you got there when you arrived. The people who were a part of that were very different from the people who are a part of the highway. . . . It was a romantic era.*

> Alan Innes–Taylor, F.R.G.S., Whitehorse, Y.T., summer, 1970.

CHAPTER TEN

Hard as Hell to Get To

THE STORY of the Alaska Highway and of east-west travel across the North began long before 1942. Trails across Alaska and the Yukon are as ancient as human life on the North American continent itself. Hunters came first. Men killing for meat tracked animals across the land bridge from Siberia into Alaska thousands of years ago, and there is evidence that long before the men came, warm-blooded animals browsed the North for millions of years. The animals and the men who hunted them traveled the banks of the Yukon and Mackenzie rivers just as the soldiers of 1942 would do. Flints, firepits, and dumps of mammoth and big-horned bison bones mark the ancient campsites along the trails which finally converged near the modern city of Edmonton. From there the trails rayed out southward over the North American continent.

In a more recent time, men built trails, or dreamed of building them, across the North and Alaska. There were the fur trails of the Northwesters in the early nineteenth century, trails opened into Athabasca and New Caledonia by men like Pond, Mackenzie, Fraser, and Thompson. These men, too, followed the waterways. They traveled by canoe wherever possible and portaged overland. After the Northwest Company merged with the Hudson's Bay Company in 1821, the Bay even won a large chunk of the Alaska trade—between 1839 and 1867—through leases with Russia and by the illegal operation of a major post at the junction of the Porcupine and Yukon rivers in Alaska. The lasting accomplishments of the Hudson's Bay Company were the exploration and mapping of the Canadian northwest and part of interior Alaska, the development of trade centers, and a system of transportation—knowledge, organization, and equipment invaluable to the settlers, miners, bush flyers, and road builders of a later day.

The gold rushes and the trails they sprouted happened well after the middle of the nineteenth century. There were numerous strikes around Sitka and on the upper Yukon and its headwaters in the seventies and eighties. The first big strike in Alaska happened in 1880 on a creek flowing into one of the narrow, deep-blue, fjordlike channels of the Panhandle. Soon there were more strikes in the same vicinity, miners rushed in, the news spread. Juneau City—earlier called Pilzburg, Fliptown, Rockwell, and Harrisburg—mushroomed. Not until the last decade of the century, however, did the really fantastic strike occur—the Klondike, the strike that created one of the maddest human rushes of all time and opened up the Alcan country to heavy travel.

In the summer of 1896, George Washington Carmack, Skookum Jim, and Tagish Charlie struck gold and staked a claim on Rabbit Creek above the Klondike River. Within weeks miners rushed in from camps at Forty-mile, Sixty-mile, Circle City, and Eagle. A tent city bellied at the junction of the Klondike and Yukon rivers. By midsummer, 1897, newspapers outside headlined the big news, and the rush, reported to amount to as many as 60,000 people, was on. Men renamed Rabbit Creek the Bonanza, the whole country the Klondike. People were either going to it or coming out. It was a place where everything happened big—rivers, mountains, lakes, snows, riches, failure, bunkum. There were mountains of blue snow with iceworms that ate each other's tails (till just the tough survived), there were rivers that ran uphill, days when the sun rose in the west, cold that shot the mercury shivering to the bottom of the tube and froze it there solid till spring. Its wealth in folklore and folk poetry—it was Robert Service country—says more for the Klondike's human wealth and drama than all the millions in gold ever carried out on river steamers. The Klondike was above all a state of mind fixed on a piece of bush country hard as hell to get to, but a place worth going to if you could arrive in time to get rich on gold. It was a spree—a binge of imaginations—that spilled over and enlivened the northern mind and economy for years to come. It caused the rapid development of the ports at Skagway, Whitehorse, and Dawson City and of ways of getting in and out—steamboat travel and a fantastic narrow-gauge railway, the White Pass and Yukon, which would be so important in the building of the Alcan Highway. Within two or three years the gold seekers spread all over Alaska, toward more big strikes at Nome and in the Tanana Valley. The gold rush, Ernest Gruening wrote, "attracted the great capitalists as well as the fly-by-night. It brought Alaska for the first time to the ken of millions of Americans."

To get to the Klondike you went by one of three main routes, all excessively costly. One was by ship to the mouth of the Yukon River on the Bering Sea in Alaska, then by steamboat upriver nearly 1,000 miles to Dawson City, the strike center. That was longer but probably safer and certainly easier than the others— over the coastal range from Skagway via White Pass, or from Dyea (pronounced "Die-ee") over Chilkoot Pass. If you took one of the mountain routes overland (some died working their way up the steep, icy, snow-filled passes, while more abandoned their gear and turned back), you had to expect a 300-mile trip from Whitehorse by boat or raft down the Yukon River to Dawson City.

Men tried other routes. One followed the Athabasca and Slave rivers from north of Edmonton to Great Slave Lake, where passengers took a steamboat down the Mackenzie. (This would become one of the main routes used to reach the CANOL oil field at Norman Wells in the 1940s.) The Royal Northwest Mounted Police also attempted to open an overland trail from Edmonton in the early days. Some of the Klondike gold hunters had tried to go to Peace River Landing, from there northwest through the bush to the Liard and Frances rivers, then down the Pelly and the Yukon to Dawson City. It was a thousand miles from Edmonton to the Pelly through the roughest kind of back country. To try to make the trip overland from Edmonton possible, the Mounted Police sent out a patrol in 1897 to find and to blaze the best way. Inspector Moodie, patrol leader, reported the best route to be through Fort St. John, Fort Graham, Findlay River, and Sylvester's Landing to Teslin Lake and from there to Dawson City. (The Alaska Highway runs through Fort St. John and Teslin, though its route between these distant points does not follow Moodie's.) A few years later the Mounties actually set out to cut the old Peace River–Yukon Trail to Dawson. Superintendent Constantine with two officers and thirty noncoms and constables began clearing a swath supposed to be 8 feet wide and clearly marked with blazes in the timber and with lines of posts across the muskeg. There were to be log shelters every 30 miles, theoretically at the end of each normal day's travel. Although the trail was open by late 1907, the rush to Dawson City had ebbed, and the police trail was still a much more difficult and time-consuming way to go than either of the main routes. Hence, it rapidly fell into disuse, and all traces of it long ago disappeared.

Most of the people who did attempt the trip from Edmonton never got very far. Ingenious inventions for carrying supplies and equipment suggest the energy and imagination of the Army Corps of Engineers and the PRA men who marched through Edmonton in 1942 and 1943. At the height of the rush, gold seekers rolled into the city at the rate of twenty to thirty parties per train, with trains arriving three a week. Men camped all over town, in the empty lots and in the fields. Horse-drawn sleds and carts, packing up for the trip north, crowded the streets. Imaginations fevered with visions of gold and riches, the men thought up all kinds of contraptions for the long haul north. The dreamers displayed more energy than good sense. One man had a barrel with shafts attached. His idea was to pack the barrel with his provisions, fit himself between the shafts, and roll the barrel across the bush to the Klondike. An American party built a steam engine on rollers to pull a string of sleds. Another had a combination boat-sleigh. Runners for use in the bush, a hull on top, the whole rig was to be turned over and floated across lakes and down rivers. A group from England brought horses with them and shipped their hay all the way from home. Wild hay grows belly deep for miles across the North.

Few of those who finally got to Dawson or to the other strike centers ever made it rich on gold. Only the fortunate or especially persistent did. Some of the talented made it on other things—supplying hopeful miners or setting up in a needed but often unglamorous business. A business that flourished and lasted for a long time, one that was important to the Corps of Engineers in 1942, was the business of steamboating. Steamboats adapted to the navigable streams of the North which branched out into the bush from the major rivers—the Yukon, the Mackenzie, the Athabasca, the Slave. Steamers unloaded and took on cargo—groceries, trappers' supplies, fur bales, construction equipment, gas, oil, and even airplane parts—right down to the end of World War II. The U.S. Army hired White Pass and Yukon steamboats in 1942 to haul men and machinery up Lake Laberge and Teslin water to Morley Bay Camp, just as they hired the services of the White Pass and Yukon Railway to bring supplies to Whitehorse from the seaport of Skagway.

After the war the old steamers tied up and smaller vessels, powered by gas or diesel engines, took over. But the river trails the boats walked, the shipping centers they sprouted, and the knowledge their pilots and owners acquired remained indispensable to people living in the bush. In many ways it was the steamboat which brought the North from the fur age into the age of mining and oil and the age of the bush plane, the truck, the bulldozer, and the Alaska Highway.

Flowers for the Wedding

AFTER WORLD WAR I aircraft were the quickest means of reaching the isolated villages and towns of the far north. In all seasons of the year, they could fly light cargo and passengers to points practically out of touch with the world except by radio. Besides their commercial uses, airplanes could be used for government surveys and forest patrols. Mining companies could use them for exploration. In 1932, the Eldorado radium mine used thirty-two planes at Great Bear Lake, 800 miles from end of steel. The aircraft made the flight to railhead in from 1 to 1 1/2 days, a trip that required two or three weeks by boat. Anyone going anywhere in a hurry in the 1920s and 1930s in the North had a clear need for airplanes, and they soon became not a luxury at all, but a necessity. Doctors, teachers, nurses, policemen, and critically ill people hurried in and out by air. Every northern villager has his story of the life that was saved by the speed with which a bush plane flew the sick person outside to the nursing station or the hospital. Without aircraft and northern airways, the Alcan Highway could not have been punched through in the single working season of 1942.

Before 1930 there were only sporadic commercial services flying the North. But by the mid 1930s, regular air schedules began to emerge. Canadian Airways, founded by Canada's great James Richardson, and Brintnell's Mackenzie Air Service, fought bitterly for control of flight operations down the Mackenzie River from Fort McMurray on the Athabasca River north of Edmonton to Aklavik on the Arctic Ocean. In all 1,676 miles of flying, 300 of it inside the Arctic Circle. The absolutely essential air route for the construction of the Alaska Highway, however, was the one mapped by the Dominion government in the mid 1930s and opened shortly thereafter by Grant McConachie and his United Air Transport, soon renamed Yukon Southern Air Transport, Ltd. Known affectionately as "Yukon Seldom," and probably often called that out of exasperation, McConachie's tiny fleet shuttled between Edmonton and Whitehorse year-round in all kinds of weather. To the Canadians who lived along the Yukon Southern air route or who used its services, and later to the men of the Army Corps of Engineers, McConachie's pilots were all well known. People called them by their first names. Ted Field, Ralph Oakes, Sheldon Luck, Ernie Kubicek, Charlie Tweed, Aleck Dame, Scotty Moir, Bob Goldie, Don "Smokey" Patry. The regular stops these pilots made were later developed by the Canadian and U.S. governments into the air bases of the Northwest Staging Route, that air route over which lend-lease aircraft flew to Russia and for whose service the Alcan Highway was largely built. The Yukon Southern route was a genuine pioneer airway.

Jack Baker

J. W. Baker was the first United Air Transport agent at Watson Lake, one of the regular stops on Grant McConachie's line. By 1942 and 1943 Watson Lake had developed into one of the main Northwest Staging Route fields along the Alcan Highway. The following selection is from a letter written by Jack Baker, 28 March 73.

The northern bush pilots were heroes to all of us trappers on the Mackenzie. Later (1938) I was running a trading post at Fort Liard N.W.T. when I met Grant McConachie for the first time. I agreed to open a station for him at Watson Lake so he could show the postal authorities he had a continuous depot system from Edmonton to Whitehorse each approx. 200 miles apart, i.e., Grande Prairie, Fort St. John [Charlie Lake], Fort Nelson, Watson Lake & Whitehorse. Each station carried fuel, was radio equipped and reported weather. Watson L. was the most difficult to service, being so remote. Log buildings and primitive accommodations. I hewed the logs with a broadaxe and whipsawed lumber by hand, tended radio and learned Morse, took weather observations 3 times daily, cooked for crews and passengers when they laid over etc. etc.

Being a bush pilot in the 1930s required an unusual amount of intelligence, experience, tactile skill, and instinct for the air.

Having to fly without the aid of modern radio, pilots developed skills that could do what the radio would later partly do for them. They literally hand-flew the aircraft by levers hooked up to cables and pulleys. Weather forecasts were primitive. A pilot who took off from Watson Lake on a clear afternoon might find Whitehorse under banks of cloud and rain. There were no modern radio beams and no modern landing fields in the far north. Pilots landed on the river at Fort Nelson and on the lake at Watson, on water in the summer and ice in the winter. They maintained contact with the station they had just left and with the one ahead by radioing every fifteen or twenty minutes.

Flyers watched landmarks on the ground below. They flew by line of sight. When a pilot heading north signed off after calling back to Watson Lake regularly, it meant he was preparing to land at Whitehorse, that the flight had gone well to that point. If the depot at Whitehorse was socked in, the flyer simply had to find his own way down, relying entirely upon his experience, his feel for the air and the weather, and upon the tiny craft with whose habits he was so intimately acquainted. There was little anyone could do to help him out in the last moments before touchdown when, breaking out from under the low rain cloud, he would see his port a few hundred feet ahead and below if he were right on course, if his knowledge and his instincts had been correct. Then with a bump the plane would be down, and everyone knew the flight had ended at that very instant. Frozen attention turned to thoughts of earth—hot bath, waiting family, winter trapline, a glass of beer, and dinner at the Whitehorse Inn.

Landings like that, in rain or snow, may not have been the routine ones. There were probably more hours spent aloft in clear weather than ones spent in bad weather with poor flying conditions. The point about these bush flyers is that they were supremely able when good weather turned sour and when normally dependable machines suddenly crumbled. Few, if any, pilots flew for many months without meeting a crisis. When they did, the whole North was with them.

Lodema George

Mrs. Arthur George was the wife of a free trader at Fort Nelson in the 1930s. She was the postmistress and handled the mail, which came in once a week when McConachie's service first began.

I remember . . . one night Sheldon Luck radioed in. . . . [He was on his way to] St. John. There was a dance or something, and he wanted to go to it, and he couldn't make it. His engine, something happened to his engine, and he radioed in and he said,

"I've got to come back to Nelson." He said, "Light up the ice."

Well, no one had electric power. . . . They had no night flying at all then. . . . It was all gas lamps, and everybody took gas lamps and they strung them on each side of the river so he could come in. And when he got in—the engine would catch fire—and [the fire] would come toward him and he'd go down, then he'd come up. And he followed every crook and turn of the river to get into Nelson. And that plane never flew again. They tried to take the engine out, and it just sort of welded in. It was just a total wreck. I don't know what happened, but poor Sheldon. His face was all oil and everything else. And that was an exciting night. Everybody was listening. Everybody was out on the ice. Everybody that had a gas lamp went down, and they strung them out on the ice for him so that he could tell where to land. . . .

Following is an account by Lodema George of Sheldon Luck's near crash on a Liard River bar. It differs somewhat from Jack Baker's account, written in a letter. The two complement each other, although Baker's account is the more precisely detailed and accurate because he was the Yukon Southern radioman talking to Sheldon from Watson Lake.

Lodema George

There was [another bad time] and that was Sheldon Luck again. He was lucky too! This was down on the Liard. There was some woman was sick. . . . And I don't know, I couldn't tell you what happened, but I happened to be over to the radio station when Chris was getting the message you see, and Sheldon said, "I'm having to land on [a bar]." And he said, "Keep your fingers crossed and pray." He said, "I'm landing on this bar and it's not very long."

And of course everybody was listening all up and down the [line]. You know, some of them had their radios so they could tune in on these. And I forget now just what it was, but he made some remark and he said, "Well," he said, "I think God was with us." He said, "The wheels are just out of the water."

Then they had to send another plane in right away that day to pick up this woman and bring her out. They sent in a smaller one. . . . But they managed. I don't know, those pilots were all very resourceful.

Jack Baker

Sheldon Luck and co-pilot Stan Emery were flying the return passenger and mail run from Whitehorse to Fort St. John. June 1939. It was an

8-passenger twin-engine Barkley-Grow, pride of the Yukon Southern Air Transport fleet, CF-BMG.

Sheldon had just crossed the Wolf Range, eastbound when he radioed in to Watson Lake—that was me at Watson—, "Watson Lake, an oil line has just blown up in my right engine. Will try to maintain altitude on one engine." Later he called again: "Watson Lake, BMG is over the Liard west of Lower Post, unable to maintain altitude on one engine, will have to pick a sand bar to land on very soon. I'm going in on the first good bar. Will call before landing."

Then shortly after: "Watson Lake, we're going in on a bar. Not much room and must make the landing at first go. Will call you on fixed antenna if it goes okay, but if you don't hear from us again we're in trouble." I call back: "Good luck, BMG." Shortly afterward to my relief, BMG called on fixed, and reported all okay. Sheldon swore a blasphemous oath, as his system shook off the keyed up emotions.

I immediately messaged Fort St. John for a relief aircraft. They were able to despatch Aleck Dame in a Waco seaplane. Aleck got in that evening and landed on the river by the bar, where he was able to ferry passengers and crew to Watson Lake, and safety. Later the company sent repairs and a mechanic to patch up the oil line, and Sheldon with Stan was barely able to fly the empty Barkley-Grow off the bar and back to base at Fort St. John.

Of all the northern bush pilots, Les Cook was probably the most widely known and admired by the men of the U.S. Army Corps of Engineers and the PRA. He was not a Yukon Southern pilot, but flew instead out of Carcross for Northern Airways, near the very center of the military highway construction project. Les had flown the North for several years before the Corps of Engineers arrived, and he probably knew its country and its weather conditions as well as any other man. During the summer and fall of 1942 he made many flights for the U.S. government precisely because he was so supremely able. Les flew food, mail, emergency equipment, and medical doctors to wherever they were urgently needed. He died in a crash at Whitehorse in December 1942. The 340th Engineers called him "a friend to the entire . . . Regiment" and placed a large black-and-white picture of him with the Norseman in which he died in their regimental history. Norm Harlin, who flew many hours with Les Cook, had become a close friend.

Norman Harlin

I started to tell you about Les at Schilsky Lake. He picked me up one time, had to go into Whitehorse, and he was flying a Norseman, and he had been flying old Fairchilds, even an old Fokker. And we were talkin' about flappin' machines. . . . He had a brand new Norseman, and . . . , "At last," he says, "I've finally got an airplane."

And it was only six months later that he was killed, with that same airplane. Oh yes. Les? I knew him well.

For bush flying you couldn't beat him. He knew the country and he'd go anyplace. Within reason. And he flew us into the trapline . . . twice every year. Once to take us in, and once to bring us out. And that was in the remotest part of Canada I guess—in the Nahanni country.

And he changed a little. He got married, and he changed a little then because Lillian was home worryin' about him, especially when he made those trips into the backwoods. But in those days that *was* remote. . . . And there was always the possibility [there wouldn't be] enough gas to get back if he run into headwinds. But he never hesitated.

Usually [a spare can of gas for his return trip] had to be part of our load. See, it was a three-hundred-mile flight, and he'd insist on takin' some gas to top his tanks in there—security to get out.

Before he was married, he, for instance, we were trappin' on Coal River and he took us in there . . . and it was sixty below or so. And he just said, "To hell with it. We'll just stay here till it warms up." . . .

But after he got married, he wouldn't go if he thought he couldn't get home that night. And we used to kid him about it of course. . . . We knew his wife well too, an Atlin girl. . . .

They all had the same attitude. If the weather was bad, and they said, "Go," and you hesitated and said, "Do you think we can make it?"—like a three-hundred-mile trip into the backwoods—their answer was always the same: "My neck's just as important to me as yours is to you." And that's the way they got by. They knew they could do it, or they wouldn't go. . . . I mean, they knew what they were doin'. No problem.

He had I don't know how many thousand hours of bush work here, and most of it in old Fairchilds, and Fokkers—he had a Waco—all old haywire 'n fabric airplanes. But he was so used to the bush . . . he wouldn't go without his axe and his rifle and his sleepin' bag and a gas can [and a box] fulla grub. And that's the way they survived. They were down lotsa times. . . . This Barr—Frank Barr—he was forced down back here someplace one time, and he broke the prop on a sandbar— broke a piece off—so he took the prop off, and he whittled that much off the other end and put it back on and took all the seats and everything out and took off and got back to Juneau. . . .

They were pretty self-sufficient. They had to be.

Les Cook made many unusually difficult flights, some of them with much trouble and success. Little wonder that he was popular with the American army men and civilian construction workers for whom he often flew. Once a man became gravely ill at a camp on the Alcan Highway at the White River. He was too sick to be moved. The medical officer on the spot wired Whitehorse—nearly three hundred miles back—for surgeons and operating equipment. Les took off at night with two surgeons, flew the Norseman up over a blizzard, got lost among the St. Elias peaks fifty miles beyond the White, turned back down a glacier he knew had to feed a major river, and found the White River camp by the headlights of rows of trucks lining a gravel bar chosen for his landing.

The building of the Alaska Highway and the development of modern air transportation mark the near end of pioneer bush flying as one symbol of the strong community spirit in the old north. In 1923 the local people had built Anchorage's first airstrip. The men used teams and tractors, the women and children used rakes. They cleared together 16 acres of brush and stumps in a day. People labored together. They helped each other out in the old north and in the days when the Alcan Highway was being built. If there was nothing they could do but listen to a pilot in trouble over the radio and radiate good wishes or carry a gas lantern out to light up the ice for a night landing, they did those things without question. The isolation of the North was made tolerable by a strong community sense.

Lodema George

And we had a wedding there, or was going to have one, at our place. And this was . . . this must have been, it was right around April, the end of March, or April . . . and Sheldon Luck was pilot. . . . And there was flowers supposed to come in for this wedding. It was a girl from Edmonton. She was from quite a well-to-do family and [it was] a trader she was going to marry. So Chris [the radioman] asked if the flowers came off, and they said, "No."

And they radioed in to Sheldon, and he was forty-five miles out toward Watson Lake—he'd already left [Fort Nelson]—and they radioed in to him and they said, "Where are the flowers?"

He said, "What flowers?"

"The flowers for the wedding."

"Oh!" he said, "No flowers, no wedding."

They said, "Sure."

"Well," he said, "I'll come back."

And he turned around and came back and delivered those flowers! Those were the kind of early-day pilots. You couldn't do that now. They were a wonderful bunch of men, all of them.

CHAPTER TWELVE

How Far Is It to Lower Post?

DOGS WERE still the major means of transportation by land in the North when the Engineers and PRA contractors cut the Alcan Highway in the summer of 1942. Many of the survey parties for the pioneer tote road absolutely depended upon good teams, and the dogs were every American soldier's pets. Every dog-loving soldier and construction worker wanted to bring a husky pup home with him. Without dogs, transportation would have been slower and less certain than it was. In the winter it would have been impossible. The military highway ground surveys like those by the Curwen and Willesen parties would have been out of the question altogether, and the soldiers would have gone without these warm animal friends. Like the bush airplane, the working dog suggests many important things in the old north as well as the North in transition—absolutely certain transportation and companionship in the back country.

Vic Johnson of Watson Lake said in 1970 that he had stayed in the North because he didn't want to leave his dogs. Other old-timers will say about the same thing. Norman Harlin, for instance. How did a man keep off the loneliness when he was running a trapline by himself? He talked to his dogs, mainly in the evening after the day's work was done. If he didn't talk to them, they got to thinking something was wrong.

The friendship between northern dogs and men is as old and as real as the North itself. Other men have been as close to horses as northerners to their dogs. Plains Indians certainly were and so was the old Texas cowboy, but it would be hard to find anywhere in the history of the world an example of a man more completely dependent upon animals for work and companionship than the old northerner was upon his dogs. It is said that the snowmobile has "replaced" the dog team. In a sense it has, but only in a very limited sense. You cannot talk to it, it won't run on moose meat acquired anywhere in the bush, and it has a bad way of breaking down in the back country. Its motor is hard to start in cold weather. One northerner observed that dogs may have been slow, but they always got you where you were going. His statement suggests the strength of the bond between men and dogs, a bond completely lacking between man and snow machine. A good team running through the bush on a crackly cold, white winter morning, its musher breaking trail ahead or pushing along behind, is a photograph of a world that used to be. It is a daguerreotype of an important thing that is past.

First and last, the good northerner was a dog man. He could pick a promising pup. He lived with his dogs, judged them, trained them, worked them. The way he got along with them was a two-way thing. He respected them, and they respected him. For like the musher and the trapper, the dogs were free spirits. They willingly gave the man their work, their playfulness, their warm tongues, their howls and choruses, their simple sorrows, and their happiness because they liked him. If the mutual respect was not there, if the man tried to make the dogs work from fear of punishment, from kicks and cuffs, they did not work well, and they left him at their first opportunity.

Henry McLeod

Henry McLeod is a small, strong man, gentle with dogs. He homestead-ed on the Peace River in 1927 and packed groceries, oats, hay and general merchandise with bobsleds and freight racks from Fort St. John to Fort Nelson throughout the 1930s. The first of those pack trips he made in 1929 required a month and a half round trip for the estimated 680 miles. Now he can drive it in six or seven hours one way on the Alaska Highway. Then, he drove his teams on the river's ice. In the 1940s and 1950s the Canadian government hired him to run a wilderness survival school for military flyers who were to be flying across the North. In this story, Henry tells of the relationship between some of those soldiers and a dog they helped.

'Nother time I went out there—that same lake again—and went out there to this lake and one o' them trappers just turned his dog loose . . . and he was thin and he played him out and he just turned him loose there—there was a little village there, you know, two or three shacks—turned his dog loose there, and this poor dog was layin' there when we got out there—we had to go past these cabins—and so then . . . I seen this dog when I went by there, I was headin' for where we were gonna camp, to get things lined up. And so some of the [soldiers], they goes to work and they brings this dog along. They took the harness off him, and they give him, I don't know, one o' the guys I think he give him a piece of a chocolate bar or somethin', they had some in their pockets you know. So they brought this dog.

And one o' them, instead of packin' his pack, he brought a little, one of them little sleighs you know, one them kid's sleighs, he brought that along, and that's where he put his pack, and he dragged that instead of packin'. . . . He had a kind of a loop, he had it around his stomach. . . .

So, then, after a while they got feedin' this dog. We set nets like I said. . . . The fish were big there you know. . . . And we had all kinds o' fish, and good fish too. So then this dog he sure got fat on that. They fed him good, and they used to use him to haul their water up from the lake you know, drinkin' water and that, put it on this little sleigh. Gollies we sure [had fun]!

We had two dog teams, too, you see, and once in a while the priest here'd lend me his dog team, and to just let [those soldiers] drive the dogs, I'd let them drive mine, and I'd drive the priest's dogs. My dogs were kinda, you know, they were quiet and easy to handle and I'd be ahead of them and then they'd listen to me and they'd be drivin' dogs too. And oh they had quite a time out of everything. And they learned a lot.

But this one here with this dog. Then he was, oh he was fat and that, in that two weeks, you see, because I told them, I said, "Just feed him all he can eat."

And a dog will fatten up quick you know, especially when they've been hungry like that. So we fattened him up all right.

So then when we come back out, the trucks'd be there at a certain time to meet us when we git back out the [Alaska] Highway. And this guy used this dog, brought his pack out, drug his little sleigh too. So when the trucks pulled in there, it was dark when they got there, and this dog knew that they were leavin' him, and he'd jump right up into the truck.

And these [trappers] wanted him back now, so when we got to the highway, it was their dog you see. They took him home, they tied him up with a rope, and he chewed the rope off and he come back again, and he jumped right up into the truck. Yah, [those trappers] sure had quite a time to get him away from there. And these guys they just thought the world of it you know after it was so skinny! And he was, you know, he just got to like them. . . . Oh Lord knows what ever happened [to him].

In the talk of old northerners there are nearly subconscious references to dogs in every possible context and in every other breath. Get northerners to talking about the past, the times that ended with World War II and the Alaska Highway, and they are soon talking of dogs. The working dog is a part of the fabric of their thought, feeling, and life. He was everywhere in the North, and he is everywhere in northern memory. *Lodema George*: "We got by nicely. . . . And in the summertime, the trappers'd come in and they'd have all their dogs staked all over the fort. . . . You had to be a pretty good sleeper to not hear the dogs."

The most important thing a dog had to be was a hard worker. Life in the North had its business aspect. If a man could not make a living for himself and his family, he had to die or leave the country. Particularly if his livelihood was trapping, his dog team was his right arm in the struggle to live. He could not do without dogs, for a trapline might be 100 miles long or much longer, and there was simply no other way of moving through the bush in the wintertime than by dog team and snowshoe. Prospectors, too, and every other kind of traveler, used dogs for packing and freighting. They were used winter and summer, by summer's sun harness exchanged for pack.

Dogs had to be well trained, and they had to be treated right. *Lodema George*: "If you baby and talk to 'em while they're in the harness, you ruin 'em. They think they don't have to do anything. It's all fun. But it isn't. It's a business. When they're traveling, it's a business, just the same as anything else." There were bad dogs too, and it was important to be responsible toward them. *Lodema*: "They wouldn't take [this one dog] in the team because he wouldn't mind. He wouldn't do what they wanted. . . . He was a worthless, no good thing. . . . But we never did sell a dog. If a dog wasn't good enough for us, he wasn't good enough to sell. It'd only mean that somebody'd be brutal with him, beat him up. This dog . . . we eventually shot him. He was lazy."

There are endless descriptions of a man's best team, his strongest wheel dog, his smartest leader. How good dogs were chosen! There was almost a magic to it. Everyone had a favorite way, a different sense. How they were broke and trained. What they ate. What kind of feet you preferred. What size you liked for wheel and lead. What color your best team was. How they looked in harness and under pack. Whether they were friendly. Whether they still could run and jump and play after a day's work. How far they could travel in soft snow or on crust. What commands they took. What hitch you preferred—fan shape or straight line (the fan was mainly used in the Arctic barrens where there are no trees, the straight line in timber). Whether you liked four- or five-dog teams (the larger the team the more feed had to be packed). Whether you ever had to whip them. How spirited they were in the morning or by midafternoon.

Lodema George

She remembers a lead dog named Diamond.

This one dog that we were offered so much for [by the Mounties] was [a strain] called a Mackenzie River husky. He was black and had a little white mark on his chest and white around the eyes, all black otherwise. Oh, he was a pretty thing! He wasn't [big]. He was a bit smaller, more like the Siberian dog. But he was a wonderful dog. Wonderful worker. He was a wonderful leader. You could just do anything with him. . . .

I broke this [Diamond]. We put him on the wheel—that's next to the toboggan—and I put three good dogs ahead that'd already been broken . . . and we started. And, of course, he'd see a little rabbit trail, and he'd think he could go, and the other dogs'd keep going and he'd get tangled up and they'd drag him. And you drag a dog a few times, and you stop and you scold him and straighten him up and go on again. And after a few times of that, why—you know it's no fun to get drug—sometimes his head was next to the toboggan, and sometimes his tail. They soon get used to it. . . .

We drove them for "Yoo" and "Cha." That's the Indian. "Yoo" is right, and left is "Cha." "Gee" and "Haw" is what a lot of them use, but I don't know myself which is Gee and which is Haw.

Henry McLeod

A dog is just like everything else. . . . If you treat 'em right, they know, and they seem to try themselves too you know. As long as you don't put too big a pack on 'em or be too rough with 'em when you're drivin' 'em in harness. . . . I've traded a horse here for five pups myself, traded a darned good saddle horse for five pups when they were small, and they were brothers like, you know, and they were all black. And then when they got grown about so big, then I just put some harness on, and let 'em drag it around. . . . So they got used to it you know. They get tangled up in everything, and pull on it. And finally I'd hook two of them together, one behind the other, till they kinda got used to it. They'd get all tangled up, and then they'd untangle themselves, you know, their legs and that.

And then you pick out which one you figure is the smartest one [and hitch him in the lead]. And you can walk ahead of them for awhile if you like, till they get used to it, and then finally you can chase them on, and they'll take off anyway. And finally, then, you have to run along on the side, and you'll start hollerin', 'Gee!' . . . and they'll finally catch on if they're smart enough, and generally they are. . . . Try it from this side for awhile, and then the other side. After they get used to sayin', "Gee," and [you] wantin' 'em to go to the right—when they get kind of onto that—then you go to the other side and keep hollerin', "Haw!" And if they don't wanta turn, a lotta times you take ahold of 'em and swing 'em that way, you know. Just, but not be mean with 'em or anything. . . . It doesn't seem to take long. They catch on.

Dogs were used for rescue work when it was necessary. Father Pierre Poullet, the Catholic priest at Lower Post on the Alcan Highway, took a rescue party out at night with his dogs to find a U.S. Army Air Corps flyer down on a lake near the Hyland River. The temperature was sixty below. Father Poullet froze his feet. He received the Medal of Freedom from President Truman for his work that night. He could not have made the rescue without his dog team or without the help of his Indian friends.

Father Pierre Poullet, O.M.I.

I think it was forty-three when a flyer was downed on a lake about twenty miles, or twenty-five miles from Watson Lake by air. . . . And this lieutenant came to Lower Post where I was livin', asked me if I thought we could find that flyer. They knew where he was, but they could not land there on the lake. He had belly landed on the lake, and would I go with my dog team to rescue him because there was no ski plane at Watson Lake, the closest was Whitehorse, the weather was bad for flying.

So it was nine o'clock at night, and we left, the lieutenant and his sergeant and myself and my dog team, five dogs. From the map they showed me I knew I could direct them to one of the Indian cabins about fifteen miles from Lower Post on the Hyland River, and I would then let those Indians lead us to the lake.

And sure enough we got there, oh, early morning, two, three o'clock in the morning. And we got those Indians up, gave them breakfast. We had all kinds of supplies, of course, more than we needed, sandwiches, coffee, and so on, and we got to the flyer in early, very early morning. . . .

So we took him to the shore, laid some spruce boughs on the ground, made a big fire, and waited for the ski plane that was to come in the morning, weather permitting. And, of course, the weather turned good, and, oh, about ten o'clock in the morning the ski plane came in from Whitehorse and picked up the pilot and myself. I had froze my feet by that time a bit. It was sixty below. No. Colder. I think it was colder than sixty. The Indians then took my dog team back to Lower Post.

Every old northerner has one particular dog that he remembers best. It is almost like having had a good wife, a true pardner. And this pardner took part in that northerner's life, nearly every aspect of it. There were joys and sorrows and a lot of hard work together and a lot of fun too. And the memories are pure silver. They are aged gold.

Norman Harlin

I had a big wheel dog, a sort of a pet, and he was the last of the dog team, I sold the rest. I had this big wheel dog, and he was with us the whole summer on the [pioneer Alcan Highway] survey, packin' stakes. And we come back to Teslin as I say on the twenty-third of October [1942] on a [U.S. Army] convoy. Of course, he was used to that because he'd been workin' part of the summer around this heavy equipment. . . .

I had a panel then, Chev panel, been parked here [Teslin] all summer, and I put Butch in that panel and we took off for Whitehorse. And he was so used to ridin' in airplanes—he'd spent half his life in planes—he watched that road all the way 'bout to Brooks' Brook, wonderin' if we were ever gonna get that thing off the ground. Finally he gave up and curled up in the back and said, "To hell with you guys. You're never gonna get off."

He'd never been in a car before, except big trucks. The guy with me sure had a kick outta him, watchin' the ground and lookin' at us as much as! You'd think he was lookin' at the instruments to see why in hell we couldn't get off.

When I got that dog, I paid five hundred dollars for him. Anyway, they shipped him to Watson Lake, and at that time they were flyin' gas in there in barrels, and there was, oh, I guess, ten thousand barrels piled up on the taxi strip, or stockpiled. Butch got off the plane, and the guy with me said, "I swear to God he peed on every barrel."

He hadn't peed since he left Whitehorse—he was holdin' it—and he pissed on every barrel on that runway.

See, these GI's when they got to Lower Post they were goin' Stateside, so they thought . . . every one of those GI's I'd run into, they knew I was a Canadian, I was guidin' the party, [so they'd ask], "How far is it to Lower Post?" I heard that a hundred times a day. . . .

[Butch] was with us all that summer, and of course I was flyin' ahead prit near every day [on the surveys], and we just didn't have room. You know, he was a big dog. He weighed about seventy-five pounds. And we'd leave him with the survey crew. And I come back one time, and the army had caught up to us . . . and here was Butch, a great big red ribbon on 'im—the [army] had steel-jacketed shells and they had rifles with them, you see, whereas the survey [party] didn't . . . —anyway, they'd been shootin' at Butch. So the survey boys they'd cut a lid off a cigar box, and they got this red ribbon and tied it around his neck. But, anyway, the sign on the cigar box hangin' on his neck when I got home says,

"My name is Butch. I am an Alaska Malemute. I am eight years old, and I don't know how far it is to Lower Post." . . .

Butch didn't know how far it was. But they quit shootin' at 'im anyway, this red ribbon on. They thought he was a bear. He was a great big black dog.

We had a lotta fun anyway.

CHAPTER THIRTEEN

The Specter of American Domination

IF THOSE who lived in the North had forever felt in their lives the daily pressure for good trails—they had been making them for years with snowshoe, dog team, steamboat, and bush plane—the decision to build the Alaska Highway across the Canadian north was not theirs to make. That decision lay instead in the hands of the army and civilian leaders in Washington and Ottawa. For years the most powerful of these leaders had only talked or listened to others talk about the need for the international highway, while the northern citizens themselves did without. If the northerners knew, because they lived in the North, that they needed good roads and trails, the distant leaders seldom knew of the need except intellectually. And when they thought of it or were told about it by a citizen or a representative of the citizens who lived in the North, they tended to see the whole matter rationally and balanced against the needs of other persons and groups. The fact was that there was a large gap between what the northerners believed would be good for them and what the distant planners thought would be good for the whole country, the larger human community with which they were concerned.

This is no doubt one of the reasons why for a decade before Pearl Harbor Washington failed to help Alaskans and other interested persons build the highway. It is also no doubt one reason why, during the same period, Ottawa failed to help British Columbia and the Yukon build the road. But there is another important factor operating in Canada. Traditionally, Canadian provinces have viewed themselves as centers of power quite independent of the Dominion government in Ottawa, while Ottawa herself has carefully avoided taking over federal powers within the provinces. Ottawa has at times no doubt used this provincial independence as an excuse to avoid helping the provinces, especially the western ones, in areas in which they suffered a financial need.

Throughout the 1930s several of the politicians and the premiers of British Columbia were adamant about wanting to build the expensive road across the North, for they believed that such a road would stimulate the economy of their province. But the officials in Ottawa refused to give them any money. At least one of the premiers was therefore driven to irregular means of trying to get the required funds. In 1938, Premier T. D. Pattullo turned directly to the United States government for aid and actually went down to Washington to try to get a loan. This action, which Pattullo had not cleared through Ottawa, had the effect in the Canadian capital parallel to what would have been the effect in Washington had the governor of Montana gone directly to a foreign government for a loan to build a highway from Missoula to Billings. It caused a fierce resentment on the part of the national leaders, especially the heads of the Canadian Department of External Affairs, the equivalent of the American Department of State. International relations were their specialty, not the responsibility of a provincial premier. Since Pattullo had gone over their heads, they seemed determined not to help him with his road.

There is another important factor. Canadians have traditionally feared American military and economic power, and rightly so, for with money there always come strings. Let the Americans put up the money to build a highway to Alaska—the road would have to cross that part of Canada which lies between Alaska and the lower forty-eight states—and Dominion leaders believed they would insist upon having certain controls over that road. Canadians had some evidence to support this fear. Seattle businessmen and west coast politicians since the early 1930s had not been sufficiently sensitive to the effects of their energies upon the Canadian mind and heart. A Seattle-based group had tried early in the decade to fund the construction with American dollars. They had proposed to build the highway across Canada with their own money in exchange for the gasoline and hotel concessions. When this news hit the papers, it seemed to Canadians to threaten economic control.

Another instance of American insensitivity was the 1933

report of the Alaskan Highway study commission appointed by President Hoover. Their report had concluded that the international highway, if it were built, would cost America two million, and Canada twelve million dollars. The Hoover Commission members had made their study without the official cooperation of Canada, and their figures were their own. The statement that Canada would have to put up twelve million dollars for the project had enraged Canadian citizens, politicians, and editors. Although later American political figures were to become considerably more generous, and the American government would actually finance the construction of the Alaska Highway after Pearl Harbor, Canadians found it next to impossible to let the old hurt and suspicion die.

Add to the fear of economic domination the fear of American military power which persisted throughout the 1930s. As the Japanese became increasingly aggressive during the decade, it appeared more likely to the Canadians that western Canada would become an important area in American defense planning if the United States and Japan were to go to war. One very important figure, Major General Ashton, Chief of the Canadian General Staff, expressed this opinion and his fears to the Minister of National Defense and to Dr. O. D. Skelton, Under Secretary of State for External Affairs. "In fact," Ashton noted, "the proposed highway is primarily a military project engendered by the U.S. fear of Japanese aggression." Ashton was worried that the Americans wanted a way "to make easy the occupation and control of the highway by American forces should it be considered necessary to disregard Canadian neutrality in the event of war" with the Japanese.

The General tied to this fear his concern about economic control. Should financial aid be accepted, he wrote, "the U.S. would have a moral right, if not a legal right, to a share in the administration and control of the highway through Canadian territory, which would be an impossible situation from the Canadian point of view." Since both Dr. Skelton and Prime Minister Mackenzie King were themselves cautious, to say the least, about American military and economic power, the Dominion government's reasons for dragging its feet in the matter of authorizing the construction of the highway in the 1930s are clear. Skelton himself had written King, after learning of Premier Pattullo's efforts in Washington, that to accept American money "would be mortgaging our independence," and King had penciled his reaction on Skelton's memo. To accept the money, he wrote, would be in the nature of "financial penetration if not financial invasion of a foreign power."

Ironically, the persistent Canadian fear of American military power had no foundation whatever in the facts of the American War Department's actual strategic planning for the defense of the west coast and Alaska in the 1930s. Until the midsummer of 1941, in fact, American military officials showed no interest whatever in the construction of a highway to Alaska. Their opinion was that the international road would be of little military value. As late as August 1940, Secretary of War Stimson wrote the chairman of the House Committee on Roads about a bill submitted by Delegate Dimond of Alaska to authorize the construction of the highway. The War Department believed, Stimson said, that "the value of the proposed highway as a defense measure" was "negligible." Thus he did not favor the bill's passage. Stimson explained that the military value of Alaska lay in the strategic areas of her southern coast, the Aleutian chain, and the Alaska Peninsula, and that these areas could all be reached by sea and air the year round. The problems of keeping a highway to Alaska open all year seemed to him difficult, if not insurmountable. He thought transportation by sea "the only practical means" of reaching installations in Alaska and that seagoing vessels could reach island installations, while a road overland could not. In general, Stimson's letter expresses the attitude of the War Department toward the construction of the Alaska Highway during the years preceding Pearl Harbor.

Nor did officials outside the War Department seem to be aware of military motives operating behind the scenes. In August 1938 newsmen reported that American Assistant Secretary of War Johnson was about to make a trip to Alaska to consider, among other problems, plans for the international highway; the War Department was at least willing to look at the matter. But the announcement of the trip caused a serious stir in Canada, and the *Vancouver Daily Province* editorialized that the trip "tears away the camouflage" that the road was to be built for its economic benefits to the North. At that time, Ruth Hampton, acting director of the Department of the Interior, wrote in a memo: "News releases from Canada indicate that military involvement is one of the chief fears which retards negotiations for the highway. Never as far as I know has the military feature of this highway been proposed as one of its major justifications." And Premier Pattullo himself said that in his several discussions with the officials in Washington about possible American funding for the Highway, "the military importance of the road had not been so much as mentioned."

Besides the War Department, which was influenced by the navy's view that the navy would be able to keep sea-lanes to Alaska open as well as by internal pressures for the development of air defense in the North, the Bureau of the Budget opposed the building of the international highway in the 1930s. At the opening of the congressional session in 1934, Delegate Dimond of Alaska introduced a bill to authorize the survey, location, and construction of the highway. U.S. senators introduced a similar bill. These bills would have authorized the President to reach an agreement with Canada for a joint survey and highway location study and for a study of the means of financing the construction and maintenance costs. Dimond's bill called for the appropriation of $100,000 for the negotiations to reach the agreement and for the cooperative studies with Canada, and $2 million for the construction of a connecting highway link within Alaska. But the Budget Bureau did not like the heavy appropriations and viewed them as not "in accord with the President's financial program." When similar bills were dropped into House and Senate hoppers the next year, Budget continued to disapprove. Daniel Bell, director of the Bureau, was a powerful figure. "I feel . . . ," he wrote the President, "that all authority to commit the United States to any program should be eliminated."

In addition to Bell's department, the Department of Agriculture disliked the bills. Rexford Guy Tugwell, Acting Secretary of Agriculture, believed that before the United States appropriated any money for joint studies or for actual construction, she should have a guarantee from Canada that the Dominion would complete her section of the highway, the link between the lower Forty-eight and Alaska.

President Roosevelt was no doubt influenced by these opinions, for while he did approve Dimond's bill in 1935, his approval stipulated that the appropriations sections be removed. Though the bill passed, and Roosevelt signed it into law that year, it gave the President the power to negotiate with and to reach an agreement with the Dominion for studying the problems of location and construction of the highway, *but without any appropriations*. And although the President then assigned the State Department the task of opening preliminary negotiations with Canada, State was able to achieve little in her frequent approaches to the Canadian government over the next several years, chiefly because the Dominion officials feared American domination. Clearly the times were not right for the construction of the Alaska Highway in the 1930s.

Nevertheless, there were a number of important steps taken late in the decade which prepared the way for the construction of the highway after Pearl Harbor. The appointment of American and Canadian study commissions and the consideration of the different routes the highway might follow were the most important of these. In 1938 the House and Senate approved and President Roosevelt signed into law a bill originally submitted by Congressman Warren Magnuson. The new law gave the President the power to appoint an "Alaskan International Highway Commission" of five members who were to "communicate directly with any similar agency which may be appointed" by Canada to study the problems of survey, location, construction, and funding. The American commissioners were to serve two-year terms "without salary or other compensation," and they were to report to the President at the end of their term. Magnuson had wisely left out any mention of agreements with the Dominion since the Canadian officials had consistently refused approaches by the State Department to discuss such agreements seriously. And he had also left out any statements about appropriations. He had clearly learned well from Delegate Dimond's disappointing experience with the Budget Bureau earlier. The point of the Magnuson bill was to provide an approach to the difficult problems of working with Canada different from that of the Highway Act of 1935. Still, the hearings on the bill in the spring of 1938 caused another terrific stir in Ottawa and the Canadian newspapers. The *Vancouver Daily Province* went so far as to cry that an international highway financed by the Americans "could be nothing less than a military highway, which, by tying us to American foreign policy would, forever, prevent our being masters in our own house."

The new American law, however, served to press forward the appointment of a similar Canadian commission. Premier Pattullo of British Columbia, who had been aggravating Dominion officials with his trips to Washington and his talk of borrowing money from the American government, thereby got another lever. In September of 1938 he met with several of Mackenzie King's Ministers in Ottawa and suggested that since the Americans had a study commission, the Canadians should also have one. He added that British Columbians revealed a great deal of "enthusiasm," that he thought the construction of the highway, if it could be achieved, would solve the provincial unemployment problem, and that the American government "ardently desired" the highway. Mr. Wismer, who accompanied Premier Pattullo to the meeting, added that the highway was the "livest issue" in British Columbian politics and that if it were not built, the citizens of that western province "would place the whole blame upon the Dominion government." Within a few weeks after the meeting, the press announced that the Prime Minister would appoint a Canadian fact-finding commission. Mackenzie King had promised Pattullo at Laurier House that he would do so, although he did not make the promise happily. But what mattered most, there would now be an official Canadian commission to parallel the American commission.

Unfortunately, however, the two commissions were to disagree over the routes they would favor. And although they were officially "study" commissions who were supposed to report their findings objectively, their efforts were to become politicized. This was especially true of the American commission, whose members, all from the west coast, favored the western route from the Seattle area, Route A, or a compromise between Routes A and B, so long as the route decided upon went through Whitehorse rather than Dawson. A western route, particularly Route A, would have linked Seattle to Alaskan defense and trade, and it would have provided a highway from which feeder roads could have been built into the isolated Alaskan Panhandle coastal towns. Route A (also called the "coastal route"), had it been utilized, would have connected Seattle with the Richardson Highway near Big Delta via Prince George, Fort St. James, Stuart Lake, Atlin, and Whitehorse. The Canadian commissioners, on the other hand, favored the Rocky Mountain Trench Route, Route B. This line lay just east of Route A, began at Prince George, went up the Rocky Mountain trench to Lower Post and Frances Lake and into Dawson City, the capital of the Yukon. It would have been much more difficult, if not impossible, to build the feeder roads from Route B over to Alaska's coastal towns, and Route B, as the Canadians desired it, would also have bypassed Whitehorse. The American commissioners insisted that Whitehorse had to be on the highway since it was the head of

Yukon River navigation toward Alaska, end of steel for the White Pass Railway from the port at Skagway, and an important center for air traffic across northern Canada.

The political nature of the American commission, chaired by Congressman Magnuson, may have slowed down the efforts to build the Alaska Highway before Pearl Harbor. Little doubt it frightened Canadian officials already afraid of the specter of American domination, and it hardened the War Department's resolve not to support the construction of the highway. The civilian American commissioners argued vocally and by letter *for the military value* of their chosen route to whatever powerful groups and persons they could reach. This they did chiefly because the Canadian government had indicated that it was not interested in cooperating in the construction of a highway to Alaska by any route unless the Canadians could be assured of its *critical* importance to the western defense of America and Canada. (Canada had suggested she would approve the highway should continental defense absolutely require it.) The War Department did not consider the international highway of major military importance. Clearly, also, the department believed it to be its job and not the commission's task to evaluate defense matters of this sort. They were therefore unfriendly to the commissioners' efforts. The Canadian-American Permanent Joint Board on Defense was also unfriendly because high officers from the U.S. War Department represented the American government on the joint board, whose task it was to make or approve decisions about important matters of mutual defense.

But the information gathered and disseminated about Routes A and B by both the American and Canadian commissions did become useful when, after Pearl Harbor, military planners decided to build the Alaska Highway. Useful, too, was the work of the famous Arctic explorer Vilhjalmur Stefansson, who testified to the importance of building the highway over Route D via the Mackenzie River to the vicinity of Norman Wells and from there westerly to Dawson City and Big Delta. Although the War Department rejected Stefansson's plan, his experience became one other source of information about the alternative lines to Alaska when the tides of war drove the department and the Permanent Joint Board to select the Alaska Highway's route.

Grave Decisions

CANADA AND THE United States carefully avoided taking measures for mutual defense until late in the decade preceding World War II. Although President Roosevelt and Prime Minister King talked about such matters privately in 1937 and Canadian and American military officers held informal conversations early in 1938, the need to avoid commitments seemed greater than the need to make them. The main efforts in both countries were to establish economic independence and to recover from the depression. Clearly, too, the Dominion wished earnestly to avoid the possibility of American economic and military domination. When the war began, Donald Creighton wrote, Canadians were "even more than the other nations of the English-speaking world . . . lamentably unprepared." They were, he thought, "what they had been in 1914, a profoundly unmilitary people."

When Hitler's tanks rumbled into Poland on September 3, 1939, Britain, Australia, New Zealand, the Union of South Africa, and then Canada declared war. The United States, however, attempted to remain neutral as long as possible. America's main concern was the defense of the Western Hemisphere, while Canada's was the active support of the British Empire. But events rapidly changed American intentions. The disaster at Dunkirk in the late spring of 1940 and the fall of France shortly thereafter suggested the terrifying possibility that Hitler might overwhelm Britain and become the power lord of Europe and the Atlantic. The Congress and the War Department immediately stepped up America's defense program, and the War Plans Division completed the top secret Rainbow 4 plan.

War Plans built Rainbow 4 upon the assumption that British and French forces would collapse and that the United States and Canada would therefore have to defend their own eastern shores. The plan assumed an agreement between the two countries under which each would hold her own territory, and the United States would use Canadian air bases, highways, railroads, and seaports to help the Canadians defend Newfoundland and Greenland. In July 1940, Canadian members of the Institute of International Affairs recommended immediate arrangements with the United States for a "single continental defence policy." Meantime, Mackenzie King asked the American government for aid and suggested that talks be held between representatives of the two nations' general staffs.

Shortly thereafter, mutual defense planning really began to go for the first time when the President and the Prime Minister created the Canadian-American Permanent Joint Board on Defense. It was this board that would have to approve the construction of the Northwest Staging Route, that chain of air bases from Edmonton through Whitehorse to Fairbanks, and the Alcan Highway, which would follow the line and link together the air bases themselves. The board would also have to approve all other mutual defense projects of importance. Hence, it was an important weekend, that of the seventeenth and eighteenth of August, 1940, when the two national leaders met in the Presidential railroad car at Ogdensburg, New York, to talk of defense matters. For it was there that the President suggested the formation of the board. "The function of this Committee should be," Secretary of War Stimson noted down in his diary, "to discuss plans for the defense of the northern half of the Western Hemisphere . . . and [Mr. Roosevelt] pointed out how vitally important it was that there should be conferences, discussions and plans made between the services of the respective countries in case there should be an attack by way of the St. Lawrence or northeastern coast of Canada, where sudden attack was very likely." Secretary Stimson noted that the Prime Minister seemed "perfectly delighted with the whole thing." To the President's suggestions, King added that he thought the board should be permanent and that its purpose should be to consider long-range problems rather than immediate crises.

The members of the board were very quickly appointed. They held their first meeting in Ottawa on August 26. Present were the representatives of each of the military services of both countries—army, navy, and air force—and the chairmen of the two delegations, O. M. Biggar of Canada and Fiorello La Guardia of the United States. The members discussed general questions of the ways of sharing defense responsibilities, questions which they pursued at later meetings and worked up into defense plans. The joint defense plans hammered together over the succeeding months and years included strategies for protecting Alaska, the Aleutians, the northwestern United States and western Canada. In the west, Canada was to press forward the construction of the Northwest Staging Route, the location of which would determine the final choice of route of the Alcan Highway. The United States was to provide army bases at Anchorage and Fairbanks and air services, as well as naval air stations, at various points on the west coast and in Alaska and the Aleutians.

Actually, the Dominion government had already planned a chain of air fields across the North between Edmonton and Whitehorse before the two nations established the joint board. The planned chain followed the same line the Dominion had surveyed in the mid-thirties, the one used by the pilots of Yukon Southern late in the decade. In 1939 Canada had authorized the planning of air fields at Grande Prairie, Fort St. John, Fort Nelson, Watson Lake, and Whitehorse, and very soon thereafter survey parties had gone into the field. By January 1940 the surveys had been completed and the planners were drawing up the details. When the Permanent Joint Board began to meet, it immediately recognized the importance of the air route, discussed the matter, and recommended on November 14 that the Dominion begin construction of the fields as soon as possible. Besides those already planned, the government was to build two others at Prince George and Smithers. The board wrote that the purpose of the bases was to provide "means for rapid movement of light bombers and fighter aircraft into Canada, into Central Alaska via Whitehorse, and into the Ketchikan–Prince Rupert area." They believed the new facilities would be "essential to the defence of Western Canada, Alaska and the United States."

Canada began construction of the air bases as early as the weather would permit in 1941. Men and equipment went into Fort Nelson from Fort St. John over a 300-mile winter road. Steamers carried supplies to Wrangell for the base at Watson Lake; smaller boats took them from Wrangell up the Stikine River to Telegraph Creek, Dease Lake, the Dease River, and Lower Post, the same route used for years by Klondikers, trappers, and traders. Meantime, the Alaska Defense Command improved Ladd Field at Fairbanks, the western end of the airway. By late 1941 the Northwest Staging Route bases were usable by daylight in good weather. Minimal landing fields, emergency lighting, radio aids, meteorological equipment, and very limited housing were in place or on the way.

Still, conditions were hardly adequate for the inexperienced American pilots who attempted to fly the route during the first winter of its use. Of a group of thirteen B-26 bombers and twenty-five P-40's ordered to Alaska in December, only eight of the bombers and thirteen of the pursuits reached the end of the line by late January 1942. Eleven of the aircraft had crashed along the way, and operational factors to which the Americans were unaccustomed had simply put the others out of commission. Northern winters were unbelievable. Oil stiffened in the cold and refused to lubricate. Metal cracked under the strain of the extreme temperatures. Part of the problem lay in disagreements between Canadians and the Americans who attempted to help with the construction of the air bases within the Dominion territory. The two governments eventually ironed out the problems so that during the war the Americans expanded facilities at the main air fields to suit their own standards, and built, among other things, eight emergency flight strips along the Alcan Highway.

The Northwest Staging Route had two very important functions during World War II. One of these was to build up and to supply the insufficient defense bases in Alaska and the Aleutians, for until after the war began the army badly neglected Alaskan defense. The air force of the Alaskan Defense Command did not, in fact, possess a single up-to-date airplane until well after the catastrophe at Pearl Harbor, and aircraft supplies, fuel, and lubricants were severely short. There was no effective aircraft warning system, and there were no well-developed bases even though at the time the Japanese struck, the Army Air Corps was supposed to bear heavy responsibility for the defense of Alaska. So badly off were air defenses there that General Buckner of the Alaskan Defense Command wrote on the day after Pearl Harbor: "At dawn this morning I watched our entire Alaska Air Force take to the air so as not to be caught on the field. This force consisted of six obsolescent medium bombers and twelve obsolete pursuit planes."

Both the Army Air Corps and various civilian air transport companies worked during the war to establish, improve, and supply Alaskan defenses. Probably the busiest month of the whole war was June 1942, when the Japanese were attacking Dutch Harbor, Attu, and Kiska. Leaders speeded up flight operations and extended them to new points. Orders went to eleven different commercial airline companies to send available aircraft to Edmonton that June. Shuttle services for cargo and passengers flew from numerous points in the United States to Edmonton and from there to Fairbanks, Anchorage, and Nome. During the emergency, flight crews suffered from fatigue, some of them having been ordered to Edmonton without time for so much as packing a change of clothing. Crews put in too many hours in the air without rest, and some flyers built up the equivalent of fifteen days flight time in three days or less. During the rest of the war, the Army Air Corps and the commercial airline companies flew steadily, supplying the Alcan Highway project, the Northwest Staging Route fields, the bases in Alaska and the Aleutians, and the CANOL oil field under construction at Norman Wells on the Mackenzie River.

The other very important function of the Northwest Staging Route during the war was to serve the American pilots who flew lend-lease aircraft to Russian crews at Ladd Field in Fairbanks. This particular air route—called ALSIB for Alaska-Siberia—had substantial advantages, and from early in the war United States military officials favored it over the others. The Americans found the alternative airways—the over-water route to Archangel and the air-water-air route through the Persian Gulf—unattractive, although pilots also used them. German submarines and aircraft infested the Archangel route, and pilots flying the other route put up with blowing African sand. Abrasive sand shortened engine life. Sea air corroded metals. But because the Russian leaders did not want Americans in Siberia and did not want to seem to be a threat to Japan, they were slow to accept the concept of deliveries via the Northwest Staging Route. It was more than a year after the Americans proposed the ALSIB delivery in August 1941 before the Russians accepted. After that, they reversed their decision, then reversed it again. Not until September 29, 1942, did the first Soviet crews fly their new American aircraft away from Ladd Field and head homeward toward Siberia. In spite of these difficulties, United States pilots flew a total of about 8,000 lend-lease airplanes to the Russians over the staging route from the southern air terminal at Great Falls, Montana, before lend-lease ceased.

Given the importance of the Northwest Staging Route and the fact that its bases were already under construction before the military planners decided to build the Alaska Highway, it seems clear that those who chose the prairie route for the highway did so correctly. High officers seriously considered the alternative routes but rejected them for sound military reasons. The army turned down Route A, which would have tied Alaska to the Seattle area, because air bases did not exist along it, because it seemed more open to attack from the west coast, because it was a long way from the industrial centers in the Middle West and East, and because the officers believed the weather along that route to be generally poorer for flying. Route B would not have supplied the established air bases; the Rocky Mountain trench through which it passed seemed as if it would present more trouble for the inexperienced American flyers than the prairie route would, and it, too, lay far from the industrial center of the country. Route D also lacked the air bases, and the army thought it considerably more indirect than the route it chose. *The planners selected Route C—the prairie route—for the most important military reasons of the time: its line provided a wider margin of safety from attack than either of the more westerly routes did, and it connected the Northwest Staging Route bases, which were already under construction and which needed an overland means of supply.* "To have abandoned these air bases in February 1942," wrote Julius Amberg, Special Assistant to the Secretary of War, "and to have begun construction anew on another air route would have meant abandonment of a usable existing airway including a large amount of Canadian construction, and dangerous delays in the entire program."

Nevertheless the decision was a difficult one. Not only did the Alaskan International Highway Commission deeply desire that construction follow the western route, but the Department of the Navy had long opposed an overland highway because it believed the navy capable of keeping the sea-lanes to Alaska open. There was also a difference of opinion among Army leaders themselves. When, in mid-January, the War Plans Division decided that defense concerns would probably require the building of the highway, the Transportation Branch of G-4 announced that it could not support War Plans' opinion because Transportation feared "diverting funds, materials, engineering talent and labor" needed elsewhere "for more pressing National Defense undertakings." Nonetheless, by the twenty-third of January, General Gerow of the War Plans Division recommended directly to General Marshall that he support the construction. Gerow argued that the road was important as an alternative supply line to Alaska in case the Japanese should interrupt the sea lanes and as a means of tying together and supplying the air bases of the Northwest Staging Route.

The army made its actual decision to support the choice of the prairie route, and it prepared its case between January 16 and February 2, 1942. At the meeting of the President's Cabinet on January 16, Secretary Ickes suggested that careful thought be given the building of the highway; he had been worried about the probability of enemy strikes on the sea-lanes to the North. Consequently, Mr. Roosevelt appointed a Special Cabinet Committee—the Secretaries of War, Navy, and the Interior—to study the matter and make a recommendation. The committee met a few days later with representatives of the Army Corps of Engineers. At that meeting, Secretary Ickes later recalled, those present "proceeded to take quick action" because they "realized the importance of getting materials into Canada while the ground was . . . frozen." They agreed also to "formulate a joint proposal to be considered again at a Cabinet meeting in the very near future."

That meeting occurred on February 2. In the meantime, Brig. Gen. R. W. Crawford and Lt. Col. James K. Tully had directed studies of the proposed routes within the War Plans Division and had decided to support the choice of the prairie route. On the second, Colonel Tully made the case for the road from Edmonton. He believed it "necessary," he told the Cabinet officers, "to connect the landing fields" at Fort St. John, Fort Nelson, Watson Lake, and Whitehorse with a road. He believed that these air bases were properly spaced for pursuit-ship travel and that the surrounding country was flat enough for easy landings and takeoffs. He added that "such spaces might be found by careful reconnaissance along the B route," but that there was "very little chance of them along the A route" and that it was an important fact that the Dominion had already built the fields at Fort Nelson and Fort St. John. Tully made it clear that the army was, therefore, completely committed to the route from Edmonton to Fairbanks, even though the officers were not yet sure what specific line it ought to follow between Watson Lake and Whitehorse.

Such matters as that could be worked out in the near future. What was certain was that the Corps of Engineers would quickly be heading for Edmonton, for at that same meeting the President's Cabinet officers ordered General Crawford to prepare his report on the prairie route. It was then that Crawford turned to General Sturdevant for a comprehensive plan. In two days Sturdevant came back with that plan. By the time fireweed blossomed again, thousands of engineer troops would be in the northern field, and when snows were November-deep at Burwash, Destruction Bay, and Contact Creek, soldiers, PRA men, and an army band would celebrate, on Kluane Lake, the opening of the pioneer road.

Gems for the Crown

AFTER THE opening ceremony at Soldiers Summit on November 14, much of the hardest work of building the Alaska Highway was yet to be done. Winter had settled down hard on the North. The first Christmas season, like those in succeeding years before the war's end, saw deep snow and very low temperatures. It also saw Canadian and American contractors working beside the soldiers to improve the primitive tote road, to keep it passable, and to ready it for the spring and summer ahead. Christmas day, though, as it had always done in the North, brought a brief halt to the work nearly everywhere—Blueberry, Trutch, Fort Nelson, Morley Bay, Slim's River, Beaver Creek, Northway, Tok, and Snag. Americans and Canadians, young engineers and old northerners, took time for dinners and talk and here and there for a little singing. There were acts of kindness, humor, and the pleasure of making simple things. There were popping hot barrel stoves and plenty of cigars. The Christmas seasons on the Alaska Highway during the early years were a fusion of the old world of dogs and trappers and Indians, and of the modern world of trained engineers and trucks, diesel engines, and Caterpillar parts. The men and women who were there find those seasons, as well as the Christmas seasons before the engineers built the highway, ones worth remembering.

Henry McLeod

Henry describes a dog team at Christmastime.

About this riggin' . . . those dog blankets, you see, they're about that square, and they're all fixed with yarn on the outside, too, this wool, different colors, right around the whole thing, and square. And this yarn is all hangin' out. See, the dog collars around the dog's neck there. And these standing irons, they stay straight. All you gotta do is slip the collars on, and these standing irons stand straight up, and the ribbons and everything . . . just different colors, bright colors, you know. And . . . the tops [of the standing irons] they're round, you see, the way they're cut . . . like a little ball . . . [and] these ribbons on there. And these bells.

And they used to, like around Christmastime or anything, . . . they'd put these on the dogs. They knew! For some reason it'd just cheer them right up.

And one day I was traveling along . . . and my brother and I was together, you know. We're out there on the trapline. So we come to a little lake, and when we hit this lake—after we got out a little ways on the lake—I started whistling, just whistling a little song, you know, and all at once they just took off and run as hard as they could, and was jumpin' around. And so finally they straightened out, and when Joe caught up with me—I stopped across the lake there, I had to see some beaver traps—and when Joe got up with me there, he says, "What the dickens did you do to them dogs?" He says, "They started jumpin' up there."

So I told him I started whistling and that, a little tune. And away they just took off and started just jumpin', you know, and playin', and just took right off. They sure were a good dog team. They were all black. They were all brothers. The guy that I got 'em from, he still lives here across the river. . . .

Lodema George

My first Christmas there [at Fort Nelson before the highway was built] I didn't know what to plan on, so we sent out and we got a dozen hens . . . for roasting. . . . And I ordered three good-sized turkeys. . . . The Indians kept coming in, and they said, "Well, we want dinner. We're coming for dinner too."

Well, I told my husband, I said, "I guess I'm going to have to cook up a lot of chickens too."

And so the trappers . . . they all turned in and they helped with everything [the dishwashing and cleaning up]. You see, I didn't have a lot of dishes. But I had enough plates . . . to serve about seven or eight. . . . And I had chickens and turkey, and I cut those up, and I don't think that some of the trappers knew whether they were eating chicken or turkey, and of course the Indians didn't know either. . . .

Well, in all, I fed thirty-five people that day, at noon. . . . I made dressing for the chicken, and we had mashed potatoes, and I think we had turnips and carrots. . . . And my Christmas pudding—and I still like it better than I do the regular plum pudding—was the carrot pudding. And I know there's a lot of people that would rather have it today . . . , and I had a lot of that made up ahead of time because you can make that up and put it out and freeze it, and that's what I had to do with my bread [too]. . . .

We had been in Fort Nelson about two-and-a-half, three years, and we had this store, and I fed the trappers, you know, and the Indians. And then when the soldiers came in, they heard there was a café there. . . . Of course, Nelson has a beautiful climate, good soil over there, and we raised all of our own vegetables, and in August we had everything. We had carrots and turnips and potatoes and cucumbers. . . . The only meat we had was canned meat, but [the soldiers] didn't care about that. It was the fresh vegetables that they wanted. . . .

There was . . . Indians that run a little ferry boat—that's a little scow boat with a kicker on it, or a canoe and kicker. And they'd bring them back and forth across the river. They got fifty cents for carrying them across. . . . And in the wintertime, they could drive across the ice. And they would come down—three or four would come down in a vehicle—and they'd come over and get pie and coffee. . . .

I don't know, maybe they were so far away from home and so homesick that they were tickled to death to come over there. The married boys told you about their families, and the single ones about their girls. . . .

They used to come and tell me their troubles. They were an awfully good bunch of boys all the way through.

Father Pierre Poullet, O.M.I.

I remember one particular instance on a Christmas morning, trying to get to a camp about fifty miles up the highway from Watson Lake. . . . Actually I was trying to get to Swift River, which was a hundred miles. There was very little traffic, of course, on Christmas, and I was on the road waiting for about four or five hours. . . . Eventually I got a ride with . . . one of those Studebaker trucks, and the driver told me, he says, "Well, I hope you don't mind the speed because I'm in a hurry to get there."

I says, "Well, that's fine with me because if I don't get there on time I might just as well not get there."

Well, what did happen we were coming down a kind of an S-curve, down a hill, and the truck kept on going straight, slid into the ditch, and we were there for two or three hours before we could get help. . . . So when I got to the Rancheria, well I was even late for supper. Too late for service. . . .

While we were in the snowbank there, we were munching on

candy that we had. All the men and . . . I got a Christmas stocking full of goodies, candies and stuff, and that's what we were eating on while we were waiting for rescue. But, of course, it didn't look too much like Christmas.

Earl Bartlett

Down at mile 300 . . . [Fort Nelson] a few families had come in by this time; I'm not sure of the year there. And they had a recreational committee appointed, going to put on a whale of a big party. But this recreational committee forgot entirely about the children that were in the camp. My concept of Christmas . . . always had to do with Sunday School concerts and plays and acts by children. And the idea of leaving them out entirely at Christmastime seemed to be unthinkable.

They did have a recreation hall with a piano in it, and one lady could play pretty well [and I used to sing tenor]. We had no music. We had no material for plays. So we thought we'd get these youngsters together and have them sing a bit at Christmastime anyway.

We started them singing. Then they wanted to put on an act of some sort. We had no plays, so the kids [said], "Well, this is the way we did it in Fort Fraser," and, "This is the way we did it in Kamloops. . . ."

They got kimonos and various colorful things that could be put on for costumes, and I raided the ragbag down at the shop, and we found some nice silk scarfs . . . that somebody had discarded. We even used such things as spark plug terminals to make gems for the crown and on the angels. And they made their own stars out of white paper.

So we put on a bit of an act there. . . . The highlight of the program no doubt was our search for a Santa Claus. And right away I thought of . . . David Irving who was on the Search and Rescue Squad. When an aircraft was lost, they would make an aerial search, and he would make a ground search. He was a tough, wiry man, of whom a book was written, telling of his experiences alone across the top of the world. . . . We used to see him frequently, and we asked him to be the Santa Claus.

So as the concert was nearing its end, he came down from up on the hill with his dog team, and he wanted to know what he could do with the dogs while he was in the concert hall.

"Well," I said, "Couldn't you bring them right in?"

And he thought maybe he could.

So while the concert was still in progress and the children were singing, the door opened and Scotty the musher came in and the beautiful team of thoroughbred dogs and the sled behind them and Santa Claus behind that. And they towed them right into the center of the hall, and Scotty said some selected word and the dogs flattened out on the floor and they stayed there. The children came along and patted them, and everything was a great day for them. . . .

So it perhaps was one of the most unique Christmas concerts. . . . Probably few places could ever boast a celebration like that one. . . .

Henry McLeod

Henry McLeod ran a survival school for pilots who were to be flying the route of the Alaska Highway. The letters he speaks of here were from some of the men he trained.

I still get letters from some of them. One Christmas here several years ago, there was 200 and some odd cards here, just one Christmas you know, that I got from them. And I didn't know they were there, you know, kind of busy all the time, and finally the old postmaster told my brother, he says, "You tell Henry to come and get these cards out of here. They're blockin' the post office."

Highway builders had to cope with a multitude of difficulties. One of them was the permanently frozen ground in the Yukon where ice was always just below the surface.

Engineering News-Record photograph

(*Top*): The road, when it was first constructed, was so perilous at many points that equipment losses reportedly were high. Witness this supply truck which came to grief on the road along Muncho Lake. *Engineering News-Record* photograph

(*Center*): Brigadier-General William M. Hoge, shown here about to board a plane to fly to a new theater of operations, was director of the project in its early stages. *Engineering News-Record* photograph

(*Bottom*): Rivers often had to be crossed before the bridge building crews arrived. Deep streams called for pontoon ferries, but all shallow waters were forded by the equipment. Here a party of engineers crosses Yukon's Rancheria River aboard a tractor. *Engineering News-Record* photograph

Sled dogs, long the lifeline of the North, were vital to plotting the route of the Crooked Road. Here John and Dennis Callison prepare their team to leave Fort Nelson in March, 1942, guiding a Public Roads Administration survey party to Summit Lake.

Dennis Callison photograph

Building one of the many log culverts on the Alcan Highway.

Department of the Army photograph

The Canyon Creek (Aishihik River) bridge which was built by the Corps of Engineers in 1942 at mile 996.3 on the Alaska Highway is the last of these original bridges still standing. This drawing was done recently by artist Craig Hudson from two sketches he made while the bridge was under construction.

A bulldozer crossing a temporary timber bridge, one of 200 built in a hurry to support heavy loads.

Engineering News-Record photograph

Jack and Norm Harlin, Canadian guides on the Northern Sector of the Alaska Highway in the spring of
1942. Author David Remley held conversations with
Norm, who is quoted often in this book.

Ada Harlin/Peggy Mobraaten photograph

Canyon Creek bridge, the last of the original bridges, as it looks today, framed in the
new steel bridge which spans the stream at Mile 996.3.

David Remley photograph

O. D. Van Buskirk, PRA member of the dog team reconnaisance during March and April, 1942, near Fort St. John, B.C.

Near the end of the trip the reconnaisance party ran out of snow. Here, they ford open water not far from Fort St. John, B.C.   *O. D. Van Buskirk* photographs

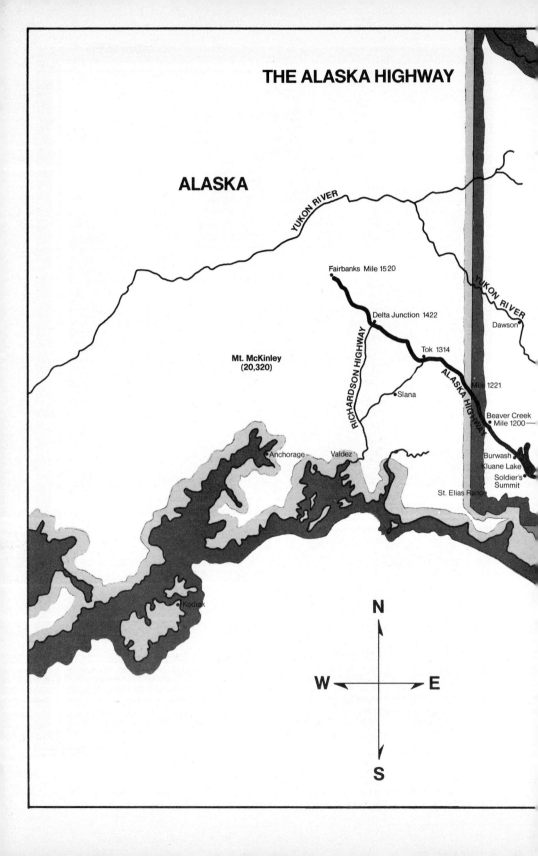

THE ALASKA HIGHWAY

ALASKA

YUKON RIVER

Fairbanks Mile 1520

Delta Junction 1422

Dawson

Tok 1314

RICHARDSON HIGHWAY

YUKON RIVER

Mt. McKinley
(20,320)

Slana

Mile 1221

ALASKA HIGHWAY

Beaver Creek
Mile 1200

Anchorage

Valdez

Burwash
Kluane Lake
Soldier's
Summit

St. Elias Range

Kodiak

N

W ◄———————► E

S

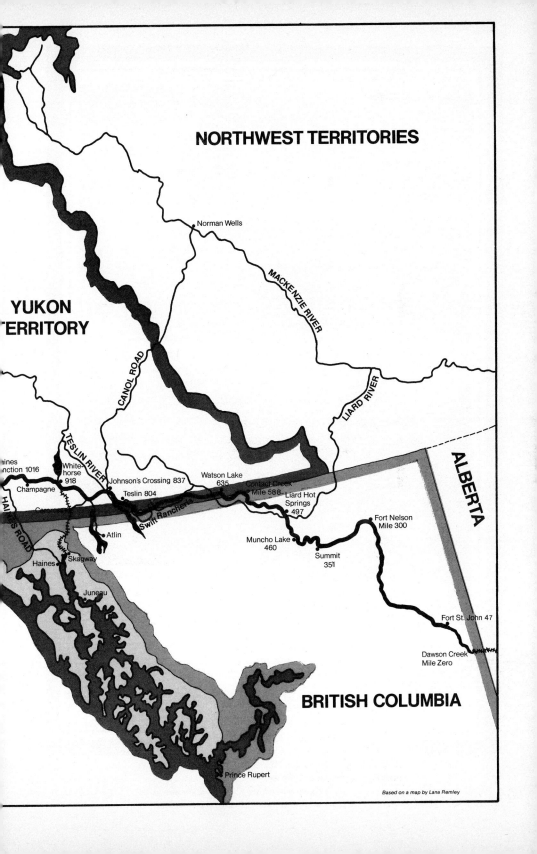

NORTHWEST TERRITORIES

YUKON TERRITORY

Norman Wells

MACKENZIE RIVER

LIARD RIVER

CANOL ROAD

TESLIN RIVER

Haines Junction 1016
White-horse 918
Champagne
Johnson's Crossing 837
Teslin 804
Watson Lake 635
Contact Creek Mile 588
Liard Hot Springs 497

Swift Ranchería

ALBERTA

Fort Nelson Mile 300

HAINES ROAD

Atlin

Muncho Lake 460

Summit 351

Haines
Skagway

Juneau

Fort St. John 47

Dawson Creek Mile Zero

BRITISH COLUMBIA

Prince Rupert

Based on a map by Lana Remley

Albeit twisting, muddy, rutted, the highway became at least a continuous thread on September 24, 1942, at the historic Meeting of the "Cats." The 340th Engineer Regiment, working south, and the 35th Engineer Regiment, coming north, met here at Contact Creek (mile 588).

Department of the Army, 340th Engineer Regiment photograph

E. L. Bartlett of Alaska, representing the United States, and the Honourable Ian Mackenzie, for Canada, prepare to cut the ribbon at Soldiers Summit near Kluane Lake, November 20, 1942, at the ceremony opening the pioneer highway.

Photograph by Gail K. Pinkstaff for Public Roads Administration

Topnotch bush pilot Les Cook carried mail, food, and anything else required, wherever and whenever it was needed, fair weather or foul. He was a particular friend to the 340th Engineer Regiment, and to a man, they mourned his death in the crash of his Norseman early in December, 1942.

Department of the Army, 340th Engineer Regiment photograph

Science and Yankee ingenuity played a big part in the building of the Crooked Road. Here a crew uses steam to melt ice around a truck frozen in on a bar of the Donjek River, February 22, 1943.

Photograph by Gail K. Pinkstaff for Public Roads Administration

Corduroy road at a Canada river crossing on the highway.

U.S. Army Corps of Engineers photograph

The steamer *Keno* prepares to tow barges of heavy equipment from Whitehorse on the Yukon River to the army's camp on Teslin Lake.

U.S. Army Corps of Engineers photograph

Flat cars at Skagway waiting to go to Whitehorse on the White Pass and Yukon R.R.

U.S. Army Corps of Engineers photograph

Pack train and Public Roads Administration survey party crossing the Donjek in July, 1943. The party was made up of local guides and packers and PRA engineers.

Photograph by Bill Ash for Public Roads Administration

In November 1942, the army was assigned to the construction of the Haines Road which formed a connecting link between the Alcan and tidewater at the Alaska port of Haines. Civilians under the PRA completed much of the work. During the spring thaw even the big bull dozers lacked enough thrust to get through the mud.

Department of the Army, 340th Engineer Regiment photograph

Bridges played a big part in the construction of the highway. The first Corps of Engineers bridge over the wide, swift Peace River near Fort St. John, B.C. washed out. Roebling and Sons replaced it with a suspension bridge which the swollen river later took out. The present bridge is a cantilever structure built by the Canadian government.

O. D. Van Buskirk photograph

Not everybody thought a highway was the best way to get from British Columbia to Fairbanks. Philip Verplanck proposed a suspended, high-speed railroad-highway-monorail combination to be built of timber pile bents. The design from which this model was built was considered by the War Department in February, 1942, but rejected as more vulnerable than a highway to enemy attack.

Philip Verplanck design
Photo courtesy the National Archives, Record Group No. 48

PART 3

W heel turning, not upon stone but saga,
Endlessly between the dead and the living.
Rider, you have begun long ago.

From coasts which knew Ulysses' oars,
Compulsion of commerce, stirring of migrations,
And how man did move upon the surface of his world.

. . . .

Each for his own dream, each for his need.
Each for the reason beyond the simple act.
One for grass, the other for gold, a third
For a thing he cannot name but hopes to find.

Norman Rosten, The Big Road, A Narrative Poem (New
York: Rinehart, 1946), pp. xvi, 46.

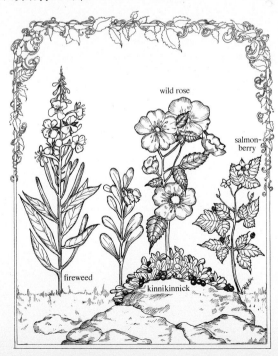

wild rose

salmon-
berry

fireweed

kinnikinnick

Too Much Too Soon

THE CONSTRUCTION of the Alaska Highway caused fundamental changes in the lives and outlooks of the people of the North. In 1942 inflation was new to them. Making big money was different for them. Fear of strangers was clearly a radical experience. In the small communities of the old north, your neighbor may have been a violent man, but you knew him well enough to be able to predict his actions. You knew what to do about them, how to protect yourself and your family from the man's violence. Now there were thousands of strangers in the land. A murder or a beating seemed more frightening because you could never tell when, where, or to whom it might happen. In the old north, men murdered people they knew. Now one man killed another who was a stranger to him. Neither the murderer nor the murdered knew each other, and both were strangers to the community.

Howard and Dorthea Calverley moved to Dawson Creek in 1936. They had come from southern Canada, she from the Swift Current District and he from the Shaunavon District of Saskatchewan. During World War II, Howard managed a hardware store, and Dorthea operated the Dominion government's rationing office in Dawson Creek. They raised a son during that unsettled period, that period of many transitions. The whole family lived through the Dawson Creek fire which destroyed the center of town in February 1943. Howard was badly injured in the explosion. As the Calverleys put it, however, they "adapted" to the strange conditions of the war and the mushrooming increase in the size of their small town.

Howard and Dorthea Calverley

Dorthea: There were about six hundred people here in 1942 when the first Engineers came, between five hundred and six hundred, and by February of 1943, there were estimated to be, wasn't it sixteen hundred? . . . I don't know, it just happened. The trains came in twice a week, and they were jammed with people standing. . . . But it was just a sudden mushroom.

Well, for one thing every able-bodied woman in town had to go to work, whether taking in washing or giving out ration books, or taking in boarders or clerking in the stores. There was nobody in this town that wasn't working. . . .

Everything went under the counter, . . . so we promptly got ourselves as self-sufficient as possible, and everybody else did. For instance, in order to get milk for our son, we had to get a goat. And we got chickens. . . . You looked after yourself. . . .

The Americans had money, and they would go out into the farms and buy every drop of milk that was available before it could be got into town. They would pay fantastic prices for it, and so, suddenly, unless you were self-sufficient, as we were—we made ourselves, with our garden and so on—you stood in queue and you did without. . . .

Oh, we made our own pleasures, and don't forget, we weren't so very far away from the depression where we'd all had to scratch anyway, so everybody was more or less prepared for that. . . . There were some good fortunes made here in those days. . . .

Howard: I'm thinking of the truck drivers came in from the prairies. All they had was a truck, and they'd been existing on what it would bring them, and then they came in here. And the difference between hauling wheat on the prairies for a fraction of a cent a bushel and getting, well, [so many] dollars per ton mile. . . . Oh, it was amazing what they would make in the space of a year! They were making *money*. . . . And this was an *experience* for a lot of those people that had come through ten years of the dirty thirties. They came in with one truck . . . and you did so well with that, you'd do your best to buy more trucks. . . .

Dorthea: The difficulties of bringing up a youngster were [tremendous]. I think the biggest one that I found was the fact that the kids had too much money. The soldiers were wonderfully good to them, and people were making money and had very little to spend it on, and youngsters were given [more than enough]. . . .

Suddenly, a kid on a paper route . . . who would offer a soldier a paper for five cents, [and the soldier would] say, "Aw, keep the change kid," and [give the kid] a dollar, was suddenly banking money and making more than his father had been making the year before. And this created a problem with children. They got an attitude towards money that has held on all the way through. It's never completely dissipated.

Howard: They got their inflation early.

Dorthea: Yes. . . . They had too much too soon, and this has been a problem. . . .

But, of course, there were some pretty rough characters around and some people that were afraid for their youngsters. People that had money . . . sent their children away to school, to private schools. Our philosophy was that if we weren't good enough parents and made a good enough home that our boy could grow up in this kind of community . . . , and if he couldn't meet it here, then he wasn't worth educating. So we just simply lived each day as it came, and we've never been sorry. . . . We have been glad, and our son has been glad, that he lived through this experience, but sometimes it was pretty grim. . . .

The thing is that, well, for instance, when the thing started, that was a barley field over there, or an oat field, and this was the edge. . . . Just outside our window here was the edge of town. . . . Well, then, suddenly they began drawing in old chicken coops, old barns, all sorts of things, anything that was habitable, and trailers, and they put them down. . . .

You didn't know what kind of person lived next to you, and, well, look at the Wilsons down there—the Gordon Wilsons—had a trailer on the back of their lot . . . , and they woke up one morning to find that a murder had been committed in there.

I opened the door one time and a man stumbled in. I thought he was drunk, and he wanted to find the police. And I directed him to the police, and he . . . stumbled off again. And then I thought, "Well, that's odd. I never did hear of a drunk man wanting to find the police."

So I opened the door and asked him if he were sick, whereupon he collapsed in the door.

Now he'd been bludgeoned . . . just outside here. He'd sent away his payroll, as it happened, so he didn't have any money in his pocket. But people thought he did, and he'd been beaten, right here, just outside, down the alley a little bit. . . .

Well, now you see our children lived with this. They saw it. They knew all about it. But it depended upon the kind of home the child came from how it affected them. Some of them I dare say it affected badly. I'm not sure whether they would have turned out badly anyway. And others learned what life was all about and took it in their stride. . . . But we lived with this. There was a tension, there was a fear all the time, because you didn't know what was going to happen next. . . .

Howard: The war [itself] was quite real to us. . . . The fact was brought home very, very forcibly to me one time. We were up to Fort

St. John, and the boy was seven or eight years of age then. He was interested in quite a number of planes on the airstrip, so he and I went looking them over.

And suddenly I was told to *halt*!

I turned around and here was an American MP with his hand on his gun ordering me off the airport.

And my first thought was, "Well, this is a fine state of affairs. I'm standing on my *own* soil and being ordered off it by a foreigner!"

Until I calmed down right away. I knew that they were in charge here because of this shuttle service that was going on [lend-lease aircraft to Russia], and . . . they were using the airport much more than the Canadian Air Force were.

Jack Baker

The disparity between American and Canadian wage scales came as a terrific shock to the Canadian mind in 1942. Here Jack Baker tells of his own experience with that disparity.

[The Americans] paid top money, you know. Wages that they got were undreamed of in Canada. Days that we saw fifty bucks in a month, some of the time, you know, that was quite a big chunk of money. Well, *they* were looking at *five hundred a month*! Astronomical figures to us in those days. That's right. Gees, I remember a fellow offering me a job pounding nails.

He says, "I'll pay you five hundred a month."

And I was Senior Dispatcher at Whitehorse for CPA at this time, and I was getting the princely sum of two hundred and thirty a month, and he offered me five hundred to pound nails. And here I was in charge of the fleet of aircraft, getting them in and sending them out into weather and that, and really had to know something. . . . [And] this was for the American air base across the field in Whitehorse—the Americans had one side and we had the other—and they were busy putting up air force buildings. . . . They needed help. So anyhow, I always remember this guy comin' in to me, and he said, "How much do you earn a month?"

You know, at first I thought, "What the hell business is it of yours?"

But I said, "Two hundred and thirty a month."

"*Two hundred and thirty a month!* And you're doin' this?" And he says, "Look," he says, "I'll offer you five hundred a month to pound nails."

Believe me, you know—I was in essential civilian service and I couldn't leave—but I believe I woulda damn near gone. Just pounding nails in boards. Somebody else'd cut the boards if I'd pound the nails.

CHAPTER SEVENTEEN

All-Weather Road

AFTER THE RIBBON CUTTING above Kluane Lake on November 20, two American soldiers gunned a half-ton truck past the speakers' stand and headed for Fairbanks. The drivers, Cpl. Otto Gronke and Pfc. Robert Rowe, had driven all the way up from Dawson Creek. Switching off, driving long hours, stopping to sleep for a while at a road camp near the Alaska-Yukon border, they arrived in Fairbanks on Saturday evening, November 21, 1942. They and their four-wheel-drive army truck were the first to run the full length of the pioneer road.

Although Gronke and Rowe told the Fairbanks newspaper reporters that the road was in good condition, it would be months before anything like a truly passable year-round highway could be completed. The two soldiers had come through in the wintertime. Muskegs and lakes were frozen over. Dry snow hard-packed long stretches of the tote road. Ice covered the bog holes and swamps. The true nature of the pioneer highway would not begin to show until the spring thaw and runoff in March. Workmen and bosses would not be able to see the size of the task that lay ahead until the coming of warm weather. When the blue light and the shadow of winter gave way to the pink and the yellow of spring and summer, long stretches of the pioneer road would become completely impassable. The big job of the Public Roads Administration and the Canadian and American contractors who worked for them would be to open these stretches again and to improve them enough that they would remain passable winter and summer.

One of the worst sections of the whole highway was the ninety-odd miles between the Donjek River and the Alaska border. This section covered the country the Corps of Engineers and the PRA locators had had so much trouble with in the summer of 1942. Permafrost. Glacial rivers. The Donjek, the White. Low ridges, muskegs, bogs quilted with blueberries, swamp, water, muck. Throughout the summer of 1943, the section remained closed, the winter trail a sea of black water. Signal Corps photographer Gail Pinkstaff, traveling on horseback with an Indian guide, made the pack trip over part of this terrain in late August. Pinkstaff reported the country tough going even for the horses. His photographs show U.S. Army trucks mired since the spring thaw. Here and there a cab and a truck bed appear above the water which stands deep in the ditches and over the road. The trucks are steel islands in an inland sea.

The Utah Construction Company wrestled with the muskeg between the Donjek and the border much of the working season. Building permanent camps for the workers and moving in heavy equipment was impossible during the summer. Small planes on floats flew men and light equipment into temporary camps, but the big machines necessary to build permanent road could come in only as workmen completed the fill. Men thought of gimmicks for moving through the soaked country. One that sometimes worked was to split spare Cat tracks from end to end with cutting torches, then to weld these half-treads to the outside of the treads mounted on the bulldozers. The welds increased the weight-bearing ability of the tractors by 50 percent. Called "swamp cats," the double-treaded bulldozers waddled along, trying to open ditches for pushing and flowing the water back. Trucks could then end-dump rock and gravel from the solid bottom of a stretch already filled and rolled down. The true secret, the construction men quickly learned, was not to remove the natural insulation of moss and bush from above the permafrost. They simply dumped and rolled the rock over the top of the plant cover. Working from both north and south, units of the Utah Construction Company met and had their own private opening ceremony at mile 285 west of Whitehorse on October 13, 1943. For the first time since the winter of 1942, the highway was passable all the way through.

ALL-WEATHER ROAD

Richard Finnie

Richard Finnie made studies of the CANOL project and the Alaska Highway for the United States government in 1943. The following selection is taken from "Richard Finnie's Report on the Alaska Highway, October, 1943," *a typescript with notes and photographs taken by Finnie for the Corps of Engineers.*

October 13 . . . It was at three o'clock that we had gone a couple of miles past Sam Rogers' Dry Creek Camp and reached the construction crews at Mile 285.

One bulldozer, supported by a flotilla of dump trucks, was working its way up toward us from the foot of a hill, another dozer was working down. The two were only 300 feet apart, undisturbed muskeg over permafrost intervening. . . .

On a leaf of my notebook I printed: AT THIS SPOT THE LAST GAP IN THE ALASKA HIGHWAY WAS CLOSED BY THE UTAH CONSTRUCTION CO. OCTOBER 13, 1943.

There was excitement in the air. Men began to gather. There were catskinners and truck drivers from the night shift. . . .

Nearer and nearer drew the bulldozers to each other, and the trucks seemed to roll faster. The driver of one became excited and forgot to release the catch on the tail gate as he raised his box, and the truck reared up on its haunches. Bystanders rushed to it and pulled it down.

At six o'clock the last remaining patch of muskeg was buried under a load of gravel, and the two bulldozers came together. As their blades touched, the skinners descended from their seats and shook hands. The skinner of the cat from the north was Bill Herman, of Oakland, California; the skinner of the cat from the south was Louis Kemmis, of Billings, Montana.

On November 20, 1942, a ceremony was staged at Soldiers Summit, Kluane Lake, to open the Alaska Military Highway. But that marked the opening of a winter road, nothing else, so far as through traffic between Dawson Creek and Fairbanks was concerned. Not until October 13, 1943 was an all-weather road linked up. This was really it, and there were no dignitaries present and no speeches were made. Appropriately, all the witnesses besides myself were men who had played an actual part in the building of the road. . . .

It was getting dark. We started back, and near the gravel pit met a BPC [Bechtel-Price-Callahan] fuel truck that had been stopped by Sam Rogers, following Colonel Campbell's order that there be no through traffic until the 18th. The truck had somehow slipped through from Whitehorse, reaching the gap at Mile 285 in the morning, and the driver had philosophically slept in his cab all day.

147

Sam Rogers called: "I guess you can go through now."

The driver grinned and headed his truck northward, the anonymous first man to take a truck from Whitehorse to Fairbanks entirely over all-weather road.

While the Northern Sector of the Alaska Highway was closed during the spring and summer of 1943, the Southern Sector from Dawson Creek to Whitehorse remained open. A fairly steady flow of traffic continued to the air bases and construction camps along the way. Here the Public Roads Administration and the contractors who worked for them carried the responsibility for the hard labor of maintenance and improvement, for most of the army engineer units who had cut the tote road in 1942 had already gone from the highway. Their job had been to open, as rapidly as possible, a road passable for military traffic. Having completed that job, they had been withdrawn and ordered to other assignments around the world: the 18th and 93rd Engineers had been pulled out in January 1943; the 35th, 95th, and 97th in February; and the 340th and 341st in May and July. Although the work of the PRA had been continuous since the very beginning (they had cooperated with the army on the survey and location, and the contractors they hired had actually cut the tote road between Jake's Corner and Whitehorse and between Tok and Big Delta and had improved the stretch of road from Dawson Creek to Fort St. John, all in 1942), the biggest job of the Public Roads Administration and their contractors was the improvement of the highway during 1943.

Their organization generally paralleled that developed by the Corps of Engineers for the work they had done on the pioneer road. At first an Alaska Highway District office operated from Seattle. But need for command in the field increased, and in January 1943 the district office moved to Edmonton. Two division offices then opened, one at Fort St. John and the other at Whitehorse. The Fort St. John office covered the Southern, the Whitehorse office the Northern Division of the highway. Other offices handled matters at Dawson Creek, Fort Nelson, and Tok. The office at Prince Rupert handled problems of shipping from that important railhead and seaport on the southern British Columbian coast.

Upon the shoulders of J. S. Bright, District Engineer, C. F. Capes, Southern Division Engineer, and F. E. Andrews, Northern

Division Engineer, settled the responsibilities for PRA management on the Alaska Highway. The problems they had to solve seem overwhelming. How to move the thousands of tons of equipment and supplies for the contractors over the railroad from Skagway to Whitehorse and onto the ends of the highway construction project at Dawson Creek and in Alaska. How to feed and house the several thousand civilian workers (there were about 7,500 of these men even before the end of 1942). How to settle disputes in the field between army and PRA locators, although theoretically the army had the authority to make the final decisions. How to organize the vast construction operation so that the companies involved could work efficiently. What to do about cold-weather problems (most of the men who worked for the PRA had never seen such extremes of temperature and did not know how to handle heavy equipment in the subarctic cold). And finally, how to dismantle the PRA and civilian contractor operation late in 1943, by which time the army expected all work to be completed.

While the locations and surveys were still under way early in 1942, the PRA began its search for contractors and equipment. PRA officials realized immediately that there was a critical shortage of construction machines, parts, and tools. Large clusters of companies pooling what equipment they had or could get their hands on seemed to be the only solution to the problem. To organize these clusters, the PRA hired five large management contractors, who in turn located and engaged the individual construction companies with their equipment and men. Next, these construction companies signed cost-plus-fixed-fee contracts with the United States government. Unit-price contracts were simply out of the question since it was impossible in the summer of 1942 to know what the extent of the job might be or where and for how long a company would be needed. The cost-plus-fixed-fee contract enabled payment for whatever work a company actually completed.

The five management contractors were the R. Melville Smith Company of Toronto, the Dowell Construction Company of Seattle, the Okes Construction Company of St. Paul, the C. F. Lytle Company and Green Construction Company—Lytle and Green—of Sioux City and Des Moines, and the E. W. Elliott Company of Seattle. In 1942, E. W. Elliott handled transportation and camp construction. The man who owned the company was the very Elliott who had created the fleet of small craft and converted pleasure yachts for shipping PRA workers and supplies from Seattle to Skagway. While Elliott labored at the task of moving people and equipment into the North, each of the other big five managed construction on particular sections of the highway itself. Smith took over the work between Dawson Creek and Fort St. John. Okes managed from Fort St. John to Fort Nelson. Dowell ran the job both directions out of Whitehorse. Lytle and Green took it in Alaska. As the work continued, the PRA had to make reassignments. Smith, for instance, also helped with the stretch of the highway west of Fort Nelson.

The operations of these five management contractors were indeed immense. In 1942 they hired forty-seven different construction companies, in 1943, seventy-seven. During the second year alone, civilian employees under their management totaled 10,400 people working for American companies and 3,700 for Canadian companies. In all, they were responsible for the construction of about 1,400 miles of the improved Alaska Highway and for shipping men, equipment, and supplies into the job. Besides the management contractors and the construction companies, several specialized contractors went into the field in 1942 and 1943. These included bridge contractors such as John A. Roebling's Sons, Bay Cities Engineering, American Bridge, and the J. E. Haddock Company, Ltd. In addition, the Utah Construction Company contracted in 1943 to reopen the impassable section of the highway west of the Donjek.

Among all the thousands of civilian construction workers on the Alcan in 1942 and 1943 there were a great many competent people. But there were also, as in any massive job requiring so many persons, corrupt people, incompetents, misfits, and men who had particular talents no one could utilize because of the circumstances.

C. D. MacKinnon

Time was a big factor to them. . . .

Certainly money was no object. . . . They overpowered it. They had so much equipment, and then they had some top-notch men on the job too. . . . I talked to several, I talked to this one, and he was a Cat operator, and he was from Wisconsin, and he was a chap that . . . he'd set his objective for a farm. And when I picked him up and I took him over to Fort St. John, he said, "Two more paychecks and I've got that farm." And he said, "I never in my wildest dreams ever expected this." . . .

See, he had gone up there with a very definite objective, and he was a good worker. . . .

When you look back and see what they accomplished, I'll tell you . . . it was a terrific undertaking! And when you think . . . that was spread over thousands of square miles! Yes indeed! . . .

[But there were the bad ones too, as there always are.] It would have taken ten Philadelphia lawyers to keep track of them up there. . . .

And then some of the expediters. See, the trucks are comin' down empty. . . . So they were sellin' rides on these trucks for fifty and a hundred dollars, all depending how anxious the guy was to get back out. . . . They were civilians. . . . Several of the truck drivers they were in on it too, but a lot of them didn't know this was takin' place.

And how we caught up on them, this one truck driver—there were five of them comin' down and two were sittin' in with him, and three out in the back. So at the first stop, the three in the back said, "Well, now we'll switch."

And so, of course, it didn't matter. The truck driver thought he was just givin' 'em a lift, but they'd all paid a hundred dollars apiece to . . . get down to Dawson Creek. And so the other kids, they'd paid as much as the two that were sittin' in the cab, and they wanted to get in there and keep warm and let the other two sit out. And so he just turned right around [and took them back]. . . .

But they don't know how much money that guy made. But he was makin' a killin'. . . . He'd be an expediter. They had expediters for everything. I think they had expediters for the expediters. . . .

[Another thing that] would happen, you see, here the craft was goin' night and day. Well, they'd fly in, say, at Fort Nelson. . . . So a plane is coming up and they've got this cargo, and the weather is turning sour. Lotsa times they'd go down to the end of the damn runway and they'd just dump it off there, and they'd close the hatches and take off again. Well, nobody knew [where anything was]. . . . I spent about a week lookin' for, oh, I'd say, maybe a half a million dollars worth of weather equipment that I found in a snowbank up at Fort Nelson. I used some big spears. You see, you'd see a hunka snow, and you'd take a wooden spear, and be shovin' in and probin'. In fact, I found a bunch of parcels—Christmas parcels—for the U.S. Signals that a guy'd dumped off out in a big snowbank when we were lookin' for the weather station. . . .

These Mounties were great guys up there, you know, and they had a tough job. And I remember one night, you know, [there was a bunch of civilian contract breakers trying to get out of Fort Norman on the CANOL project] and, of course, they weren't workin', they were just eating, and they wanted to get 'em outta there. And there was a big guy from California that was their spokesman. . . .

[Well, finally they flew them down to Fort Nelson. And the army operations officer there] he said to me, "What have you done to us here?"

"Well," I said, "What on earth's happenin'?"

"Why," he said, "We're gonna have a riot on our hands. That gang arrived."

And they were all civilians, you see. So the military didn't know just what control they had over 'em. And oh man!

So I said, "Well, they were told very definitely by Captain Westling [at Fort Norman] that they'd git the lift into Nelson, but they were on their own from there on out."

Well! Of course! Once they got in there, then they were just, "Where's the cookhouse? Where do we sleep? Let's git goin' here!"

And so [the officer in charge] didn't know what to do. "Well," I said. Then all of a sudden I remembered; they had a big, tough Mountie down at Fort Liard—it was just about five miles from the air base—I said, "Go down and get the old Mountie."

Oh, and he *was* a *tough* old baby! And I said, "He'll fix yuh."

Well, sir, the old boy comes up, he was tickled to death to help them out anyway, and he come up, and I'll never forget, he come in and he was just throwin' these guys right and left as he waded through them up to get up on the top. He said, "O.K. All 'o yuh, line up on the sides. Git yer stuff, we're goin' down to Liard."

And the old Californian was yellin', "You can't do that to us."

And he said, "Oh?" He said, "You know, you're up here, and if yuh don't work, yuh don't eat. And I've gotta lot of logs down there that need cuttin', and you're goin' down and cut 'em."

Well, that was different. They said, "How do we git outta here?" . . . And this [big Californian] said to him, he said, "We're United States citizens."

[And the old Mountie] said, "You're in Canada and *I'm* the *law* here, and you'll do what I say. When yuh get down there, somebody else'll take care 'o yuh."

"Boy!" . . .

[But] they had some top-notch [men]. Well, I'll never forget this youngster came in, and he was on the faculty of a school in Virginia, but he got in the service, and he arrived in Edmonton, and they gave him a desk in my office. And, you know, he was a youngster that wanted to do something, and a capable boy. But he sat around there, and nobody said anything to him, nobody told him what he was to do or anything. And I used to feel sorry for the poor kid. He'd go out in the morning and get the morning paper, work the crossword puzzle, maybe

go down to the PX and go out for a walk. But . . . it upset him fearfully.
And then you had others that it was just a big gravy train for them. It was funny. . . . Some were quite dedicated, and others didn't care whether school kept or not.

One of the most critical of the jobs during 1942 and 1943 was completing the bridges. In the summer of 1942 the army had built temporary pontoon bridges and had used ferries for crossing the biggest rivers. In many places the Corps and the PRA contractors had constructed timber trestles which were set on mudsills or on driven piles. They had also used box culverts made of logs or lumber ripped from local timber. The army engineers had not intended the wooden culverts and bridges to be permanent, and PRA designers did not expect many of them to survive the spring runoff in 1943.

Wherever possible, the PRA left those timber bridges alone that stayed in place during the second season on the highway, but they had to rebuild many others. By late in the summer of 1943 contractors were at work from one end of the Alcan to the other on a wide variety of bridges, including I-beam, steel truss, timber truss, and plate girder. They built two suspension bridges, one over the Peace River near Fort St. John, and the other over the Liard about two hundred miles west of Fort Nelson. Workmen began constructing the foundations of this Liard River bridge during the winter, but spring runoff and its heavy ice flow severely injured the cofferdam. The river's swift current for a time prevented divers going down to make repairs. Men could not make the repairs until the river dropped, and contractors were not able to begin putting up the steel framework until summer. When the weather cleared, they rapidly completed the job and opened the bridge to traffic in November 1943. At the Liard, as elsewhere on the Alaska Highway, when the country dried out and the weather improved, workmen labored hard for long hours to finish their work.

The northern winters did have several advantages. Dry snow and ice hard-surfaced the highway until breakup so that the heavy trucks and carriers moving cement, bridge steel, and long timbers did not cut the road into deep ruts. In addition, the frozen surfaces of the rivers made natural platforms for the heavy construction work. All winter long the men labored at the bridge sites, cutting timber, erecting falsework, putting in piers and trusses, moving

153

heavy equipment and steel beams into place. The Peace, the Liard, the Kiskatinaw, the Sikanni Chief, the Muskwa. Workmen did much of the winter's work in darkness or semidarkness because in November, December, and January there are only four or five hours of daylight, and even these are long-shadowed and blue, the sun merely rising above the horizon and setting again after a short arc. Much of the winter's work, too, occurred in long stints. The shift on the Peace River bridge was ten hours. The men worked two shifts, a twenty hour work day. Knowing well that all the falsework and the erection towers resting on the rivers' ice must go out within minutes when the breakup came, construction companies drove themselves with the permanent bridges in the winter of 1943.

Transportation of materials was one of the major problems the contractors and PRA professionals had to solve. They had to ship fabricated steel bridge sections, many of them up to eighty feet long, by rail from the United States or Canada to access points on the highway. At these points men loaded the sections and trucked them up or down the Alcan sometimes as far as five or six hundred miles. They moved pile drivers and derricks in the same way. Bridges on the section of the Alaska Highway managed by Dowell, a 480-mile piece running north and south from Whitehorse, required an estimated 1,650,000 miles of truck hauling from July 1943 until Dowell's men completed their work. Dowell estimated that its drivers made five thousand truck trips to serve this bridge construction project during the July-until-the-end period.

Of all the bridges built on the highway in 1942 and 1943, the Peace River suspension bridge at Taylor, near Fort St. John, was the most spectacular and the most trouble-ridden. The Peace River here had been a serious bottleneck when the Corps of Engineers had used the ferry during the summer of 1942. Men, equipment, and supplies going north by land had had to cross the river at this point, and the ferry simply had not been able to handle the loads efficiently. Engineers had constructed a timber trestle bridge in October 1942, but the river had taken it out in November. It was essential that a permanent steel bridge be completed as soon as possible because no timber structure could withstand the strong and twisting current of the Peace here near the mouth of the Pine River. Ice also was too much for timber structures on the Peace.

An ice cover 4 to 5 feet thick forms near Taylor in the wintertime. In the spring the ice goes out in chunks sometimes as large as 700 by 2,000 feet.

Workmen began laying foundations for the Peace River bridge in December 1942. Shortly afterward Roebling's Sons engineers arrived to plan and oversee the construction of this 2,130-foot bridge. By early March, the men had completed the foundations. Then they skidded the erection tower out onto the ice. Now was the most crucial time. Breakup would come in early April, only a month away. The whole bridge had yet to be assembled, and the river's ice must serve to support the erection tower and all the heavy construction equipment and bridge steel.

There were delays. Necessary material did not arrive on schedule, an epidemic of colds and flu hit many of the workers, and in late March the sun warmed the country. Heavy rains followed. The men who were well worked hard. They began erecting the south main tower on March 27. Rapidly completing that, they slid the erection tower across the river and carefully placed it for raising the north main tower. Another delay. Three cars of steel for the north tower had checked through Edmonton, but had not arrived in Dawson Creek. Men had to locate these, unload the steel, and truck it up to the Peace River before they could complete the tower.

Finally by April 5 the workmen had located the cars, assembled the pieces, and put the north tower in place. The ice had held while the contractors erected 700 tons of steel in 5-1/2 days. They were then able to dismantle the erection tower and skid it off the ice just in time. Breakup came on the eleventh. Then the men went to work to place the cables and do the steelwork for the roadway. By the end of July they had finished the concrete roadway, and by early August they opened the Peace River suspension bridge to traffic. Workers had completed in exactly four months and one week a job which probably would have taken eight months or more under normal conditions.

As one would expect, there were serious accidents along the Alcan during the crush of labor in 1942 and 1943. There were those which killed several persons, and others in which many people were injured—the drowning of eleven men on Charlie Lake, for instance, and the Dawson Creek fire. There were also lone inci-

dents of death or injuries to one or two. Here and there along the
highway today tiny stone monuments mark the places where men
died among the black spruce and the aspen. You can find them if
you search the borders of the highway lined with fireweed in
summer or blown with soft snow in winter. There were plane
crashes too, and C. D. MacKinnon remembers one of the bad ones.

C. D. MacKinnon

There were twenty-six of them went down this night. In fact, I was on
the manifest to come in with a chap on the Northwest Airlines, at Fort
Nelson, and that night there were three aircraft went down. . . .

We were coming right on into Edmonton, nonstop, and just prior
to Colonel Knight comin' in they brought in two accident cases, one
boy was supposed to have had his back broken, and the other boy with
his shoulder . . . and they were on stretchers, both on stretchers, and
that meant they would have to come in at Fort St. John to the hospital
there.

And I turned to this Northwest Airlines guy and I said, "You
know, I think now I'll stay here tonight. I can do some more work, and
then I'll go on into Edmonton tomorrow because if they come in at Fort
St. John that means they'll be an hour or so delay and we won't get into
Edmonton till about three or four in the morning and you'll have a
deuce of a time gittin' a car out of the pool to git home." . . .

Now the American CO there was a very personal friend of
Colonel Knight's, and he tried to talk the colonel into staying. And
there were twenty-six GIs coming out that had been selected for
officer's training, and two of them had little huskies. I'll never forget
that. Oh they were the cutest little rascals. And these kids.

And they were gassing up, and the colonel took on more
gas . . . and the chap who was the CO there was tryin' to talk 'em into
staying overnight. The weather was bad, it was fearful, and I think
actually it was on account of these two injured boys. If they hadn't
been there, I think the Colonel woulda pulled in, but he wanted to get
them to the hospital. . . .

And he took off. And I remember . . . it was within a half an hour
after they took off, oh hell it was less than that, hell it was fifteen
minutes, they got word that she was socked in up and down the line and
all over! And they tried to call Colonel Knight, tell 'em to come back
into Nelson, but they couldn't raise 'em. . . . It was storming, and it
was a fearful night out. Anyway, they were unable to raise 'em. And
they went down.

And there was a hunting party—it was in 'fifty-six or 'fifty-seven,
I remember readin' it in the *Journal*—and they were going down this

fire break, and the fella happened to see metal shining, and they went over, and here was the plane. It had gone down in under, and the trees had fallen over it. . . .

Oh, and it was fearfully cold, about sixty or seventy. They weren't actually off, very little off track. They were just making their turn to get on the beam to come into Edmonton. But something must have malfunctioned. They never did find out. . . .

But we searched, oh they brought in all the aircraft, brought aircraft in from Edmonton, and everybody was up looking, you know. But it was so cold that there was a ground haze, so the visibility was nil, and you couldn't git down too low, and they never did find them. And it was snowing too, and it was fearful out. But there were three aircraft down that night.

By the early spring of 1943, the world situation began to change. The Allied strategic position in the Pacific improved. In January United States military forces occupied Amchitka in the Aleutians and prepared for attacks upon the Japanese at Kiska and Attu. The main thrust of the Japanese appeared to be toward the South Pacific, rather than the North. Air and sea-lanes to the North Pacific and Alaska had remained open since Pearl Harbor, and there seemed little danger that they might now be closed off. These facts seemed to relieve the pressing need for the highway as an emergency supply route to Alaska. Hence, the War Department wished to reduce its commitments there and to transfer its forces to other war zones where military duties were more urgent.

The Corps of Engineers had borne the final responsibility for the management of all construction and maintenance on the Alaska Highway since the beginning of the project. The Corps officers and the PRA engineers who worked with them had often disagreed on the standards to which the road ought to be built, and now as war pressures lessened and the army wished earnestly to decrease its responsibilities in the North, the Corps began to insist more firmly upon faster work and lower standards. On March 25 the Chief of Engineers announced to the heads of the Federal Works Administration and the PRA at a conference in Washington that he wanted to reduce standards considerably, and on April 5 the army's Northwest Division Engineer told PRA District Engineer J. S. Bright that all plans for a safe, high-speed modern highway must be abandoned immediately. He added that the Public Roads Administration and its mass of private contractors must complete their work by no later than the last day of December 1943. General Worsham stressed to J. S. Bright that an all-weather military truck road was the only kind of road that could be justified. Among Worsham's stipulations were orders that no bituminous surfacing be done, that for the sake of economy one-way stretches of road and one-way bridges must be utilized, and that PRA plans for relocations to improve curvature and sight distance must be dropped. Two days later, on April 7, the army sent out a formal directive confirming Worsham's words to Bright.

PRA contract work in the field in the summer and fall of 1943, therefore, consisted mainly of completing the Alaska Highway to the army's standards for expediency. There were, nonetheless, certain compromises enforced by circumstances. The rains and heavy floods of early June entirely washed out the pioneer road in some places so that relocations were the only practicable way to rebuild. Workmen had to reopen the impassable stretch from the Donjek to the border; necessarily, they made many relocations here. The steep cliffs around Muncho Lake also required relocations. Construction men, too, completed the stretch of nearly finished modern highway between Dawson Creek and Fort St. John. Otherwise, the PRA contractors spent the summer and early fall in widening the road to 26 feet in some places, in laying a gravel or crushed rock surface, and in completing as many of the bridges as they could.

By September, the PRA began to close out its work up and down the highway. In the Fort St. John sector, for instance, contractors completed their assignments, packed up, and began moving down the road toward the railhead at Dawson Creek. The Northwest Division Engineer took over all government equipment needed for maintenance and opened negotiations with the contractors for the purchase or rental of any equipment the army needed for keeping the highway open. The Corps also selected camps for road maintenance centers. The contractors were to leave these fully equipped for occupancy by military and civilian maintenance units. They were to dismantle all other camps and return government equipment to the agency which had originally issued it.

In the fall, the army ordered the five large management contractors to complete their work and evacuate by October 31, two months earlier than the original deadline of December 31.

Throughout October, a crush of men, supplies, and equipment all across the snow-covered country shoved its way down the highway or out over the railroad to Skagway. On October 30, all but absolutely essential PRA construction ceased. A handful of PRA engineers under Raymond Archibald stayed behind to oversee the completion of bridge construction, but men working for the army engineers did the actual work of finishing.

In mid-October, the PRA District Office at Edmonton moved to Chicago, and by the end of the month the seventy-seven construction companies and the thousands of civilian workers hired to complete the Alaska Highway had packed up and gone home. Only skeleton crews to close up camps and do other essential jobs remained behind. The end had come to a very complex attempt at cooperation between the army engineers and the professionals of the Public Roads Administration in a time of world crisis. What remained to be accomplished was a minimum maintenance program. The United States Army Engineers would direct this maintenance program until six months after the end of the war. At that time the Dominion government would take charge of the 1,200 miles of the Alaska Highway stretching across the mountains and muskegs of northern Canada.

Something in the Nature of This Clay

THE PERIOD of American construction on the Alaska Highway officially closed on October 31, 1943. From then until the Canadian takeover after the war's end, the United States Army Corps of Engineers kept up only the simplest kind of maintenance program for the road. The Northwest Service Command and the Northwest Division Engineer maintained that part of the highway crossing Canada, and the Alaska Department of the Army and the Alaska Road Commission that part in Alaska after June 1944. From the several-thousand-man force working on the Canadian section in the fall of 1943, the number used for maintenance plummeted to 385 by September 1944. In February the tiny maintenance force was up to 514. Except for a handful of supervisors, however, all the workers were Canadian citizens, and these men concerned themselves with little more than keeping the road open to military traffic.

Actual traffic over the highway during World War II was far lighter than it would have been had air or sea-lanes to Alaska been cut off. Tonnage hauled all the way through to Fairbanks was small. Most of it went to intermediate points such as the air bases. From the northern end, freight went south to the border. From Whitehorse, it went up to the border and south as far as Coal River and the Liard. Trucks packed tonnage from railhead at Dawson Creek up as far as Muncho Lake, the drivers getting relief and refueling at relay stations kept at intervals along the road. During this period the government limited civilian use to a strictly military function. Civilian employees of the army moved when necessary up and down the highway, and there were various civilian investigative bodies as well as the occasional photographer or journalist, but all traveled by special permit.

Icing continued to be one of the biggest problems during the maintenance period. In the North, as engineers and workers from the lower Forty-eight learned the hard way, icing is a whole field of study in itself. Known locally in the early days of the highway as "glaciering," icing most often happens around seeps, springs, or along shallow streams or rivers. The process occurs something like this: ground water flows out on top of ice surfaces already formed, freezes, and builds up a fan-shaped ice formation over the roadway. More water flows over the top of the ice fan and freezes, leaving an air space between the layers of ice. The fords then become difficult to cross because unsupported crusts of ice break through under the weight of the truck or tractor making the crossing. Narrow mountain road shelves where seeps flow over the road from the upper side are the most hazardous places of all. Seeps in such locations form an icy slope toward the downhill side of the roadway, toward the side over which the truck driver dares not slip. Such icy places stop all traffic until maintenance men blast or pick the ice away. The shapes of the ice fans are often fantastic. Ice shelves grow like deadly cancers.

What causes such icing? What keeps water flowing in subzero temperatures? One important factor is the insulating layer of peat, moss, or snow from under which the flow occurs. Water moving under such insulation simply does not freeze until it seeps out into the lower temperature of the outside air. Another factor is the depth of the stream or river in which the seep occurs. Icing happens readily on the braided rivers of the North where the water is fairly shallow. In these rivers, the bottom tends to freeze first. This freezing forces the flowing water up and over the top of the ice into the cold northern air. Heat transfer of several kinds is another cause of icing. Radiation is the transfer of the sun's heat. Convection is heat transfer as the result of circulation. In convection, the water and air just below the surface of peat or moss, since they are warmer than the cold atmosphere above them, tend to rise toward that cold air. Upon contacting the cold air, the water freezes. A third kind of heat transfer causing icing is molecular vibration. In this kind of transfer, heat conducted by subsurface water, when it reaches the surface of the ground, is lost directly into space by radiation, or it may warm the air it contacts and be carried off in convection currents. Whatever the type of transfer, the result is the same—the water freezes due to heat loss.

Engineers and PRA contractors had tried all kinds of methods to prevent or at least to combat the icing. Around bridges one answer was to build the superstructures high enough over the stream bed to avoid ice buildup underneath. When ice did build up around the piling, workmen tried to blast it away before its grinding and shoving took the bridge out. On southerly slopes where water seeped and iced over the road, blasting with dynamite, trenching ruts to guide the wheels of passing traffic, and covering the ice with insulating layers of corduroy and gravel were all partially effective. Another method of removing the ice fan was to break it up with a heavy rooter pulled by two tractors. A small tractor on the ice fan held the drawbar steady while a heavy tractor off the ice exerted the power. Men also used steam jets to open flow-channels under ice or under the insulating covers of peat and moss by the side of the road. Engineers, too, tried deep and very narrow ditches: the high walls and the insulation of plant life growing along such ditches helped to keep the flowing water from freezing. Proper placement of culverts was another means of preventing the icing.

Permafrost continued to plague the roadbuilders. Known also as "frozen ground," "blue ice," "black ice," "ground ice," and "ice lense," the ice and permanently frozen ground underlies the topsoil and matted ground cover of all of North America above the Arctic Circle and of southward reaching fingers of it below the circle. Engineers in 1942 had had to learn quickly that when they uncovered the permafrost, melting inevitably began and did not cease. Ground ice was the North's great topic while the Americans worked on the Alaska Highway. Roadmen dwelt on the matter nights before bed as they sat around crackling barrel stoves. Like Mississippi riverboat pilots experimenting and talking among themselves of the mysteries of bars and crossings, cutoffs and wind reefs, Cat skinners and engineers with experience on permafrost experimented, questioned, talked, and experimented again. Ancient trappers spoke wisdom about permafrost to privates fresh from Texas, cheechakos before the sourdoughs. Some northerners said permafrost was the remnants of age-old glaciers; others said it was ancient lakes frozen in place. Some said they had seen lenses of it a thousand feet high and five or six times as long extending along the sides of valleys. But all the old-timers agreed, "Where tundra is thickest, you'll find ice."

After extensive research, engineers learned that the permafrost often extended to great depths, in places down to 300 feet or more. Often the frozen subsoil contained masses of nearly pure ice lying in horizontal planes, called "lenses," and merging into vertical "wedges" or "veins." The deep freezing happened in the early Pleistocene period, perhaps a million years ago, and although some of the areas have thawed and refrozen since that time, most of them have probably been frozen solid ever since. Much of Alaska and the Yukon Territory in permafrost country are covered with dense growths of mosses, grasses, shrubs, and trees which, in turn, are underlain with decayed plant matter, peat. The combination of living plants and the peat acts both as a sponge, holding water and preventing rapid runoff, and as an insulator, preventing thawing in the summer months for more than a few inches below the surface. If drainage happened to be good where the highway crossed permafrost, the road eventually stabilized itself as the soil moisture drained away and the ground dried out. But if the land was poorly drained, as it usually was, especially in muskeg country, engineers rapidly learned that the only thing to do was to go around, to bridge, to corduroy, or to fill on top of the layers of natural insulation.

Silt and muck also caused severe problems. Engineers, contractors, and workmen spent nearly endless effort and knowledge to solve these problems, as well as those caused by permafrost and icing. Often, bumbling trial and error were the only ways to get results.

Earl Bartlett

There were a lot of problem areas in which money had to be poured in just on the solution of problems. One of the most prominent is called the Mud Hill at [mile] 368. The Americans did very many things to stabilize this hill. They piled great masses of stones on the downhill side trying to stabilize the bank, and these endless tons of stone all showered down and ended up in the valley. They took and drove piles fifty or sixty feet in length and tied them together to hold up the road embankment, and the piles and all tipped over and went down into the valley. So they discovered that there was something in the nature of this clay, or river silt is what it was, glacial silt, that was retaining the water, and they just had to keep the water out of it.

They went up the hillside, scraped the trees off, did considerable amount of trenching, finally they worked out a system. They've stabilized that hillside. It slides a little bit, but only on the surface. Money expended in a place like that should never be charged to that one location. It was a workshop in which they were developing techniques that would be applied in many similar situations.

During the period of American maintenance there were many washouts on the road. The new, raw subgrade and bridge approaches gave way easily to the rush of water in rivers and creeks, especially during spring runoff and the rainy seasons of summer. In July 1943, more than forty bridges went out on the highway in a single day, and while bridges were much improved by 1945, men labored constantly to keep them in good shape—to keep the highway open. While Walter Williscroft was superintendent of the maintenance section headquartered at Destruction Bay on Kluane Lake, he and his men worked around the clock until washouts were repaired and the traffic could move again. Williscroft designed a movable bridge after the big slide at mile 1058 on Kluane Lake took out the road. He got his idea from the principles of the farm push rake and the stone boat. He was a practical man using his imagination.

Walter Williscroft

I've been on all these washouts, day and night, and I've been on 'em for a week at a time. I never had my boots off. . . .

I think one of the worst things we had was the Kluane Lake slide. . . . We lost a Cat in that slide. . . . In 1945, July. . . . And boy that thing come down, I'm tellin' ya! It slid every half hour, on the hour. . . .

Up on the top of the mountain was a big pocket. . . . And this stuff would slide off the mountain and fall down into that crick and plug the crick up, and then the water would build up behind it until it got enough water pressure to just swush! Away she'd go. It'd just take that long . . . it was rainin'. . . . About [every] half an hour it'd slide. . . .

I was there when this Cat got buried up, and I told [the skinner], I said, "Don't get your back towards that slide." . . .

I was on foot. I had a car there. . . . And you know with a Cat runnin' you can't hear anything. I said, "You watch me, and if you see me beltin' them lights, you get outta there." Because I had to stay back where I could hear the slide building up, you see.

Well this guy got up there, messed around, and the first thing he had his back towards me, you see, and I heard the thing was goin' to go.

Well, no use to shout. I started to run in there, and I thought, "No," about half way there, "I'm on foot. He's better on that Cat."

Well then when he did notice me, he jumped off the Cat—he got outta there—but a guy from the other side run in to get the Cat, and he just about stepped onto the Cat when the first shot of the slide hit him, and he just went down on his back like that right to the lake. Good thing it hit him in the heels, that he fell on top of the slide. And he had white coveralls on, and I could see him going. He was right on top of this muck and slop, and it dumped him right in the lake.

And we rushed down there and give him a hand to get out. He wasn't hurt, although he was black and blue from bouncin' on these boulders. [And *scared*!] Oh yes! . . .

For a long while we didn't know whether we were goin' to put a ferry in there. We brought a scow up. We didn't know what we was goin' to do. . . . The darned thing would change. There was about five channels, and this time it'd come down over here, see. Well then the next time it'd come down over there.

We built this little bridge, and we had a Cat on each end had a cable on it, see, so that if it went down over there, we'd put the bridge on there. . . . We'd run the traffic over it for a little while. About time it was goin' to come down, we'd haul the bridge off, see, and let her go. . . .

We built [the bridge] on skids—big skids—and we'd just snake it onto the Cat. . . . And we had to watch pretty close for the time that that thing was goin' to slide. . . . We didn't want to get caught. We never did get caught with traffic on it. . . .

We made it plenty sturdy. . . . We designed it, and it worked. We had a cable on each end of it, and just hauled it back and forth from one washout to the other. . . .

The bridge was about twenty-four foot long, you see, and that would cover the channel, and we could build some on the ends and run the traffic over. . . .

Actually, I think we learnt that from the farm of using a push rake for a haystack, you know. We used to use a timber like that with teeth on it, and then just skid her up the poles with a load of hay. I think we more or less got the idea from that. Or [from] a big stone boat [as] we called it. . . .

We didn't run anything really heavy over it . . . because we might have busted it. . . . [We were kind of fussy about running heavy traffic over it] because that's pretty slow, and we could get caught. When we moved that traffic, *they moved fast* because maybe you'd have twenty, twenty-five, or thirty lined up on each side, and they had to go quick because you only had a very short time to get 'em over.

Although there were tensions between Canadian and American workmen on the highway until the Americans pulled out, cooperative performance remained generally high. The Canadians did resent the much higher American wage scale, however. The Dominion government did not want Canadian citizens to receive American wages, and Canadians were paid less than Americans for comparable work. Canadians also chafed over American wastefulness. The Corps of Engineers and the PRA contractors revealed, it seemed to northerners, a total disregard for equipment. Saving money and machinery seemed unimportant to the Americans; they discarded worn-out or damaged equipment upon leaving Canada as if the supplies of new machines back in the United States would be endless. More often than not, however, the period from the end of 1943 until the Canadian takeover was harmonious. The American engineers were officially in charge of work on the highway, but the Canadians did the labor and were left the responsibility for working out most of the practical details of repair and maintenance. Many Canadians remember this period with nostalgia.

Earl Bartlett

It was very gratifying to be able to help them out in a situation, give a fellow a little feeling of importance in a world that was in trouble. . . .

I did have some work on American aircraft, twice, three times. One of them, I remember that when one of their big Globemasters, four-motored job, was held up because of trouble in one of the starting motors, the captain of our establishment told me that they were bringing over one and that he wanted me to give it my best attention.

My shop was upstairs in a long building then, facing the road, and when I heard footsteps up the stairway, I thought the whole American and Canadian army was coming. The captain of the garrison and the commanding officer of the air base was up first, and behind them all the lower ranks, and finally the two airmen carrying this defective part. There were no less than fifteen high-ranking personnel came in to request a civilian to get their blasted aircraft repaired.

So we made some tests and some attempts at repairs, and when it became apparent that we would be able to get them going again, the rest of them left and the two airmen stayed there. They were perhaps the most unpretentious looking chaps you'd ever see, with flop-eared headgear and clothing that was designed for warmth rather than for style. A delightful pair of chaps.

I got this starting motor repaired for them. Otherwise, the ship would have been grounded for two or three days getting one in through Great Falls. They were on a mission in which time was important to them.

Oh, three o'clock in the afternoon I heard the roar of an aircraft, and the old Globemaster was in the air, and the fellows came along over the shop and dipped their wings in salute.

Norman Harlin

Although Norman Harlin's account covers a period before the American contractors left late in 1943, it is representative of the good feeling that existed and remained between many of the Canadians and the Americans who worked along the Alaska Highway during the war.

Actually, we got along pretty well—Canadians and the Americans. We had a lot of hard work and a lot of cushy work. . . .

Oh, I had a little trouble with guy's never been in the woods before. There was one young fellow up here. . . . Well, he was with us two months I guess, but he was more trouble. And the poor little guy, he had thick, thick glasses. And all these creeks in June, they're pretty high you know. We had to fall trees to get across 'em. And we never made one crossing that he didn't fall in. Someone had to jump in after him. And a hell of a good little guy!

And finally there where Brooks' Brook is now, I told him, I said, "You're gonna get hurt. You're gonna drown. Cut yourself with an axe, and no way o' getting you out." I said, "I'm gonna have to put you on the plane and send you back."

"Well," he says, "I was gonna suggest that anyhow."

He'd been a postman, a mailcarrier in San Francisco. But he says, "I been thinkin' the same thing." But he says, "I got no money."

Well, I had a government check in my pocket for a couple-hundred bucks, and I pulled it out and I said, "Well here. Get on the plane and . . . pay your fare back to San Francisco and send me back the money."

And by God in three weeks that money was back. Nice letter. He still writes to me at Christmas. But I knew sooner or later he was gonna [get hurt]. He couldn't see properly. You know, walkin' a log across a little canyon. . . . Bad enough for us to have to walk across. He couldn't see. Lose his balance. He had no sense of equilibrium at all, poor little guy. And an axe, he didn't know which end to use. And I was so afraid he'd cut his feet.

Throw a Barl Out

By THE TIME the PRA contractors left Canada late in 1943, the Americans had assembled mountains of equipment and supplies in the North for the construction of the Alaska Highway, the CANOL road and pipelines, and other closely related projects. The problem of disposing of all this material then became very complicated. Rapid transportation out by bus, air, truck, rail, and sea for the thousands of workers was difficult in itself, but disposing of the things sent in for the construction task was quite another matter. So large was the job of accounting for, of inventorying, the stocks of such items as clothing, sleeping bags, foodstuffs, and surpluses of large and small machines and parts—all stored in dumps and warehouses—that the Northwest Service Command did not fully attempt it. Instead they set up common pools for the materials and stated in a report that it was simply "not practicable to keep a record of the surpluses resulting from each construction project."

The officials responsible drew up a plan for handling these things. It was meant to work as follows: property belonging to private contractors was to be returned to the owners or cash settlements were to be made with them; all United States government property that might be located and accounted for, on the other hand, was to be inspected and placed in one of four categories depending upon condition. Category 1 was for items so badly damaged or worn out that they had no value. Category 2 was for items having some salvage or second-hand value. Placed in category 3 were those materials or parts in critically short supply, and category 4 was for those which were new or lightly used and in very good condition. Items in the first category were to be dumped, and those in the third and fourth categories were to be saved for use elsewhere. Machines, supplies, and parts in the second category, however, seemed to cause the most trouble. The original American agreement with the Dominion to build the highway had made no provision for the sale or disposal of any United States matériel in Canada. The value of items in category 2 did not warrant the cost of transportation back to American territory. Canadian merchants did not want the local market flooded with any surplus parts, machines, and other stocks which they themselves would be in the business of selling to Canadian citizens after the end of the war. The Dominion government, therefore, opposed the sale of these things in Canada.

On June 23, 1944, the two governments themselves signed an agreement for disposing of the immovables—buildings, airstrips, and the like. The Canadian government might now purchase these, while the United States government retained the right to use them until the war's end. Disposing of the movables, however, was far more complicated. Finally the Permanent Joint Board on Defense took the matter in hand, and on September 7, 1944, adopted as their Thirty-third Recommendation the principle that the U.S. government should remove from Canada all items it considered of value, that the Dominion government should arrange to purchase from the United States whatever other items it wanted, and that all remaining movables should be transferred to an agency of the Canadian government for sale. Proceeds from the sales were to be paid to the American government.

There was a gap of approximately ten months between October 31, 1943, when nearly all the Americans had to drop the highway construction project and leave Canada and September 7, 1944, when the Permanent Joint Board adopted the Thirty-third Recommendation. This was a most troublesome period. During that ten months officials had little more than a plan for categorizing and arranging the American matériel in the North, and the Dominion government had not reached a final agreement with the United States for purchasing any of it, or for allowing the Americans to sell or give it to interested Canadian citizens, although representatives carried on negotiations throughout the spring and summer. Reportedly, men destroyed large amounts of material along the Alaska Highway in Canada during this period. People who lived along the highway in late 1943 and in 1944 still tell of the dumping, burying, and burning of goods as small as mosquito netting and down-filled sleeping bags and as large as trucks and Caterpillar parts.

Two Canadian newspapers—the *Vancouver Daily Province* and the *Edmonton Journal*—also carried stories of this destruction. B. A. McKelvie reported in the *Daily Province* that he had gone to Fort St. John and Dawson Creek where he had seen large dumps of things thrown away. One dump "was littered with cans, debris and decaying food." Another was on fire, "burning night and day." Still another contained barrel heaters, water heaters, and "hot-air chambers for furnaces." McKelvie also reported that the local people were busy trying to salvage what they could of the usable items, but that many of the goods had been intentionally damaged. One man told him that someone had smashed good cast iron stoves with a sledgehammer before throwing them into a dump. "War devastation to a surprising degree is being witnessed here and at Fort St. John," McKelvie wrote. "Destruction of property is not being done by enemy action, but with deliberate purpose." There were also stories of destruction farther up the highway. The *Edmonton Journal* reprinted a letter on July 11, 1944 from a woman in Whitehorse. The writer said that she had seen, near Whitehorse, "a barracks between two and three city blocks long, packed with winter clothes, overshoes, parkas, pure wool blankets, comforters, chairs, office desks, and almost everything you could imagine. They stacked them up, poured gasoline over them, set them on fire. Guards stood around with fixed bayonets so nobody could get anything."

Officials attempted to prevent salvaging or taking of goods from dumps and storage depots by placing guards over them. They also denied that destruction was taking place. The *Edmonton Journal* reported on July 6, 1944, that both Maj. Gen. W. W. Foster, Canadian Special Commissioner for Northwest Defence Projects, and Col. Frederick K. Strong, Jr., in charge of the American Northwest Service Command, had denied McKelvie's charges. And on the fourteenth, the *Journal* reported that Maj. Gen. E. B. Gregory, U. S. Quartermaster General, had said that: "he knew nothing of the destruction," but that he was quite aware that "disposal of clothing and equipment no longer useable by the American army 'is becoming an increasingly difficult problem.'" During this same period, however, the Americans were making sincere efforts to haul a lot of their equipment out of Canada. McKelvie had reported in the *Daily Province* on July 6 that he had himself seen forty-three carloads of American freight and that thirty to forty carloads of heavy equipment were rolling each day through central British Columbia on their way back to the United States.

In the fall of 1945 an American army captain personally went out to check for and if possible to locate "lost" heavy equipment supposed to be strewn along the Alaska Highway. The *Edmonton Journal* carried the story of Captain Carpenter's search on February 19, 1946. Carpenter had flown the length of the road at an average altitude of 500 feet to study anything that might look like abandoned equipment. He had marked the suspicious-looking areas. Ground parties later went in to investigate. According to his report, Carpenter located no more than thirty to thirty-five pieces. These had all been "cannibalized," that is, stripped, and had no value whatever. The House Roads Committee of the United States Congress also investigated charges of corruption and waste along the highway. After a four-month study, they concluded in March 1946 that, considering the wartime circumstances, the PRA and the Corps of Engineers had done "a splendid job" and that the "rumors of abandoned equipment, wild extravagances, fraud and corruption" were not borne out by the facts.

There the matter seemed to rest, though the legends never quite died and people in the North continued to talk. The reality of the matter must lie somewhere between the fabulous stories and the official denials. It is correct that the Americans tried to haul out what they could, but it is also true that goods were wasted. Many Canadians saw these things happen. They could not be entirely wrong. Nor could the newspaper accounts be completely inaccurate. The *Edmonton Journal* spoke of "the wholesale and spectacular destruction of American supplies in the summer of 1944" in an editorial it published on January 12, 1946, and it blamed both the American Army and the Canadian War Assets Corporation, that corporation which by agreement between the two countries was to handle the transfer of unwanted American goods to the Dominion. It was this "wholesale" destruction as well as additional destruction of surpluses by the War Assets Corporation, the *Journal* said, which had "helped create a psychological atmosphere which encourages looting."

There is little doubt that much of the blame lies simply upon the changing circumstances of war. By 1943 the Japanese war was clearly focusing in the South Pacific rather than in the North, and the American army correctly shifted its forces accordingly. But the decision to slash American commitments in the North and along the Alaska Highway in 1943 had its price. It meant that contractors had to go on a crash program to get out by the October 31 deadline, that they did not have time to pack much of value out with them. Even had there been more time, however, there would still no doubt have been waste. The Americans had shipped a superabundance of machinery and supplies into Canada; they had "overwhelmed" the task. They were rapidly becoming a production-oriented, rather than a repair-oriented society. Their leaders would very likely have thought it economically wiser to order new machines and supplies than to salvage and reuse the old. Indeed only a very wealthy industrial society could have created all those surpluses in the first place. Besides, there was the consideration of the manpower and money required to pack all the surpluses out. The army needed the manpower elsewhere, on other war fronts.

Probably the most important factor, however, was that during the period in 1944 when the waste along the highway appears to have peaked there was no final agreement with the Dominion for transferring the matériel to Canada. That meant that the Americans had to look out for it until an agreement could be reached. They had to store it or ship it out. Storing it meant collecting, sorting, preserving, and guarding it effectively, but the numbers of men needed to accomplish these things were unavailable. Shipping all of it out was also impracticable, if not downright impossible. Many an officer in the northern field lacking manpower for inventorying and adequate means of transporting the stuff, yet faced with the immediate decision of what to do with the excess of matériel under his charge, probably thought of the only other alternative—destroy it, get rid of it, maybe even "lose" the records. Rather than destroy, he would have liked to give the stuff away, but he could not legally let the local people have it. Canadian Customs would not permit that. So the officer was trapped.

The puzzle remains today as to precisely how much new or usable material the Americans and Canadians did discard or destroy in the months following October 1943. Perhaps no one can ever clear up the puzzle since official denials differ from oral accounts and newspaper reports. However the matter may at last be settled, if settled at all, the stories of the waste and destruction are very much alive among those people who lived along the Alaska Highway or worked for the project managers during the war. There are, of course, second- and third-hand accounts, but there are many persons who tell of seeing the destruction with their own eyes. If one listens to these people, one cannot help wondering about accuracy. But the informants talk with vigor, and the events they describe have become as real to them as their memories of trapping and steamboats, working dogs and classic bush flyers. The accounts are a vital part of the oral literature of the Alaska Highway. Importantly, they suggest the changes in northwestern Canadian attitudes during and after the war—the changes that happened in the minds and feelings of a people accustomed to making do with little when they first sensed that a new and affluent industrial age was at hand, when they first met another people who could afford to throw things away.

Many of the Canadians who saw these events were honestly shocked at the extent of the waste. Though some no doubt took things in order to sell them, most simply picked up what they could use or give away to their friends. Nearly all those northerners who spoke to me in the summer of 1970 still were aghast as their memories came alive. Having been taught as children that waste was wrong and that taking things that belonged to someone else was stealing—was evil—they could not bring themselves to lift anything at all without a terrible wrenching of conscience. And they could not fully approve a people whose lives were already so rich in goods and machines that they could allow themselves to destroy or to leave things behind in the bush. The stories of the oral informants suggest the shock waves that began when an affluent society with a superabundance of things came face to face with a tested old community which had made a virtue of economy.

C. D. MacKinnon

The construction of the Alaska Highway produced, as one would expect, cases of inefficiency and personal corruption. C. D. MacKinnon, in charge of inventorying and placing priorities upon shipments up the line from Edmonton, remembers such instances. His account suggests why many people in the early days called the Alcan the "Oilcan Highway."

They had some top-notch men that were just as dedicated! . . . It was a tremendous project. It was a terrific feat of engineering, but . . . you are going to experience dissipation in a big project like that. . . . That's what used to bother me more. . . .

[One time] I saw where they were ordering five cars, to be attached to the Twentieth Century, of empty drums to get up to Dawson Creek right away. Five carloads. To be hooked onto a passenger train. Express.

So, Holy Smokes, the minute I saw that—I'd just come back from Fort Nelson, and in and around Fort Nelson there I'd seen about 15,000 empty drums just lyin' on the side of the highway.

So I rushed into the colonel's office and I said, "Colonel. Holy Smokes. Has this [order] gone out for the drums?" Back to, someplace in New Jersey.

And he said, "No. Not yet."

Well, I said, "Holy Smokes, there's enough empty drums around Fort Nelson there."

He said, "Are you sure?"

And I said, "I am positive." I said, "I was down to Camp Zero, and I'll betcha I counted five hundred drums."

See, what would happen, the truck drivers would take a drum of gas with them as an emergency item, and they'd . . . fill their tanks, and then when the drum was empty, they'd just throw it off, throw it over to the side of the road.

So he said, "We can't slip up on this."

I said, "I'm positive." I said, "They were there, and I'm sure they'll still be there. . . . "

And I said, "We can put [the empty drums] on and these trucks are comin' down empty, so it's good ballast for 'em, and the trucks'll ride easier, and everybody'll be happier." And I said, "We can give 'em a dollar a drum. They'll lug 'em down to the railhead if that's where you want 'em."

So Holy Smokes, I had to get in an airplane and go up there and make sure they were there. I knew damn well. We picked up about twenty-five thousand of 'em, just lyin' around there you know. . . .

I had a funny one. . . . You see, number one priority on the aircraft was blood plasma. An accident, a bad accident, [and] everything else was dumped off, and you put the blood on, and it went down. . . . And cigarettes were number two. They were very important. . . .

I'd caught them cheating, you know. They'd consign it and say it was mukluks, and you'd look at the package and you knew it wasn't mukluks, it was somethin' else for some guy up on the project, you know. Maybe a fancy parka or something. And so, that was taking up space, and I wasn't playing it that way. And I used to go out to the airport in the middle of the night, and I'd check the manifest, and I caught them three or four times.

So, I went in to the colonel, and I said, "Look, Colonel, you back me up on this, because I have to be backed up, and I'll give the priorities." . . . And I told him why I wanted it.

So he said, "Fine."

I said, "Now. If they want [number one], you send 'em to me, and I'll guarantee you there won't be anything goin' on that aircraft that's not supposed to be on there, or that we can be condemned or criticized for."

He said, "That just suits me fine."

So. They called me up. They had twenty-seven hundred pounds of *critical*! *Had to have* number one priority.

I said, "Have you had a bad accident up there?"

"No."

"Well," I said. "What is it?"

He said, "I'm not at liberty to tell yuh."

This at ten o'clock at night! And we were loadin'. We had three of 'em loadin' that night.

"Well," I said, "until I find out what it is, you're not getting a number, that's for sure." And I said, "I'll make damn sure. I'll call out to our guys out there and tell them."

So in about a half an hour then another guy . . . he called, and I said, "No. Until I find out what it is, you're not getting any number. . . ."

So he said, "Well, we'll call Colonel Lockridge."

"Well," I said, "you shouldn't disturb the colonel at this hour o' night, but if you do, I'll tell you, he's gonna tell you to come back to me. So this'll save you callin' the colonel."

Well to hell with it. So he called the colonel, and then they called back, and I still wouldn't give it to 'em.

So the next morning I arrive over at the office, and the colonel's secretary said, "The colonel wants to see you."

So in I go to see the colonel, and he said, "What was this? Did you get a phone call last night?"

I said, "Yes, I did, I got *three* of them." And I said, "The last one was about one-thirty at night, and I just hung up on 'em and told 'em I'd see 'em today."

And he said, "Well, I had a phone call from the project manager." . . . He said, "I just told 'em they had to clear through you." So he said, "What are you gonna do about it?"

I said, "I'm on my way out there right now to find out what the hell this twenty-seven hundred pounds is."

And so, out I go, get over there. And you know what it was? *Twenty-seven hundred pounds of bricks. Brick*!

So! I got ahold o' this expediter, and *I told him to get his fanny over there*, I wanted to talk to 'im. And then I started looking at them. I thought maybe they were firebricks and they needed them for . . . forges or somethin'. But they weren't.

So I got this guy over, and I said to him, "What is this going into CANOL camp for?" . . .

"Well," he said, "They're building this guy a fireplace in his chalet." He had a big chalet up there.

I said, "Do you mean to tell me that they're putting a *fireplace* in for that guy up there?"

"That's right."

So I said, "Okay, that's fine." I said, "You might as well bring a truck over here. They can go up in the goddamn barge this spring."

So I get back to the office, and so in I go to see the colonel. I said, "Well," I said, "I found out about the bricks, Colonel."

He said, "What about 'em?"

"Well," I said, "you know, they're to build a fireplace for this guy up there."

"A *fireplace*!" he said. He said, "You mean to tell me they call me up in the middle of the night and they wanted a number-one priority for some bricks to build a fireplace up there?" He said, "What the hell are we doin' here!"

He got on that phone, and he had *them* over there, and if he didn't take! . . .

So, after the meetin' he said to me, . . . "Well," he said, "You know, I can see your point about the number-one priority and why we have it."

Norman Harlin

It was amazing to us, of course, the stuff that [the Americans] had flown in to us that, as trappers, we'd never think of ever takin' anything like that junk. These glass jars of, for instance, cranberry sauce, stuff like that. The whole country's full o' cranberries!

Sure! And flew it to us.

And guys goin' out for a day's work would take a lunch, a can o' these cranberries, and cans o' stuff that we'd never seen before. And you'd see the cans layin' all through the bush. Just *waste* of course! I've seen 'em sit down and have lunch and take one spoon o' cranberries and throw the can away full. . . .

We missed too many meals in the bush, livin' on bannock and moose meat, to ever waste anything. . . .

On the CANOL line when we were surveyin' it, they brought a reefer of meat up there, whole reefer, probably twenty tons, and the medics—their refrigerating plant had gone on the hog—and the medics opened it up and took a look at it, and the meat . . . on top had started to lose the frost. It hadn't thawed much. The frost had gone off . . . and they took a look at it, and: "Dump 'er!"

Twenty ton! Mostly big, choice pork loins and sides 'o choice beef. And they dumped 'er.

Johnny Dewhurst was right up there with a four-by-four he borrowed from the army and loaded 'er up and packed it to his cabin.

But they thought nothing o' that. Imagine what that load o' meat cost to get it in there. That was way up beyond Lapie Lakes. Fact, it was on the Macmillan River, Northwest Territories. . . .

Money meant *nothin'*!

"After we [Norman and Jack Harlin] started contractin' for them, logging and buildin' cabins, they assigned us a brand new truck, my brother and I. . . . And we were flyin' to Fort Norman, and I didn't know what to do with the truck. We couldn't take it. . . . And I took the truck into U.S. Engineers and told them I wanted a receipt for it. We'd had it four years, and it had a new motor every year. Just pull it into the motor pool and get it. And tires.

And, no sir, they wouldn't take it. They said, "We've looked all through the files. We got no fifty-three tens."

"Well," I said, "It's sittin' out in front o' your window there."

"Well," he said, "We can't do anything about it, it don't belong to the army."

No record.

[I said], "I'm gonna leave it there, and you can do what you like with it. . . . "

After the war, they came up here and spent . . . a whole summer tryin' to find this equipment that was missin'. They found a shovel under a sawdust pile at Koidern. Boom was stickin' out, and they happened to find the [clamshell] laying out on the ground, and they tried to pull it out to see if it was U.S., and there was a shovel on the end of it. . . . [Somebody'd] set a mill up, blew sawdust on it, buried it. . . .

At Fort Norman they left warehouses full o' Cat parts, brand new, it wouldn't pay to ship them out. . . . [Later] the Canadian Customs were after them . . . to git that stuff outta here or destroy it. No duty paid on it. The American government weren't strict, but the . . . Canadian Customs were, because the merchants would be kicking, of course, if you could pick up that duty-free stuff for nothing. You wouldn't be buyin' *their* tires. So the Canadian Customs . . . I mean, they had to lower the boom.

Earl Bartlett

When the American army left . . . there was a tremendous disorder that can probably properly be called a shamozzle. . . . The identity and the location and the quantities of so many different items were hopelessly lost. Some equipment borrowed by one department and still on loan and all of this . . . so it was inevitable that they would lose track altogether of a lot of . . . equipment. . . . This condition was a very ripe one for anybody who wanted to engage in thievery of any kind.

When I was at [mile] 375 . . . we found out that they were gonna shrink [the camp] still farther and move . . . down to Zero. . . . We moved out and left a lot of supplies. One box I came to there in a warehouse that had half the doors off I guess, and there must have been fifty brand-new mosquito nets in that. I grabbed a couple for myself and a couple more thinking that somebody might need them and brought them down with me. I gave . . . the others away and kept one for myself I guess.

And there was all of this stuff. They just drove away and left it. One warehouse had four or five lighting plants in it. . . . And [there was] a great mass of new electrical parts and equipment just stored in there. No inventory. No shopkeeper. I don't even know whether there was a lock on the door. They just moved out of the camp and left the whole shebang there. . . .

One friend of mine worked down at mile 300. . . . He had some time off . . . and he was at the dump where a lot of very valuable clothing . . . was being put on the bonfire and, among other things, eiderdown sleeping bags that are now worth something like eighty or ninety dollars. A truck had just brought a truckload and thrown it on there and went back for another load, and a guard was standing there, walking up and down and a rifle over his back, and this fellow . . . said to the guard, said, "What would happen if I went down there and rolled off a couple those sleeping bags off into the bush there?" He said, "I could use them."

Well the guard says, "Just don't let me see you do it, that's all."

So the guard started in the other direction on his regular beat, and Bill went down and rolled 'em off into the bush, and by the time the guard had turned, he was back up on the level again. So the guard didn't see him, and [when] the bonfire was over, Bill went back and got a pair of beautiful sleeping bags. Some of the inconsistencies, of course, that are associated with war.

Jack Baker and Pen Powell

On the evening of June 22, 1970, I taped a talk between Jack Baker and Pen Powell at Pen's home on Charlie Lake, British Columbia. We were in the yard outside, almost within sight of the place where the soldiers from the 341st Engineer Regiment had drowned on May 14, 1942. I have reproduced a part of their talk here in the way they talked to each other, rather than to me. While the events they described were occurring, Pen Powell was trucking on the southern end of the highway and Jack Baker was working as Senior Dispatcher for Canadian Pacific Airlines in Whitehorse.

Pen: Beer came bottled, packed in big wooden barls. It was rationed after the war begun. . . . [The beer was trucked in], and at that time the road was so damned bad, you know, between here and Dawson and, . . . the big trouble was they were always short a barl or two when they got here or Fort St. John. . . . They'd hide in the bush, see, and then they'd run up behind the truck and get on—and the [driver] can't see in the rear view mirror, you know, in that dust the way it was . . . climbin' the hill—and get in the back and throw a barl out—out the back end—and when he'd get to Fort St. John . . . you know, short a barl or short two barls. Oh they had a hell of a time with that! . . .

Jack: Oh Gee, I'll tell you, the amount of material that the Americans brought in here, though, talk about rationing, that's one thing, but the amount of material they brought in here, foodstuffs and machinery! Oh! It'd just astound you!

I remember Whitehorse, there was an area there, there was two blocks, two whole blocks, and it was just covered with cases upon cases and bags upon bags and then covered over with great big tarpaulins. . . . There's no one looked after it. . . . The machinery! Oh Gee.

Pen: They buried hundreds o' tons o' steel down here, and they had kids goin' around here gatherin' up the damn tinfoil offa the cigarettes.

Jack: For the Red Cross, you know. This galls. Oh, this galls you. As Pen said, these kids'd be picking up tinfoil wrappers off cigarettes to turn in, and the old girls would bundle it up, you know, and the Americans were just throwin' this stuff away. Steel. Tons of steel. Tons of, oh all sorts of materials were just thrown away. . . .

Pen: Diggin' big pits down here south o' town, down here with those bulldozers and just buryin' it . . . , just wallin' it in there, and then still had these damn kids to make people war conscious, apparently, goin' around gatherin' up these little bits o' tinfoil. . . .

Jack: Durin' the war, too, but after the war it was fantastic what you saw. You got a wool sweater on, see. And the old girls used to knit these for the Red Cross, you know, and weep a little bit about the boys at the front. I've seen just bales of those things destroyed in the fire up at Whitehorse. They had great pits, burning pits, oh, from here over to those trees there bulldozed out, deep pits, and they were throwing this stuff in . . . eiderdowns. . . . You couldn't buy them. They were taking them and slashing them and throwing them into those fires. . . .

Pen: You see, if you got caught with any that stuff, hell, you got [picked up]. Walt . . . and I got a buncha radiators one time. They had 'em all sittin' there ready to go to the dump, see. We stole 'em, I guess you'd call it stealin'. We took 'em. Took 'em. By God, they picked us up, and they charged us with bein' in possession of stuff that the duty hadn't been paid on, you know. . . .

Jack: Canadian Customs.

Pen: *But they were gonna bury it! But nobody could have the damn stuff!*

Jack: The Americans would willingly have given us this stuff. The Canadian Customs said *no*! We weren't allowed to have *anything*. . . .

And I saw, after the war, I saw machinery going out of Whitehorse. It was loaded on that little railway, that little narrow-gauge White Pass railway. Day after day after day. There was miles o' this stuff down the road. It was loaded on flatcars and taken down to Skagway and dumped in the ocean at Skagway. And the Americans offered to sell our government those things at one dollar a unit. Shovels. Bulldozers. Cranes. All sorts of good machinery. And they wouldn't buy it. Of course, what would they use it for? But we weren't allowed to have it. I'd have given anything to had a bulldozer. I'd a given a dollar for a bulldozer. Umm. And it's out off Skagway, dumped into, into the briny ocean. *Waste*? Hahh! . . .

Pen: [After the civilian contractors began working on the highway], apparently the local people here were . . . startin' to steal, you know. . . . After seein' all this waste apparently goin' to the dump, well, they started to steal, you know. Christ, didn't matter what it was, you couldn't dare go to sleep in your cab for fear they'd steal a tire off the damn thing, or anything like this.

And I talked to this one American. . . , "By God," he says real funny, . . . "they're worried about the Russians . . . comin' down," he says, "to the United States . . . raisin' any hell down there." He said, "There's no way they can get there. Those Goddamn Canucks," he said, "steal 'em blind." "There won't be a wheel," he said, "on a wheelbarrow . . . before they git through Whitehorse!"

"There's no way," he said. "They won't ever get there," he says.

Jack: But you know the reason for this, of course, is that *we saw all this material*! We'd never seen *anything* like this in our lives before! We didn't even know it existed! We saw it all. We saw it being destroyed, needlessly. . . .

Most people that lived in the early days in this country here had to be adaptable. They had to do improbable things in order to get by. We've all done, Pen here's done many improbable things, too, in order to survive, you know, and I've done some myself. You know, you had to. . . . But making things . . . , making things do that you wouldn't hardly expect. You know, it's surprising how you can get along with very little when you have to. . . .

Pen: [The Americans weren't so good at making things do], especially the PRA part of it [the PRA contractors]. By God they were just the opposite way. . . .

Jack: Course, they had equipment and all, they had lotsa everything, they had stuff that we never dreamed existed. So they didn't have to. They didn't need to improvise at all. They had it.

Jack Baker once described to me how he and Vic Johnson at Watson Lake had devised an electromagnet to remove a piece of steel from an injured man's eye. I later asked Vic about it.

Vic Johnson: There's nothing to it. Anyone can make an electromagnet. Actually, I had no idea just how it should be except I knew it had to come to a point, you see, so as to get [to] a small part of the eye. And furthermore, the point couldn't be too long or you'd lose the strength of the magnet. There was nothing complicated about it. And then all we had for voltage, you see, was thirty-two volts. We didn't have wire enough to handle thirty-two volts, so we had to put in a resistor there to cut it down, keep it from getting too hot. We had to cut it down. Put a resistor in between. It worked out all right though. So far as I know I think the fellow still has his eye. I'm sure his eye was okay when he left here.

An RCMP officer in Ottawa who had been stationed in the Canadian Northwest as a young man told me of watching a bush pilot fashion a set of electrical distributor points for an old truck out of two nails. The party was out in the bush, and their truck had broken down, the points had burned up. The Mountie officer said, "But Danny put it together using the points of those nails, and it got us where we were going."

They Can Have It for the Asking

DURING THE FIRST WEEK of April 1946, the Royal Canadian Army officially took over the main stretch of the Alaska Highway, the twelve hundred or so miles from Dawson Creek to the Alaska border. A celebration near Whitehorse paralleled the service for the opening of the tote road which had been held in the snow at Soldiers Summit in November 1942. In April the country was still very wet, but the days quickly lengthened. Plant rootlets were coming to life. Already, geese were on the way north. Ray Atherton, U.S. Ambassador to Canada, and General A. G. L. McNaughton, Canadian Chairman of the Permanent Joint Board on Defense, were present at the ceremony. McNaughton stressed that the highway would continue to operate essentially as a military road, and that civilian travel must be strictly limited because of the lack of such facilities as restaurants, overnight stops, and gas stations.

The Royal Canadian Army was to maintain, not only that part of the Alaska Highway crossing Canada, but also the 200 miles of connecting roads to the airfields, the 120 miles of the Haines Road in Canada, and the land-line communications system to the border. In addition, the Canadian Army was to operate seven landing fields along the highway. It was also to haul freight for the RCAF, repair RCAF vehicles and equipment, and run the utilities for the Dominion departments located in Whitehorse. "We took over," wrote Lt. Col. J. R. B. Jones, new Senior Highway Engineer for the Canadian Northwest Highway System, the military organization managing the Alaska Highway lying in Canada, a strange unknown ribbon of road covered with snow. We knew the vehicles and equipment left us were old and worn and needed immediate replacement. . . . It looked grim. We read the records of how the rivers rose suddenly in the spring and took out dozens of bridges, we were told of flash floods that sprang from mountain slopes to wash out miles of highway. It looked grimmer. We took another look at the old and decrepit road machinery, the tremendous task of sorting out warehouses full of unlisted tools and spare parts, and the way our proposed establishment had been pared down. It looked hopeless.

First commanded by Brig. Gen. G. A. Walsh, one of those vigorous men like Generals Hoge and O'Connor had been, the officers and men of the Northwest Highway System started immediately upon their task.

While the highway was passable in April 1946, at least for rugged vehicles, there were still very poor pieces of roadbed. The dust was bad everywhere. Many bridges needed to be replaced. Log culverts were rotting out. The stretch from about mile 207 to mile 270, for instance, was a twisting section of roadway winding through bad curves and over undrained muskeg underlain with permafrost. This section required constant watching and heavy maintenance as the foundation of the highway settled and slid continually into the soggy bottom. The muskeg and the braided rivers between Kluane Lake and the border made for another formidable section.

The Canadian army had many of the same problems the Americans had had in keeping the highway open. Cold-weather operation of machinery was one of them. The winter of 1946 and 1947 was exceptionally cold. Beyond Watson Lake the temperature stayed at 50 degrees below zero for more than a week at a time. It often plunged to 70 below. Near the border the men recorded a temperature of 83 degrees below zero. In such temperatures gasoline became slushy, grease hardened so that turning gears cut paths through it and could not lubricate themselves, oil failed to flow through bearings, batteries had to be taken inside at night to prevent freeze-up and bursting. And the Canadian workmen had other problems in common with the Americans. Permafrost and icing were continuing headaches. There was the need to improve drainage, to bridge streams and washouts, and to eliminate the most deadly of the curves and hills.

But there were also new problems which the Americans had never had to face. For one thing the Canadian Army in the North did not have and could not get new construction equipment. They were saddled with worn-out scrapers and bulldozers and cranes, for the Americans and the Canadian War Assets Corporation had removed most of the valuable United States machines and parts. Hence, the Canadians had to rely upon their long-tested capacity to make do with little, to repair and fix and even hand-make usable parts. They had, as always, to make one machine do the work of ten, one dollar do the work of twenty. The Dominion government at that time could not or would not finance a program of serious improvement for the Alaska Highway in Canada. Maintenance, not improvement, was the key word for the operations of the Northwest Highway System.

There were other new problems. Given the lack of money, the Canadian army had to pare down the number of workers. They had to get rid of incompetent people and do it at times with a hatchet. They also had to manage and plan for the coming of civilian travelers and tourists on the highway, even though they hoped to maintain the road mainly for military purposes. American citizens wanted to go through to Alaska, and the Canadian government could hardly justify preventing that. Hence there was the problem of making the road available to civilians at a time when there were few or no adequate facilities and no tax money to pay for building them.

Brigadier General J. R. B. Jones

General Jones, in 1946 Senior Highway Engineer for the Northwest Highway System and from 1957 to 1960 Commander and Chief Engineer of the operation, clearly remembers and comments upon the problems of operating the highway in the period immediately after the war.

By that time [the spring of 1946] there was really nothing much but an engineering and a small administrative staff left. Nearly all the equipment had been shipped out. They left us a bunch of junk. Not deliberately, because they thought we were going to buy new equipment. But we couldn't get any. Civilian supply had come in, you see, and it had the priority. . . . So we had to keep these damn junk pieces operating for three, four years before we could get replacements. I don't know how the hell we did it.

CROOKED ROAD

It was interesting in the first whack we had at it. The road was closed, you see. I mean it was not open to the public at all. And there was a gate—this was at the time of takeover, and it existed for a period after the takeover. . . . And there was a gate across the highway just north of Fort St. John with Mounted Police, or civilians employed by them. And every car that was heading north had to have spare tires, spare wheels, spare carburetors. They had to have spare tins of gas. The car had to be in good shape. They had to have a certain amount of money. . . . And they had to have proper clothing. They had to have an axe and a shovel, sleeping bags, and the main reason was there weren't any gas stations along the highway, and there were no private hotels, except at Watson Lake . . . and at Whitehorse.

So the army . . . had to run filling stations for the buses and for these travelers. We had to run hotels for them. I think I had four hotels. Godawful hotels too. They were just, you know, bunkhouses transformed. We had some private rooms, of course, because there were ladies traveling the highway as well. And we had to provide them with meals, blankets, and sheets. What a damned nuisance all that was. . . . We charged them, not very much, but also we didn't give terribly good service either.

But . . . that's one of the things I got rid of fairly early, as I was determined. For one thing, Ottawa just wouldn't have understood the Corps of Engineers running hotels and service stations and restaurants. So we induced the White Pass and Yukon railroad [to take over the hotels], cooking equipment and everything. . . . And then we got the oil companies to come in and start taking over the filling stations. . . .

So we couldn't open the road up until all this had been looked after. So, for I guess over a year, we had this gate over the road to check people in and out, and the same was true at the north end. . . .

[In the first years after the Canadian takeover] we were never given . . . authority to do more than maintain the road. . . . Not improve it. Just maintain it. However, as the traffic kept increasing, you see, you have to maintain it at a higher standard, so we had to put in improvements. So under that rather funny policy of just sort of maintain it, but do it on the minimum amount of money, we managed to replace all the bridges [and culverts]. . . .

[The reason Ottawa said maintain but don't rebuild the highway was because there was no long-term policy for it.] . . . We had evacuation plans for Alaska. . . . [But] during this period nobody would . . . say for sure . . . whether they really needed a highway. . . .

So, as I said, it was difficult. The army budget was not very large, and the highway portion came out of the army budget, and some of the Chiefs of Staff said, "To hell with the highway. I need some new guns." Or, "I need some tanks. Why should we put this money on a road up to Alaska?"

186

In 1946 and 1947 civilian travel restrictions on the highway were severely kept. In early 1948, the government lifted restrictions for a time, but soon had to reimpose them. So many vehicles were breaking down en route to Alaska because their drivers were poorly prepared for the rugged journey that many travelers were stranded, their decrepit autos abandoned along the way. As a result, Canadian Customs imposed a cash deposit or guarantee of bond for export upon every old model car or upon any vehicle in poor condition. This deposit had to be made at the border and could be returned only when the driver crossed the border again or could show proof that the vehicle had been exported. Ten years later, Canada still had the same problem. In August 1959, the *Vancouver Sun* reported that the highway was beginning to look like a "vast junk heap" from the abandoned American jalopies. The Canadian government had instituted what the *Sun* called "a kind of 'pioneer insurance'" in order to make it more likely that Alaska-bound drivers would get to the end of the road. Each driver had to prove that he had a minimum of $250 for the car and himself, $100 for each driver, and a valid credit card before the Dominion would permit him to begin his trip.

Americans attempted to drive to Alaska in the late 1940s and early 1950s in all kinds of vehicles and for all kinds of reasons. The old rush to the promised land somewhere in the West was on again. The Pacific transition continued. There were, of course, military men being transferred to Alaska stations—Ladd and Eielsen Air Force Bases, and the army's Fort Richardson. Many of them towed their families and their furniture with them, most of the men dreaming of the seemingly limitless hunting and fishing the North had to offer. Civilians drove up to look for jobs or to homestead. Adventurers went up to see the sights—Mt. McKinley ("Denali" in the native language, the highest mountain on the North American continent) and the Alaska brown bear, the world's largest carnivorous animal. Others went apparently just for the hell of it. Three college students from the University of Oklahoma drove back the 2,162 miles from Fairbanks to Edmonton in fifty-nine hours in August 1949, believing that they had established a speed record. A five-ton refrigerator truck made the haul in November 1946 with a load of 14,000 pounds of fresh meat. One family drove five new buses to Fairbanks for the university bus lines. Big trailer trucks packed six helicopters from Dayton to Fairbanks early in 1948. An outfit called "Happiness Tours" arranged sight-seeing trips from Chicago in the summer of 1947. People applied for permits even to go by motor scooter and bicycle. In 1947 two brothers, James Benjamin and Joseph Albert Stubbins, tried to go through Edmonton in a three-wheeled motorcycle towing a 7-foot, two-wheeled trailer. The Mountie traffic control officer refused them a permit. He reported that the rig was loaded with gadgets. The *Edmonton Journal* described it as equipped even with a set of deer horns, a portable table, and a desk lamp. It looked, the *Journal* reporter wrote, as if "it had just crashed through a second hand store."

Edmonton very soon collected a small contingent of profiteers out to take the money off the suckers. Drivers headed up the road claimed they had been told they would have to buy all their spare parts and tires before leaving the city, even that they would have to pack all their gasoline with them. One woman, driving alone and apparently acting on someone's advice, reportedly bought a drum of gas which she had to tow behind her car in a trailer. When she got to Dawson Creek and learned that fuel was available along the highway, she sold out and drove on. A trucker said someone told him he would have to buy 1,700 gallons of fuel for his truck convoy because it was not to be had beyond Edmonton. There were even imaginative plans for luring American hunters and fishermen into the great wilderness along the road. A hunting lodge near White-horse proposed a dude trapper plan. The dude was to be taken out on an actual trapline by dogsled, and would be allowed to take a pelt for himself. The *Edmonton Journal* quipped that the dude would then "be able to put his silver fox, beaver or mink pelt around his wife's neck and tell her great big lies about the hardships he suffered to trap it."

Psychologically, the whole movement up the highway was something like the Klondike gold rush—seekers living on fantasies and being taken in by a handful of operators, but mainly by the rugged circumstances of this difficult northern road. Fortunately, however, most of the people who lived and worked along the highway went out of their way to be friendly. Northerners had been brought up to help out in emergencies. Generosity was a part of the upbringing of those who had long lived in the bush—flyers, guides, trappers, trailmen, and road builders. The demands of the cold and the snow and the backwoods and the blue distances required it.

Walter Williscroft

One time I think one of the nicest things that happened, we were travelin' the highway . . . and we met this chap. He was a sergeant . . . in the U.S. Army, and he had three little girls. . . . He was cold and he was havin' trouble with his car. . . .

And the next time [we] met him in Whitehorse. . . . And we had gone over to the liquor vendor, and comin' back, and he kind of waved us down. Well, we [had seen] him that morning in the café, and I said to my wife, "He wasn't havin' very much of a breakfast."

He had three girls . . . and him and his wife and they were kinda dividin' a milk shake up between them. . . .

But when we came back . . . from the liquor vendor, he waved me down and he said, "I hate to ask you, but . . . I was supposed to have some money and I didn't get any," and he said, "I'd like to borrow . . . twenty . . . dollars."

And I said, "Well," I said, "I've got lotsa twenty dollarses up and down the road and all across Canada and the United States." But I said, "Just a minute."

And I went to talk to [my wife]. . . . They had a small family like us; we had three girls. And to be broke is not very nice.

So we decided we'd give 'em the twenty dollars, and he thanked us. He give us his address. . . . He was stationed in Fairbanks, and so he said, "I'll have it back to you by Christmas." . . .

Anyway, Christmas come and Christmas went, but the money didn't come, so we just said, "Well, we just helped somebody out again. . . .

But after New Year's a letter come from St. Paul, and he'd upped it five dollars. If I loaned him twenty, he give us twenty-five. And a very nice letter. We still have the letter, thankin' us. He'd gone to Fairbanks, [had] enough to eat, and all the rest of it. . . . And I think them's the kinda people that made it worthwhile bein' on the highway, to know that he appreciated it. . . .

One of the main problems for the men of the Northwest Highway System in the 1950s was building bridges. Wooden trestles, piles, and log culverts all rotted out or went out in spring runoff and had to be replaced. The Canadian Army built, for instance, large new steel and concrete bridges over both the Donjek and the Peace rivers. The first crossing of the Donjek, mile 1130, had been about three miles wide, over a sticky mud flat with several channels. The original U.S. Army Corps of Engineers bridge at this point consisted of seven separate wooden spans, each for a different channel. Since such a structure could not last for long, the Canadian Army completed a permanent steel bridge in 1952 after hauling eight spans up from Whitehorse on sixty-ton carriers. Each span was 200 feet long. The new bridge made eight crossings for a total length of 1,600 feet.

The Peace River suspension bridge built by Roebling and Sons during the war had had its own troubles. The river where the highway crossed it near Fort St. John was deep and troubled water. In the spring, great chunks of ice weighing tons piled against the bridge's foundations. The unceasing current of the Pine River, which poured into the Peace just above the suspension bridge, pushed against the east bank of the Peace, recoiled, then roiled backward and downward into the bridge's west pier. In 1949 and again in 1952 Canadian workers tried to build huge cofferdams to save the piers. In the winter of 1949, they dumped 4,000 tons of five-ton boulders into the river above the piers in an effort to block the current. In 1952 they tried to do the same with 25,000 blocks of concrete weighing 300 pounds each. All their effort was finally to no avail, however, for the currents of the Peace and the Pine worked like termites at the shale bottom along the west bank.

At last the rivers had their way. In the early morning hours of October 16, 1957, local people heard loud popping noises made by steel snapping from the immense strain as the whole west pier began its slide toward the water. Bridge men ran out to halt all traffic immediately, and Royal Canadian Engineers rushed to work upon the failing bank, trying to hold the pier in place. By midmorning there was clearly not much left that could be done. Hundreds of people came in from the little towns and the countryside of the Peace River Block. Hundreds more, waiting in line to get across the river—drivers and freight headed up toward Alaska or going Outside to the States—cut their engines and walked ahead to watch the end. In the face of certain failure, engineers with puny machines kept up their work as the bridge of steel and cable and concrete, undermined by its river, slowly pressed them back and forced its way downward toward the gray water. By noon the west pier had slipped about twenty feet. Suspension cables sagged. The deck began to buckle. At 12:39 P.M. girders slipped off the pier, and a 600-foot span went into the river.

Immediately, Canadian engineers went to work to find another means of getting the traffic across the Peace temporarily. Soon they were planning the new bridge itself. Workers had to rebuild piers and approaches, and they had to haul the old suspension towers and the other junk out of the river. By the end of January 1960, the Dominion opened the new Peace River cantilever bridge to traffic.

The decade of the 1960s brought the final step in the changeover of the Alaska Highway from a wartime, military project to a peacetime, commercial road managed by a nonmilitary department of the Canadian government. There had long been talk of making this changeover. In the late summer of 1954 a team of Canadian engineers had toured the highway and made recommendations for the future administration of the road, and in the fall of the same year a Defence Department official announced that the army did not consider it its duty to maintain a highway during peacetime. Three years later, the Minister of the Department of Defence complained in public of the responsibility. "They can have it for the asking," he said, "anyone who wants to pave and maintain it."

Not until the fall of 1963, however, did Canadian officials announce that the changeover was soon to become a fact. In late October Defence Minister Hellyer told the Commons that the Canadian section of the Alaska Highway would be turned over to the Department of Public Works in the spring. In the West, reaction was favorable. Some Canadians there believed the transfer was to be the first step toward getting the highway paved. Others thought the changeover would be a good thing for western business and for the local contractors. The date set for the transfer was April 1, 1964. William Koropatnick, the new chief of the Northwest Highway System for the Department of Public Works, told the press that all the army's civilian employees were to be retained. He added that Whitehorse, whose citizens had long feared the day the army would at last leave the highway, need not be concerned. "The army supports itself, but we'll buy our services and goods locally as much as possible."

On the first of April, eighteen years after the Royal Canadian Engineers had assumed a maintenance operation that was supposed to have been temporary, Lt. Gen. G. A. Walsh, the first commander of the army's Northwest Highway System, returned to Whitehorse to hand the highway over to the Department of Public Works. It was nearly twenty-two years since the opening of the pioneer road on a snowy day at Soldiers Summit above Kluane Lake almost 150 miles farther up the road. On the first, brilliant sunshine lighted the country. Though fireweed—now the territorial flower of the Yukon as well as Alaska's flower—was yet to bloom, spring runoff had begun. The celebrants gathered on a knoll outside Whitehorse. There were speeches. General Walsh honored the United States Army Corps of Engineers who had punched the pioneer road through in the summer of 1942, and he spoke of the services which, as he saw it, the Alaska Highway had brought the citizens of northern British Columbia and the Yukon Territory. It had already provided one essential facility, he believed, a rapid means of transportation for new mineral, oil, and gas exploration. Another speaker talked of the importance of paving the highway as soon as possible.

A new element had entered the thinking of northern leaders. Their people could and should have, they believed, the supposed benefits of a modern industrial society, and these could be acquired by exploiting fully the North's nearly untouched natural resources—gas, oil, minerals—with the aid of modern vehicles and a rapid-transit roadway. Wage scales, growth, industry, and time schedules were soon to become important factors in the northern life. For good or for ill, the people were trying to take on different values from those of their pre-World War II society, the old one of more natural rhythms—of slow crossings by dog team and pack string, of the timeless sense of steamboat travel, and the certain generosities of guides, trappers, and bush flyers. In the process, the old ways of life would begin to go as new classes of people came in and as natives tried, but often failed, to adapt to the alien requirements. The trapper, the trader, and the dog man were soon to be replaced by the Cat skinner, the trucker, the roughneck, and the prospector who moved by chopper and hunted by electronic metal detector. In spite of continuing economic ills, the North was now beginning to take on standards of progress, organization, and efficiency, those standards which had already become the patterns for life in the United States and the industrial areas of Canada.

CHAPTER TWENTY-ONE

Always on Their Way

JUST OVER three years after the April 1964 ceremony, local leaders sponsored a twenty-five-year Alaska Highway anniversary celebration at Whitehorse. A bronze plaque mentioned "the glorious future of both Alaska and the Yukon Territory." But only minor officials appeared, and few enough of these. The *Edmonton Journal* called the ceremony a "lonely affair." Edmonton leaders and Alberta and Dominion officials had not even been invited. Keith Miller, Secretary of State for Alaska, and Yukon Commissioner James Smith were there, but the celebration was not a serious international affair at all. Instead, it was a local affair, a joining of hands by two economically neglected brother regions—the Yukon Territory and Alaska—for an incantation. The speakers called for the paving of the highway. If it took one world war to get the road built, they said they hoped it would not take another to get it paved.

Since the 1940s a few people had talked of paving the Alaska Highway, and interested politicians in western Canada and in the United States had pressed the matter. Leaders from Alaska, the Yukon Territory, British Columbia, Alberta, Saskatchewan, and various American states had formed an Alaska Highway Paving Committee in the 1940s. In general, those who wished to see the road paved argued that paving would substantially enlarge the tourist trade, that it would increase the military value of the highway for Alaska and the United States, and that it would improve the flow of truck freight and boost the mining, oil, forest products, and agricultural industries in the North. Officials attended conferences on the subject in Whitehorse and in Edmonton, and the two national governments intermittently held talks on paving for several years. Senators Mansfield and Metcalf of Montana introduced bills in the United States Senate in the middle 1960s to offer half the cost of hard-surfacing if the Dominion would arrange for the cost of the rest.

Interested leaders sponsored several feasibility studies. The Batelle Institute completed one for the United States government, and the Stanford Research Institute another for the Dominion. The Stanford study, released in 1966, concluded that paving would be a losing proposition for Canada. Tourism would be the only industry to benefit greatly, Stanford believed. Paving would not substantially help mining, forest products, or the oil and gas industries. It might help agriculture slightly, but it would not significantly increase truck traffic all the way through to Alaska. The study seemed to convince Dominion politicians who were not already convinced that the government ought to avoid any commitment to paving the whole highway across the Yukon, although Canada has paved or is paving those sections where traffic is densest, such as the one from Dawson Creek to Fort St. John and beyond toward Fort Nelson and the approaches to Whitehorse. In the meantime the Americans have paved the stretch of the highway in Alaska.

In fact, political leaders in Ottawa have never shown much interest in the paving, and the Stanford study seemed only to confirm their negative views. Senator Mansfield reportedly remarked in 1964 that "the major obstacle" to paving was a "lack of interest on the part of the Canadian government." A year earlier, in 1963, the Dominion's federal Minister of Forestry, John Nicholson, had clearly suggested the reason for this national lack of interest. The paving of the highway, Nicholson thought, would mean much more to Alaska than to Canada. The highway provides a link between the lower Forty-eight and the forty-ninth state, a link very important to the United States and to Alaska. The Dominion government simply cannot afford to lend financial aid to an interest essentially American. And while paving is important to many of the businessmen and citizens who live along the highway, their views are not shared by all the people of Canada whom the government represents. Hence, the Dominion has engaged in piecemeal paving and in spending limited sums on maintenance, relocation around bad hills and curves, and experimentation with solving the problem of the poor visibility caused by dust.

Actually, the difficulties of driving the Alaska Highway sound worse than they are. Tourists and travelers coming in off the interstate highways and the paved roads of the United States and of heavily settled parts of Canada complain about the dust, the curves, and the slow speeds on this two-lane gravel and crushed rock highway. They complain because they are accustomed to cleaner, wider, and straighter roads, or because they are not interested in slowing down and looking at the landscape the highway crosses. They wish simply to get to Alaska or to get back. Many of them miss what the Canadian north has to offer that heavily populated areas do not—large and small game, incomparable mountains, rivers and prairies, and a strange feeling of timelessness and of unlimited space. Spruce forest. Jackpine. Fireweed. Wolf. Moose. Graveled road and dusty curves seem like obstacles to fast travel, rather than means of getting into uniquely beautiful country.

Earl Bartlett

One of the most fascinating animals was the cross fox. He was about a fox-and-a-half long [with a] beautiful bushy tail. West of here, between here and Steamboat Mountain, places there these foxes used to be along the roadside at night, and they'd get confused with the lights of the vehicle, of course, and they'd race along in front of the car. And my, it was a beautiful sight to see them! They run so pretty, and they seem to be waving all the way from the head, point of the nose, clear to the tip of the tail. . . .

In spite of the lack of pavement, traffic on the Alaska Highway rolls on in the summer's dust and the winter's snow. The truckers are one group of drivers to whom the road seems mainly an obstacle and a challenge. They are a class who have become identified with northern driving and with the coming of the industrial consciousness since World War II. More than a class or a group, they are a breed for whom driving is a serious and demanding business. Tourists, known among the truckers out of breed arrogance as "pilgrims," usually are not aware of the trucker's concentration upon the task of driving. The tourist is out for pleasure of a kind, and he inevitably gets in the trucker's way. The local people, on the other hand, understand that the trucker must have the right of way on the highway. He has to run hard on the flats to make the hills and the mountain slopes. He has to meet a tight schedule, to get his load home on time. He cannot be leisured while in his cab. When he drives, he kicks up a long pillar of dust or snow, and tourists hate to let him pass. But pass he must and will, or he will ride without mercy on the impenitent pilgrim's bumper.

Father Leo Boyd, O.M.I.

Father Boyd, of the Sacred Heart Cathedral in Whitehorse, has spent years at various mission churches along the Alaska Highway. He is well acquainted with some of the old truckers, the men who have been driving the highway since the early 1950s.

They get a tourist in front of them that sits in the middle of the road and goes forty, forty-five, and these big trucks carrying twenty tons, I mean they have to run the hills . . . , and in the flat stretch they have to pick up speed, so they get a little annoyed.

I remember one of them telling me that he followed this [tourist] toward Fort Nelson for . . . fifty to a hundred miles anyway. And this truck . . . tryin' to pass this car, and the car was stayin' in the middle of the road. So when he got to Fort Nelson, the tourist pulled into one of these café stops, and the trucker . . . pulled in behind him, and [as he told it], "I just walked over to the car . . . and the fellow had these big [rear view] mirrors on." . . .

And so he said, "I tapped the window, and the guy cranked down the window," and [the trucker] said, "What in the hell do you call this?"

And he grabbed [the] mirror, of course, and the fellow said, "Well," he said. "You know what it is."

So [the trucker] said, "I just grabbed it." He gave it one wrench and tore it right off and threw it away. He said, "Well, you're not usin' this thing anyway."

Like other breeds—the cowboy for instance—truckers are exceptionally loyal to each other, for they must depend upon their fellow drivers when they are tired or in trouble. The drivers normally run in pairs, one on duty while the other rests in the sleeper. They keep the rig rolling twenty-four hours a day and may drive twelve hours on and twelve off, or eight and eight, whichever suits the particular pair. The driver on duty knows there is a man behind him in the sleeper, and he slows down for bumps or bad curves so as to avoid disturbing his companion. Often the trucking companies have a senior driver hire his own second driver. Since they live together around the clock, it is essential that the two get along.

Tom Mickey

Tom Mickey trucked the Alaska Highway for several years. In 1970 he was manager of Gordie's Trucking, Ltd., in Whitehorse. Gordie's was a Canadian company running between Edmonton and Whitehorse.

Like I've had one of our drivers come in to us and say, "Well, the marriage is dissolved."

In other words, the boys weren't gittin' along. And if they're not gittin' along, there is no sense leavin' 'em together. And the worst thing I think any company can do is take and hire two strangers and then throw 'em together in a truck for a twenty-five-hundred-mile trip. Because some of 'em are gonna git along, and others aren't.

We find it a much better arrangement where you git the one driver and then say, "Okay. Now you know a bunch of guys. You probably know guys you've driven with before or something. You git your own driver."

The professional driver is not essentially a threatening man, even though tourists often exasperate him. He can be helpful to drivers other than truckers when asked. He gives good advice about the weather. No one knows the driving conditions of the highway better than the trucker who has just been over the road. He has occasionally driven for nontruckers who were in trouble, and he will tell an Outsider how to keep his car running and warm in the subzero temperatures of winter. Put a piece of cardboard in front of the radiator to keep out the freezing wind. Drive slower in cold weather to conserve the engine's heat. Carry tire chains. Put them on if the trucks coming down the highway are chained up. Carry a load in the rear end of the car to improve traction in snow or mud.

The loyalty of truckers to each other is largely the loyalty of the risk taken in common. All truckers risk their health. They run hard for long hours. They get sleepy. Sometimes they get sick. Drivers try to meet tight schedules, and sometimes there are disasters. Each trucker must face the possibility of a wreck as a part of his professional life. Knowing that he may himself need help, he helps out other truckers in emergencies.

Tom Mickey

We run into, for instance, an American trucker here a couple of years ago that mortgaged his house in Anchorage and went down to

California and bought a whole load of produce, nice fresh watermelons, all kinds of fruits that you could think of.

And after mortgaging his house to raise the money to do this, he neglected to put insurance on the load, and he proceeded to come up the road, and he got to mile 933 which is just past here. And it had been a wet summer, and some of these curves are pretty slippery, and he didn't make 'er. He got around the curve, but he couldn't get straightened out again, and it laid down on him. And here he was with forty thousand pounds of fresh vegetables all scattered all over the place.

And there was nobody that was around here that was really in the business of being able to help him too much. I mean, we can go out and set a rig up again, but when you got a load of produce on, it's gotta be unloaded first.

Anyway, he couldn't find nobody, so we undertook ourselves here to supply a crew and go out and do this. We packed all the produce out, loaded it into one of our vans, and brought it back to town here and then set him up on his wheels. And his truck would probably run, but he didn't want to try it, take a chance on it, because I don't think he had too much insurance on the truck either, so he could have been faced with a ten-or twelve-thousand-dollar motor job if the motor was bad.

Well, anyway, we went ahead and pulled his load into Anchorage for him. And he did salvage some, but he lost a heck of a lot of it when he got all squared away. With no insurance and what not, plus the recovery and plus what the insurance would pay, it wasn't too good. But it happened, and that's one of the sadder ones.

If the trucker's life is risky and the Alaska Highway is especially dangerous, why do drivers choose to run it for years and years? First, there is the money. The wages for driving the Alaska Highway are somewhat better than those paid almost anywhere else. Then there is the challenge. Drivers thrive on extending themselves and practicing self-restraint in meeting the demands of their work. There is more to know and more to do in driving the Alaska Highway than in driving the interstates of the lower Forty-eight.

Bill Shannon

Bill Shannon, a trucker nearly his whole life, was in 1970 the Alaska District Manager of LTI, Lynden Transport, Incorporated. He lived in Anchorage.

Driving the highway is a good job. There's no question about it. . . .

Most all of our drivers are all the same drivers. They've been with us for years. . . . I really honest to God think that the . . . drivers themselves like to drive the highway. I know I did. I enjoyed it, myself. And I think that every driver that we got likes to drive it. It's different. Something different. I wouldn't want to be down in the States drivin' those freeways, because you just set there all day long in the same gear doin' the same speed, you know. It's not like the North.

It's a challenge to drive the North.

Tom Mickey

I think that it's something that gets in their blood. They like it. I'll tell you, you take especially the American trucker comin' out of the States. They're trucking between the south Forty-eight and the forty-ninth State, Alaska, and this makes good stories, which truckers are great for. There's no two ways about that.

And I think it's a challenge to them. . . . I know a lot of these American truckers personally. I've known 'em for years, well, since 1957, and some of the same ones are there and some of 'em are dead now, and some of 'em have retired, but there are some of 'em that are still drivin'. These men aren't young anymore. You know, they're gettin' up in years. They got lots of gray hairs to prove it too.

Keeping the time schedule is part of the challenge of driving the Alaska Highway. Truckers push themselves. It is all-important that they get their load to its destination on time. LTI drivers are a good example. Lynden Transport, Incorporated, started out with one truck, hauling eggs from Lynden, Washington, north of Seattle, to Alaska in the early 1950s. Then they added meat and, shortly, freight. Finally they received the contract to haul the United States mail between Alaska and the lower Forty-eight. In 1970 LTI had twenty-four units on the highway, and nearly every rig checked into Fairbanks or Anchorage once a week. They were running, that is, close to twenty-four trips a week, the rigs carrying about 22 tons apiece.

Each LTI unit makes the round trip in six days, the drivers hooking onto their northbound loads at Lynden after the freight and mail have been packed out from Seattle. From there they drive through British Columbia and up the Hart Highway to its junction with the Alaska Highway at Dawson Creek. Then they run the more than 1,500 miles to Fairbanks or the more than 1,600 to Anchorage, most of it on gravel. They make the trip, one way, in three days, driving around the clock. Restraint is essential to their success.

Tom Mickey

Those guys, they work, the two of them work twenty-four hours out of the day. . . . On our run here—we're on a twenty-five-hundred-mile round trip to Edmonton—and we usually don't like to see them run more than four to five trips without taking one trip off. . . . There's many, many times when they leave Edmonton, come to Whitehorse. They're here for three or four hours. They get back into Edmonton. There's another load waitin' for 'em, and they have to come right out that night.

So, in effect, this ends up to be a five-thousand-mile trip. They can't make too many of those, because I don't care, there's some guys that can sleep good in these trucks, and there's others that can't. But I don't think that anybody gets the same sleep as they do in a bed sittin' still in a bedroom because these things are movin' all the time. . . .

Bill Shannon

If [a driver gets into Lynden] say at six o'clock in the mornin', and if he's the only truck in there . . . they'll service his truck, and he'll go back out that night at midnight. That'll give him from six o'clock in the morning til midnight [that] night . . . off at home. I have seen one guy in here [Anchorage] the same day in every week. He used to arrive here every Thursday, and he was in here seven trips straight, every Thursday right down the book. . . .

Most of our trucks'll pull in here every night about between eight and ten o'clock, at night. Some of those drivers, they git so tired of stoppin' up and down that road, they'll just ball right through, and they'll git in here around four and five in the afternoon. But most of 'em all get in here around eight and nine o'clock at night. . . . And then we pick up the mail at ten. So they usually eat and everything, and then they're back out of town by midnight. . . .

[The ideal driver] is a steady man. I've got teams of drivers that I can tell you exactly one hour—I can be within one hour of where they're at down that highway. And lots of times I've picked up the telephone here, and I'll call twenty-four hours away from here, as far as Whitehorse, and catch 'em settin' in a café. Might wanta talk to 'em. Or maybe we've got another schedule broke down, might want them guys to turn back with that load or somethin' like that, see. We can turn our southbound trucks and pick up a northbound load which is [broke down]. We've got a time limit on 'em to git 'em in here, you know, and we can coordinate our loads like that. Just switch tractors and bring a load back up. . . . "

LTI and the other major truck lines have regular tire and fuel stops and regular full-service schedules, and all the drivers know how to make minor repairs. Regularity and efficiency are the keys to correct trucking as they are the keys everywhere to a successful industrial operation. LTI truckers made fuel and sign-in stops in 1970 at Prophet River Esso (mile 245), the Circle T (mile 408, near Summit Lake where Curwen and the Callisons marked the high point on the pioneer survey line in the spring of 1942), Riverview Esso (mile 543, on the Liard River), McCrae Inn (mile 910, near Whitehorse), Destruction Bay (mile 1083, on Kluane Lake at the center of Walter Williscroft's country), and at Forty-mile Road-house, about ten miles east of Tok, Alaska.

Bill Shannon

Each truck is equipped with certain items which fail more regularly than anything, like a water pump for instance. . . . Each truck carries a set of fan belts. And sometimes they carry two or three head bolts, which sometimes a head bolt will go out and you hear it right away. And you stop and the driver'll raise up the cab and [in an] hour, hour and a half, he's got it out, new head bolt in, and he's gone, see. To where, if we didn't carry these few extra parts, he'd have to call a mechanic out from the nearest place that had a garage, and he'd have to come down and fix the thing . . . and we'd lose a lot of time on the road.

So all of our drivers know how to change a head bolt, they know how to change a water pump, know how to put on a new set of belts . . . and so they're always on their way. . . . They watch their trucks real close coming up the highway, and somethin' goes wrong, well, right away they know it, and they know exactly what to do. And if they don't, immediately they can call me or call our head shop manager there in Lynden and we can all coordinate, see. . . .

[After each round trip a truck gets] a complete service. And after so many trips—we have it set up on a schedule—we pull all the component gear boxes out and completely go through 'em. And each driver when he gets in, he writes up a crash sheet, what we call it, puts down everything that's wrong with that truck, and a mechanic takes that truck. . . . They pull it right in the shop. Completely serviced all the way through. Oil changed. All your filters are changed.

And a guy starts right at the front bumper underneath it and goes all the way completely through it underneath, greasin' it, checkin' everything, making sure everything's tight, right straight on back to the back. Another guy starts on the top of the engine and comes back this way with it. . . . They're excellent mechanics. We have real good mechanics. We can change an engine completely, pull one engine out and put another engine in and have a truck ready to go in four hours. . . .

With the demanding regularity of their lives, truckers have to have their fun. Besides the regular sign-in stops, they can pull off anywhere they please if time allows. There is room for pleasure. Truckers enjoy pie and coffee where the people are friendly, and they also enjoy telling stories. Many of these are about drivers. Listening to a group of them talking and laughing at a coffee stop may mean hearing stories like the one Father Leo Boyd remembers about two truckers and an Indian. These are tales in which someone, usually an inexperienced driver or a nontrucker such as an Indian or a tourist, is the butt of the humor. Other stories involve bears or other animals that live in the North. Such tales are an important part of the oral literature of the Alaska Highway.

Tom Mickey

[The drivers select the stops they like depending] on what kind of staff they got. If they got a nice young girl there, well that usually draws the boys just like flies, you know. They like a pleasant face, they like somebody they can kid and joke with. Fact, you find most of the stoppin' places along the highway . . . they're pretty genial people. . . . They know each other by names, and . . . you put in a ten- or twelve-hour shift of drivin', and . . . you like to come into a place where you're known. . . . The thing that makes a trucker feel good is he walks in and gets called by name. You know, it makes him sort of feel at home.

Especially on the long runs like these . . . out of Seattle. Those guys are . . . something like . . . sixty and seventy hours on the road, each way, and that doesn't leave much of the week for being at home. So usually the key to the highway stops is the people that run it. . . . If you get people that don't care, well that's about the kind of help they get too. And it doesn't take long for the truckers to find out these places, and they just naturally avoid them.

Father Leo Boyd, O.M.I.

This trucker always told [this one], especially when he'd have a couple of drinks.

He was hauling lumber out from a sawmill, and he had this Indian with him. And it was quite a sharp rise onto the highway from this bush road, and it was a long stretch of the Alaska Highway there, coupla miles anyway. That's about as long as they get. And as he pulled up this hill, he had quite a drag to it, so he asked this Indian, "Is anybody coming?"

And he said, "No."

He said, "For sure?"

"No."

And so when he just got the tractor up on the highway, this Indian said, "*Big truck come!*"

So he . . . didn't wanta stop. So he just gave it all he could. And he got across the highway, and this . . . big transport just whistled, just skinned 'im.

So the [other driver], one of the oldest . . . on the Alaska Highway, a fellow by the name of Lennox, he's between here and Dawson Creek, he's an old, old timer. Anyway, it was him drivin' the truck. . . . He's one of these million milers for sure, very, very fine fellow.

But anyway, he picks up a wrench or something, he walks back, he's gonna crown this Ken Pryor who was drivin' the lumber truck. And he came back, of course, and he said, "What's goin' on here? Crazy apple! Pulling out like that right in front of me!"

"Well," he said, "Talk to this Indian here. He's the guy that said '*big truck come.*'"

J. T. Bell

J. T. Bell is a fictional name, and this is my own version of a story I once heard somewhere along the Alaska Highway. I have no memory of who told it or where I heard it or even when, except that it was told by some old northerner probably in a coffee stop on one of my several trips up and down the highway. I repeat it here because it is such a story as truckers relish and retell many times.

A guy was tellin' me one time about this guy and an old bear. I guess it was when the army was buildin' this road. I don't know for sure.

Anyhow, they were sleepin' in big tents, you know, those big wall tents settin' on a platform, and they had little bunks inside the tents.

Well, anyway, this Cat skinner come in one night late—he was wore out and probably had to git up in about a couple hours to go back to work. So he just pulled off his boots and rolled into his bunk ready to git some sleep.

And his buddy in the bunk next to him was snorin' to beat hell, so this guy, it woke him up I guess, and he got mad and he yelled at his buddy to roll over on his side and quit the damn snorin', it was keepin' him awake.

But his buddy—he thought it was his buddy—anyway he just kept right on snorin'. Fact, it got louder.

So anyhow, this guy reached over the side of his bunk and got one of his boots and throwed it at his buddy, he thought, and be damn if that guy didn't keep right on snorin' louder'n hell.

Well the old guy was really mad then. He wanted his sleep. So he just got up and he stepped across to his buddy's bunk and he kicked that bunk about hard enough to make a tree rattle, and boy the bunk raised right up off the floor about six feet and something said "*hoot*" and it was a damn big old bear that'd crawled in there under this guy's bunk to get some sleep where it was warm.

And scared? This guy that told me this he said that old guy that kicked that bunk he run clear outta there, said he pure left the country right now. Said he run right outta his socks. Said by Jesus they found 'em layin' there the next mornin'.

And that's a fact, because this guy told me.

The truckers too have their views on paving. None of them likes the dust, nor do they like the bumpy character of the road. The best of trucks shake and rattle all the way down the highway, and crushed stone and gravel are tough on tires. Rubber wears thin. Bolts loosen. Truckers' backs ache, their lungs get raspy from dust. Still, driving the highway is the northern trucker's thing, and he does it with care and with pride. He likes the challenge, and probably even grows dependent upon the regularity of the time schedule. At least he works hard at keeping it. Most of all, he likes simply rolling along on top of a big steel rig up and down the highway to Alaska. "People that drive that highway," says Bill Shannon, "come up, they'll gripe about it and this and that and the other, you know, all the dust and everything. But still, all in all, if you boil down to it, you haven't been anywhere until you've been over the Alaska Highway."

CHAPTER TWENTY-TWO

Just Like Cuttin' Grass

"HISTORY," SOMEONE SAID, "is about all those dead people." At least one of the speakers at the opening ceremony at Soldiers Summit in November 1942 had that partly in mind. General O'Connor spoke there of Alexander Mackenzie and Simon Fraser and other explorers who had helped open the North to the Europeans and ultimately to all white Americans and Canadians. The Alaska Highway and its people and landscape clearly suggest the continuing human struggle begun by these restless and ambitious early intruders. The present-day highway and the stories of the people whose lives it has changed are the result of the efforts of the explorers and pioneers coupled with the energies of modern men and women, people born of a technological society and laboring first under the pressures of war and more recently, since World War II, under the burden of an ambition to turn the North into a place of industrial profit and progress.

Among the changes the construction of the highway caused or speeded up, those in the lives of the Indians are the most obviously painful. The highway brought Cats and trucks and cars and all the things that go with modern transportation and industry. It made technological civilization available, and the Indian as well as the white natives of the old north took it up. It gave the Indian a fast road to travel. It produced new towns and small cities—places where the Indian could settle down. However, once he settled along the road, he began to lose the will and the knowledge to live as he had done before, off the land, in the bush, keeping his family alive with moose and fish, furs and berries, all taken by hand.

For many Indians, the changes have been very bad. There has been much suffering and there will be more. The Indians are not immune to all the white man's illnesses, physical and mental. They drink heavily. It is not pretty to see a northern native village on a clear fall morning, a scattering of people already drunk in the paths and trails. These are men who in an earlier time would have been out on the fall hunt or preparing themselves for the winter trapline, and women who would have been cutting fresh meat into strips for drying in the sun, or tanning the moose hide and drying the sinew for stitching moccasins, mukluks, and warm clothing. In August the people would have been picking salmonberry, blueberry, red raspberry, and currant. No one would say, of course, that the building of the Alaska Highway alone caused these changes, but it rushed forward those which had been occurring little by little since the nineteenth century and, indeed, ever since the first days of contact with the white man. That the changes were and are traumatic one cannot help but see.

Father Leo Boyd, O.M.I.

It's most important in regard to the Indian part of [the history of the highway], and that is the phase from their life until suddenly, you might say, civilization, right now. . . .

[The Beavers and Slaves] had a little camp set up near the Prophet River. But one of the old, old Indians there by the name of Jumbie told me this.

At the time, they were out—it was I believe in the spring, anyway, I'm not sure, whatever time the Alaska Highway went through there. But they were all out camping, or hunting, and they were moving back to the Prophet River.

And the whole tribe was moving, most likely packs, dog packs . . . and as they came along on their way to the river . . . suddenly they noticed the trees were knocked down. And they couldn't figure this out at all. And here was the Alaska Highway. The bulldozers had gone through, and they'd cleared it while they were away.

And ordinarily that particular group, the only contacts they had with any other people were through a few of them going to a trading post in Fort St. John or Fort Liard to get a few supplies. But otherwise their contacts were nil, except with the priests that would come through. . . .

And anyway, this [Jumbie] told me that when they came to the clearing . . . they were all astounded. So they chased all the women and children back, and all the men walked ahead. So they were peering through the trees, and they . . . loaded their rifles, and they were quite afraid. . . . And suddenly [they] saw a man standing by the side of the road . . . and it was a Negro. And one of them picked up his rifle, and he was going to shoot. He thought it was the devil himself, so this Jumbie tells it. He always told me that. He told me that story time and time again.

He'd say, you know, "I tell 'em! You know what Father tell you? You 'member? In the world there's white men, red men, yellow men, and black men. . . . Don't shoot 'im!"

[He said], "And then that man turn around . . . and he called us and we came out."

And I guess he gave 'em some cigarettes or something. And along came a truck, and they gave them a ride in the truck, first thing. Never heard of it before, of course.

And they got in. And then he describes [the sense of the speed], "You see those trees? They're like that apart. Then they're closer, closer, closer, closer, closer." Describing the speed of the truck. And it's important to realize . . . how far they've come, really, in a short . . . while. Eh?

Father Pierre Poullet, O.M.I.

I have known the Indians in 1937 and I know them today, and I cannot say that they are better today than they were in 1937. I must admit that they are not as good. They have lost their way of life. It's no good today. You can hardly make a livin' trappin', and they have not adjusted to the white man's way of life. They are used to working when they feel like it or when they have to, and they are not used to this eight o'clock to five o'clock time schedule for working. They are not used to saving money for another day. They live for the day. And they find difficulty in adjusting themselves: employment of an Indian is a problem. Takes a lot of patience. You have to be ready to have him today, gone tomorrow, back the next day, and so on. . . .

The earlier age was one that knew little of time as a technological society defines it. Hunters lived by the change of seasons, not by the tensions of the wristwatch, the clock, and the trucker's tight schedule into Fairbanks. The Indians' daily life was much like that of the people who appeared soon after the ice age ended. They traveled on foot and used dogs for packing and hauling. Sometimes they used big canoes. They lived in the bush and followed the game. When they needed meat, they killed and moved camp to the site of the kill. The kill eaten, they went to another place and killed again. In the summertime they fished, in the wintertime they trapped. People watched the sun and the clouds, and in fundamental ways knew what the coming of early snow or the suddenly frosty nights of late summer meant. It was not always a happy life and certainly not an easy one—the people often felt afraid of freezing or of starving—but it must have seemed a full life. More than anything else, their old life was a way of *being*, rather than of *doing*. They worked for no one. They did not make payments or keep appointments. Time did not run them as it runs us.

Lawrence Willard

Lawrence Willard is a fictional name for an Indian man I met in the North. I asked him what the life was like for his people before the army engineers cut the road and technological society began to come with a rush to the old north.

Nothin' to do at all. Just life. No work. Nothing. Just do the trappin' and you fill your life. For the winter. That's all. No business. Nothing. . . .

Way long before, we use to go down to Dawson when the trappin' finish. We go down to Dawson for sell fur. That's what we use to do. I'm only kid dat time. Then, all way down the Yukon, with runnin' boat. Circle. Eagle. You know dem place? My daddy use to cross there with paddle, with big size canoe.

Some people see positive aspects in the Indians' efforts to change to the new ways. Everyone in the North and in the government either has or has had his views of the Indian "problem" and how it should be solved. The experienced—both Indian and white—know that the changes must be slow in coming and that they will require much patience and effort on the part of the Natives. Bureaus and Indian policies will not of themselves effect the changes. In the meantime, the Indians survive, some of them better than others. A few work and adjust. Many more drink and smoke and wait. Life is full of sickness and death for them. The old life, they see, has been cut off, the old people cut down.

William Wolf

William Wolf is a fictional name for an Indian man who has seen the Alaska Highway and the other roads bring a new age to the North. My fictional man hitchhikes near Ross River, the junction of the CANOL

Road and the Robert Campbell Highway, but he might be found on any
of the roads of the North. The sickness he speaks of may have occurred
before the U.S. Army came to northern Canada, perhaps while Canadi-
an soldiers and civilians worked on the Northwest Staging Route air
bases.

In six months' time the highway all pushed through. . . . Well, of
course, [the people] they like it all right, but I'll tell you it cause us lot
of bad. We lose lot of people, you know, when the army come through.
Lot of people die off, just like cuttin' grass. Some kinda sickness. Git it.
In here. We was just lucky that the army got good doctors, you know.
That's what helped us.

Yes, there's pretty, pretty danger when the first army come
through. There's two guys save my uncle's life. They find him sick on
trapline. By Toobally Lakes. They're only men save my uncle, those
fellows.

They wrap him up in bedroll, you know. Build little fire. Give him
rubbin'. Stay two, three days. Keep him warm. When he git better, they
keep comin' out. With dog team. Keep comin' out with him. When they
git out, he's better. He's lucky to live, that uncle. He die just six, seven
years ago.

Another man drop sick too. He's too far gone. Couldn't save him.
They got that sickness, you know.

That's the one the people die off with it. Lotta them die off. The
doctors give them shots for it, you know, and this is how they pull
through. Someone they go too far, and they just only, just like cuttin'
grass.

Some of the Indians who have lived on are unbelievably tough.
Hardship has become habit to them. It is this capacity to stand
things that would kill a man or woman used to the comforts of the
new age that may at last be their main hope. Father Leo Boyd tells
a story.

Father Leo Boyd, O.M.I.

Those [Indians] are tough! . . . I knew the guy personally that was
driving the truck, near the Liard. He was driving a truck for Christie at
Watson Lake, an oil truck, or a tanker.

And along the highway he picked up this Indian woman. And it
was one of those winters, you know, it got fairly cold. It went right
down in fact. And he picked this woman up to give her a ride. She
wanted a ride to the Liard or to Watson Lake. It was about fifty-five,
sixty below in there. He got about ten miles from Upper Liard—driving
this tanker—and this woman said to the driver,

"You stop!"

Well, he wasn't very fussy about stopping, so he thought she wanted to go to the bathroom, you know. He says, "O.K. Fine. Don't take long."

[And she] said, "No. I won't take long."

He stopped the truck, and she walked out of the truck, and . . . over [to] the side of the highway. And where they made the Alaska Highway, they just . . . knocked down the bush and then bulldozed it to the side, and there's always a ridge with the fallen trees. Have you noticed?

Well, this woman climbed over . . . the top, through the snow and all, over the top this little ridge. He thought she was just being very, very modest.

Anyway, oh she was there for not very, very long . . . but long enough that he blew the horn a few times to hurry her up.

And finally she came back to the truck and got in, and he started driving down the highway. And he got going about, not very far, and he heard this "Whah! Whah! Whah!"

She had the baby, and wrapped the baby up in her parka or coat and brought it back. . . .

It is Lake Frances on the Campbell Highway several miles north of Lake Simpson. There are scatterings of wind across the blue surface of water. Brief rain showers. Then the sun shines out. A worn, gray canvas tent on the beach by the edge of the spruce woods. A grandmother, a wrinkle of a woman, sits quietly in the tent, her head down. Fish, and strips of fresh-killed moose meat dry on a rack in the sun. It is midmorning, and the breakfast fire smolders. A new moose hide, rolled up, is yet to be cured. Another, stretched with thongs on a frame, is curing. A woman has fleshed the hide and removed the hair. Then she has mixed one can of grocery store lye and two to three parts of lard and worked the mixture into the hide with a flat stick. Later she will rub it or work it back and forth over a wooden frame. It will come out soft and white. She can then stitch it up the side and hang it like a glove over a very slow fire of rotten wood and spruce or pine cones. The smoking will give the new leather its odor and its yellow-brown color.

Frances Lake is North. When I stopped for coffee from the thermos a few miles back down the road, a Canada Jay perched on the top of my car's radio antenna. He perked sideways and eyed me while I lined up a fly rod. Then he hopped from the antenna to the tip of the rod as I held it in my hand. He wanted a closer look.

Mary Fox Thomas, the keeper of the tent and the daughter of the wrinkled old lady, is a middle-aged woman. She speaks quietly, shows me her moose hides, talks of her childhood and of the present. Her father and her grandfather were trappers on this lake before World War II. They raised her here, in a cabin. The parents, grandparents, and children all lived together. They worked and played together. "When I was a child," she says, "I thought it was pretty tough. Now it looks very good."

For eight or ten months of the year—for the winter's trapping—the whole family stayed here on Frances Lake. Each year in the spring they went to the nearest post, but they came back in the summer for the fishing. They were not village people. They were not hang-around-the-post people. They traveled to and from the post on the river, using a boat and kicker. Their dogs went too, running along the shore and stopping for licks and pats when the family beached to rest and to eat. "It was really very good before the Alaska Highway came," Mary Fox Thomas says. "Everyone was healthy. Since then, there is much sickness."

Occasionally she got some schooling. When she was a child, there was a teacher at the post for a few weeks every summer. "I have," she says, "a third grade education."

Now, during the winter, Mary Fox Thomas and her family live at a trailer court in a town on the Alaska Highway. Her husband is a Cat skinner. This summer he works on the Campbell Highway above Finlayson Lake, many miles north on up the road. "You will pass him as you go north," she says. "Stop and say hello."

I meet him in the late afternoon—after quitting time—along the Finlayson River. He is headed south in his pickup, going home for the night at the camp on Frances Lake. He is in a hurry. He will eat, and then I can imagine that he will fish for a while before he goes to bed on a cot in the tent. Fifteen or twenty miles beyond where I meet him on the road, he has parked his Cat for the night. It sits like a shadow at the edge of the bush, popping and cracking occasionally as its steel cools from the heat of the day's work.

Mary Fox Thomas has a daughter who works for the government in Ottawa. Her daughter has urged her to come for a visit. She could fly, she says, or she could go by bus. She would like to go. She would like to see Ottawa and the East and visit her daughter. But there is the expense of the travel, and she is afraid. Mostly, she is afraid of the travel itself. The fear shows in her dark eyes when she speaks of the long flight or the bus ride and when she thinks of all those strange people, those Outsiders. She wants to take up beadwork again, too, but most of all, she says, she wants to summer here on Frances Lake with her husband and her children and her mother. Especially the children. She wants them to know how it was with her and the old people and the lake and the bush before the highway came. It can never, she assures me, be quite the same again.

All those dead people. But history is more. It is the stuff of a people's usable past, that part of it they must remember in order to know where they have been and who they are. It is a people's self-knowledge, the panorama of growth out of trial, failure, and occasional victory that thrusts itself into the present and toward the future which no one, not even a man or woman of great prescience, can foresee. History is one means of preparing for the unknown that is still to come.

The history of the Alaska Highway is about that human panorama, well focused in time and place. Some of the men who were active in the planning or the construction of the highway have recently died, Ernest Gruening for one. Few if any were as active as Gruening in trying to arrange the building of the international highway before Pearl Harbor. His death makes the period of the 1930s, when the idea of a highway to Alaska was incubating in many good minds, and that of the 1940s, when leaders actuated the idea, seem for the moment absolutely, irretrievably past.

But many others live on. The voices of some of them speak in this book. Their minds are full of the memories not only of how things used to be, but also of how things might have been different and even better. Walter Williscroft's kind of knowledge of the natural damage construction in permafrost can do is essential to other roadbuilders. Those who build the pipeline to Prudhoe Bay must learn from experiences like his. The voices of men like Earl Bartlett and George Nelms, Norman Harlin and Jack Baker say much of the hopes, the frustrations, and the values of the people whose lives were changed radically by the building of the highway. Their voices suggest something of who we too used to be, and of what we have become. The truckers tell us of our scheduled lives, the Indians and the priests of lives that were nearly ruined by the new technological society. The voices increase the human sympathy, expand the consciousness and the understanding.

The Alaska Highway, too, is clearly the last of the great westward overland trails. Though its conception was altogether different, it belongs in a class with old lines of human migration like the Cumberland Road, the Ohio River, and the Oregon and California trails. Since World War II men and women by the thousands have gone off to Alaska, driving the highway to homestead and to mine. They have pursued the ancient dream of the future, the good life to be found in the West, the dream that has driven American history since the Spanish came for gold and the French for fish and beaver. The Spanish sought the substance of their dreams in the Caribbean Islands, the Florida swamps, the deserts of Sonora and Chihuahua, New Mexico and Arizona. Eldorado. The Seven Cities of Cibola.

Frenchmen, led by Jacques Cartier, hoped their wealth was to be found in Saguenay, the western kingdom of Canada. Englishmen and their American descendants pursued a wealth in land—in the Appalachians, the Ohio Valley, in Missouri and the Far West. Men driven west by their dreams performed acts of faith and hope, not essentially of reason. They believed that somewhere toward the sunset they would find at last the freedom and the happiness they desired. Those who have driven the highway to Alaska since World War II have been no different in that respect.

Jesse Hubbs lives near the Alaska Highway not far from Tanacross. He went to Alaska in 1922. In 1973 he is seventy-seven years old and lives alone in a cabin. He keeps a garden and traps some in the winter. Blue eyes. White hair. Jesse has the odor of rawhide and smoked moose. What he says suggests some of the reasons why so many others, thousands upon thousands of them, have headed west over the last 400 and more years, and why that westward movement has continued over the Alaska Highway down to the very present.

"We was minin' gold, workin' fer the company. I've stood in it big as that (Jesse holds up a thumb to indicate the size of the nuggets), shoveled it into a box fer the company. But we quit the company and took out on our own. That's why we was hittin' the wilderness so damn hard in them days. Wanted to git some fer ourselves."

For others, "gittin' some" for themselves in the West meant the chance to realize a dream of wealth in land, or timber, or fish and furs, or political power, or simply to have a better home. For some it meant the chance to roam at will, to try out this or that, to be restless, to take things as they came. But for all those people, it meant a search for freedom from something they did not like—the restrictions of government or family or church; the confinement of poverty or prison; and often from the ruin of a spoiled farm and the wreckage of a past life. In our time it has often meant escape from cities, miles of tract houses, monthly payments, and the necessity to work for someone else.

Do such centuries-old acts of faith—faith in the promise of a free future that lies to the West—end now in our time or in some time soon to come? Our own acts of greed—greed turned loose ironically by our very hunger for individual fulfillment and enterprise—have depleted the natural resources Europeans came to the American wilderness to grasp and trap, and to mine and take. The world becomes increasingly organized and technological, human beings ever more interlocked in industrialized systems. Others have taken up the mineral wealth and the open land that once in its availability identified the West to hopeful immigrants. A man can no longer homestead a good place in Alaska or anywhere in the lower Forty-eight. Realtors, investors, big operators preying upon our own greed have put the price of productive land everywhere out of the reach of the poor, the dispossessed, and the hungry man willing to work. Land for us is not a place to be and to grow; increasingly it is an investment in dollars and cents. Even though most of the trappers, traders, and miners depleted the resources they sought, even though most of the homesteaders ruined the very land they staked and cleared and plowed because of their own impatience and their ignorance of its demands, so long as the animals, the minerals, and the land were there to take, individual hope and faith in the West could live in the minds of men.

Perhaps such acts of faith may soon end. There is evidence that the Pacific transition is reversing itself. The American wilderness—in an earlier time seemingly unlimited and always available—so essential to the working out of the Pacific transition, has come to its end. The frontier as we knew it is dead. Men turn eastward, disappointed. They drive the Alaska Highway back to the lower States, thinking that the homes they once left in Kansas or Kentucky may be better now than the discouragements of being landless and jobless in Alaska. "Might as well starve in Arkansas," said one man, heading back with his family after several years of disappointment. He had once driven hopefully west over the Highway. Now he went east, ready, he thought, for a compromise. The Pacific transition may be superseded by a transition to the East. If so, the Alaska Highway will have served the movement of humanity, hopeful and discouraged, both ways.

One can drive the Alaska Highway in search of relics, believing that they record something of the lives of the men who designed them, built them, used them. One can find short stretches of the old pioneer road cut off by relocations, pieces of the CANOL pipeline which once carried oil from Norman Wells into Whitehorse and westward toward Alaska, the remains of wooden piling at a Corps of Engineers bridge site, the door of an old truck cab with U S E D or P R A painted on the side, building foundations, tin boxes of rusted transmission gears, bolts, nails, parts of army cookstoves. I return time and again hunting such relics and looking up old-timers who were in the North in 1942 and who helped with the building of the highway. But year by year the relics disappear in bush growth and in weather rot, and the old-timers die off. One wonders what in God's name endures.

For one thing people do continue to come, though the flow long ago slowed and the state of Alaska has tried to discourage them. Most of them will be disappointed if they hope to find productive land, gold, or easy freedom, but it is good to know that some still dream—kids with long hair, hitchhikers, men and women displaced, or just tired of somewhere else. I remember an ancient straight truck, Dodge. Job-rated. Montana plate. It was loaded from the axles to the top. Stopped on a hill. Power trouble. Couldn't make it. The driver put out reflectors and looked anguished. Up the hill ahead, already out of sight, going west, his wife—tired woman with glasses on, head scarf tied tight—drove a fifty-four Chev panel, towing their old house car. In the mountains already there was snow. Ground birches glowed gold.

But I return for other things. Mooseberry. Red currant. Alder, willow, cranberry. The blue-green sweep of distance in spruce country, sweep of uncluttered time. Denali is *my* West. Mt. McKinley. I had been in and out of Alaska three times between 1954 and 1970 before I had the luck to see the mountain, highest on the North American continent, a mountain over 20,300 feet. On all my trips it rained. Denali generates her own weather. In summer it is usually bad. Fog, cloudbank, unending gray drizzle.

In 1973 I went again. Again it rained for weeks. I drank coffee and waited, kept the watch at McKinley View on the Fairbanks-Anchorage Highway 29 miles from the peak. I made the trip across the park to Wonder Lake, saw caribou, grizzly, ptarmigan, but in the distance a wall of rain and cloud. It must take still another trip, something in me said, and I turned east, stopped one night with friends near Tok, listened to the weather reports.

Sunday. Eleven P.M. Glennallen radio said the weather would clear from the West by Monday night. I started back, drove west again over the road I had just traveled, 200 and more miles to Fairbanks, another 125 to the park. Late Monday night I pulled off to sleep. At 5 A.M. on Tuesday I awoke to see the mountain at last, her peak cloudless. Pink-trimmed white cloud layers curdled across the lower mountains which surround her. Original mountain. Ultimate mountain. Mountain big enough for human dreams. West. By 9 A.M. wind began to pick up scarfs of dry snow, whipping them around her peak. Gold. Silver. Northwest Passage. Beaver bales. Land for the taking. Cibola. Eldorado. The Klondike.

I studied her until long past noon, then turned east again, this time down the Denali Highway toward Paxson, stopping now and then to pick blueberries and eat them with fresh milk poured into a pan. Always I looked backward toward the mountain. This time she was good to me, stayed clear for as far as I could see her, clouds here and there blown into changing shapes by scuffing winds, colors pink, orange, red as sunset came on.

Paxson. Rapids. Donnelly. Delta Junction. Dot Lake. Tok. Always when I start east from Tok my mind is full—planning in fantasy the next trip West, wondering if I shall ever return. I drive a few miles, stop to study the country, try to fix it in my mind, see in it a mirror for myself and for western man. I repeat that pattern again and again. Can't get enough of it. Would too much ever be enough? Silence. Space. Unticked time. Wealth. This West is all the unknown and sought-after, all the unexplored and desired distances in the human mind.

I sit there somewhere along an Alaskan road trying to place these things and writing in a journal, then look up to see the Talkeetnas or the Wrangells, the Chugach or the Nutzotin or the Alaska Range on a sunny, still fall afternoon, the mountains all topped with fresh snow, winter not far away. A fly buzzes. No other sound. No wind. Birch and aspen gone to gold. Fireweed petals fallen. Fireweed stems purple in wild meadows the color of spawned-out Sockeye. Quilts of spruce forest spread away in dark green distance toward mountain sunsets, and I turn east again into my future, into my past.

Light cover of snow on the highway near Beaver Creek. White wolf at the edge of the bush above the Donjek. Burwash. Destruction Bay. Williscroft country. Aurora borealis plays all over the sky at night this time of year. Fall sky. Early winter sky. Canyon Creek. Champagne. Classical music at night on CBC. Two half-grown wolves put a rabbit across the road near Teslin. Swift River. The Rancheria. Norm Harlin's country. The Liard. Alexander Mackenzie passed its mouth on the way to the Arctic. Moose on the highway above Muncho Lake. Enough rain between the Summit and Fort Nelson to keep the dust down, pack her good. Headed home at last I can really fly.

Is going to heaven like this? Where are the LTI boys?

Notes

Notes

I HAVE RECEIVED the oral informants' written permission to quote from
their contributions. I quote these informants from the tapes I made of their voices,
inserting ellipses to show omissions or slight rearrangements of material for the
sake of sense or coherence. In the course of my travels up and down the Alaska
Highway, however, I spoke briefly with many people and listened to still others.
From most of these I did not ask or receive permission. Probably they did not
even know I was listening or recording things in my mind, and the use of the
battered Sony was out of the question. You can't ask a hurried camper, a
hitchhiker, or a couple of truckers telling each other stories if you can tape what
they are saying. That would intrude enough to spoil their talk and to end the flow
of their memories and their impressions. Hence, some of the characters who
speak in this book are fictitious, as are the places where they speak. Such
characters are not "real" people, and the things they say are not "real" since I
only remembered and partly imagined their statements in later months or years.
These fictionalized speakers are meant to be representative rather than actual.

To discover the oral sources, I drove the highway and questioned editors,
priests, policemen, librarians, and other important persons who had lived in their
communities long enough to know the people. These men and women did
invaluable service in directing me to those whom I taped.

I have also studied literally thousands of typed, printed, mimeographed, and
written sources, mainly primary. To avoid an overly elaborate system of notes, I
do not attempt to cite each source wherever I have used it, nor do I clutter the text
with footnote numbers. My intention is to make the notes readable and useful to
students who wish to pursue subjects in more depth, but not to burden other
readers with wearisome numberings.

Most of the primary sources are to be found in the National Archives in
Washington, the Federal Records Center at Suitland, Maryland, and the Public
Archives in Ottawa. The Bureau of Public Roads library, now consolidated with
the Department of Transportation library, has some primary and secondary
materials of the PRA, although, to my best knowledge, the records of the various
Alaska Highway offices of the PRA for 1942–1943 have, unfortunately, been
destroyed. The Roosevelt Library at Hyde Park also has some important primary
items. Other items, mainly secondary, are to be found in the scattered libraries in
Alaska and along the highway in the Yukon and British Columbia. In these distant

places, the state library at Juneau and the library at Whitehorse have the most extensive collections of secondary materials. The Library of Congress has a large collection of secondary oddities—books of Alaska Highway lore and literature. The Office of the Chief of Military History, in Washington, has some useful items and books. The National Personnel Records Center at St. Louis has the rosters and the morning reports of the regiments who worked on the Alcan in 1942 and 1943. The National Archives has a large collection of photographs taken along the highway while the American services and the PRA were there.

Feeling overwhelmed by the number of documents available and by the problem of reading and making notes on them, I had the good luck to think of providing my own portable copy machine. I rented one, took it with me to Washington for two summers, read through the materials, and copied those things which added detail to my stock of information. Without the use of this machine, I would no doubt be in Washington yet, taking notes and tearing my hair. Instead, I was able to bring copies of the documents I wanted home with me—several thousand in number—and to catalog and study them at my leisure.

Newspapers are also important sources of information and points of view. Western Microfilm, Ltd., in Edmonton provides microfiche sheets of the Alaska Highway file of the *Edmonton Journal*. The Press Library in Vancouver provides copies of articles which appeared in the *Daily Province* and the *Vancouver Sun*. The *Seattle Times* provides on microfiche the Alaska Highway file from their newspaper. Copies of Fairbanks, Anchorage, and Juneau papers may be found in libraries in those Alaskan cities, at the state library in Juneau, or at the University of Alaska library in Fairbanks. Editors of the smaller newspapers at Whitehorse, Fort Nelson, and other towns along the highway dig out their own files for the serious student's use.

Of the many, many dedicated archivists, librarians, Alaska Highway buffs, and others who helped me locate the information I needed, the persons I remember most often are John Wiltz, professor of history at Indiana University; Thomas Hohmann, of the Modern Military Records Division of the National Archives; James Quong, of the Department of Public Works in Whitehorse; Brian Stafford, manager of Western Microfilm, Ltd., in Edmonton; and Jack Baker, who lives in Fort St. John, British Columbia. There is no doubt that to the student of primary historical sources, such persons are the noblest works of God. The writing of history would surely be difficult without them, for they are the keepers who stand at the gates of the historical mines. The good ones know the lodes and veins of their diggings, and in Christian spirit they advise, facilitate, and freely give information as the student prospects, probes, and scratches his head. May the world bring such men as these big nuggets of golden luck. May the curves and grades of their roads be easy, the dust of their highways light.

CHAPTER 1

Some of the characters and places described in this chapter are fictions suggested by people I listened to or talked with briefly as I drove the Alaska Highway. Others, such as the Streepers, the Moulds, the highway towns, and the lodges specifically named are real. Overall, this chapter is, I believe, an accurate description of characters, scenes, and attitudes almost anyone might observe or experience if he were to drive the highway. The chapter is, of course, based upon my own observations made on several trips over a period of years from 1964 to 1973.

"Outside" is the northerner's word for anywhere but in the North, although it usually refers to someplace to the south or east. A man from Whitehorse goes Outside to Vancouver to enjoy the warmer weather for the month of January. An Anchorage businessman goes Outside to Minneapolis to purchase equipment. Almost anywhere in the North, one might hear a person ask, "Have you heard whether the Christofersons are goin' Outside this winter?" Or one will hear someone emphatically state, "By Gollies, I'm goin' Outside this winter. Gonna git away from the cold!"

CHAPTER 2

For a brief history of the special Cabinet committee's work, see the following three books: Stetson Conn and Byron Fairchild, *United States Army in World War II: The Western Hemisphere, The Framework of Hemisphere Defense* (Washington, D.C.: OCMH, Department of the Army, 1960); Karl C. Dod, *United States Army in World War II: The Technical Services, The Corps of Engineers, The War Against Japan* (Washington, D.C.: OCMH, Department of the Army, 1966); and Colonel Stanley W. Dziuban, *United States Army in World War II: Special Studies, Military Relations Between the United States and Canada, 1939–1945* (Washington, D.C.: OCMH, Department of the Army, 1959). The notes and bibliographies to these books are useful for locating primary and secondary sources on a wide variety of subjects having to do with the Alaska Highway. The Conn and Fairchild bibliographical note is admirably annotated.

For Sturdevant's plan see memo, Sturdevant to Assistant Chief of Staff, War Plans Division, 4 Feb. 42 (in the National Archives, Modern Military Records Division—hereinafter NA and MMRD—AG 611 Alaska 2-4-42). See other documents in the same file.

Copies of subsequent orders attempting to clarify the relationship between army and PRA locators may be found in a typescript, "Alaska Highway Completion Report . . . 6 April 1945" (in NA, MMRD, WDSBU 611 Alaska, box 167). In Appendix 1 see especially Sturdevant's letter to the Southern Sector commander at Fort St. John, 29 Apr. 42. Sturdevant writes: "Both the final decision as to location of the pioneer road and the specifications therefor will rest with each Sector Commander since the mission requires Engineer troops to push through a pioneer road during the present working season, regardless of desirable specifications." Sturdevant adds that wherever troops may be used to work on the improved road, PRA locations are to be followed, but only after conferences between PRA "field representatives" and the sector commanders. Clearly, the army engineers intended to remain in command of all location work whether it was done by the army or by the PRA.

For primary accounts of the PRA part in location and construction on the pioneer road, see the following typescripts: "The Alaska Highway, First Year: A Condensation of a Report by Theodore A. Huntley, Senior Administrative Office [sic], Federal Works Agency, Assigned to the Public Roads Administration" (Edmonton, 1943); and "Construction Activities of the Public Roads Administration and Their Contractors in Cooperation with the War Department, Corps of Engineers, on the Canadian-Alaska Military Highway, by Thos. H. MacDonald, Commissioner of Public Roads," et al. The latter, a paper read at a meeting of the American Society of Civil Engineers in January 1943, later appeared as an article: Thos. H. MacDonald et al., "Alaska Highway—Organizing $30,000,000 Job," *Western Construction News*, **18** (February 1943), 55–58. Both primary documents may be found in the Federal Records Center at Suitland, Md.—hereinafter FRC— (OCE 611 Alaska A52-434, file 30).

For the disagreement in the earliest days between Sturdevant and MacDonald over the standards to which the highway should be built, see letter, MacDonald to Sturdevant, 4 Mar. 42; and Sturdevant, "Specifications for Alcan Highway Construction," 29 Apr. 42 (both in FRC, OCE 611 Alaska A52-434, file 30). Mr. Schott's telephoned message giving Roosevelt's approval of Sturdevant's plan is dated February 11 and typed in the margin of a memo, Generals Crawford and Gerow to Chief of Staff, 6 Feb. 42 (in NA, MMRD, AG 611 Alaska 2-4-42). Copies of memoranda concerning orders for General DeWitt and other commanders to ready troops for the construction of the Alaska Highway may be found (in NA, MMRD, AG 611 Alaska 2-4-42). The diplomatic agreement between Canada and the United States permitting the beginning of construction is printed in "Agreement between the United States of America and Canada, Effected by Exchange of Notes, Signed March 17 and 18, 1942: Military Highway to Alaska, Executive Agreement Series 246" (Washington, D.C.: USGPO, 1942).

As soon as the word leaked out that the army and the President's Special Cabinet Committee had chosen the route from Edmonton, criticism of their decision surfaced. Various persons had long supported other routes for the Alaska Highway (see Chaps. 13 and 14 of this book), and now these persons raised their voices. Especially involved in America were the members of the Alaskan International Highway Commission (AIHC); Congressman Warren Magnuson, Chairman of that commission; Ernest Gruening of Alaska, also a member of the commission; and Senator Langer of North Dakota. Their arguments may be summarized as follows: a "western route" linking the Seattle area and the west coast to Alaska (two western routes, called Routes A and B had been proposed and studied) would be shorter than the "prairie route" from Edmonton, and construction and supply problems along it would be easier to solve. Thorough studies had been made of the proposed western routes A and B by the AIHC and its Canadian counterpart. Such studies, the critics argued correctly, had not at that time been made of the route from Edmonton. The western routes (especially Route A) would provide more efficient transportation arteries to the defense outposts in Alaska. Air defense of the west coast would be difficult from bases along the Edmonton route (known also as Route C), but relatively easy from one of the western routes. Route A, and, with considerably more trouble and expense, Route B could serve the Alaskan coastal ports via stub roads, while the Edmonton route could not. Canadian air bases along the latter route were inadequate for the American pilots who would be flying it, inexperienced as they were in the bad weather conditions of the North.

Governor Gruening proposed building another highway into Whitehorse over a line from Fort St. James through Atlin, British Columbia. Senator Langer implied collusion between those who had chosen the route and the Canadian Pacific Railway. Canadian Pacific, Langer said, stood to profit by the choice of the route from Edmonton.

Delegate Anthony Dimond of Alaska submitted bills in the United States

House of Representatives in 1942 and again in 1943 to authorize construction of a western linking highway to Whitehorse. But the Federal Works Agency, the Bureau of the Budget, and the War Department all opposed the Dimond bills. Responding to Delegate Dimond's bill of 1942, Secretary of War Stimson wrote to Congressman Cartwright, chairman of the House Roads Committee: "In normal times the War Department would offer no objection to the construction of Route A in addition to the current undertaking. . . . However, the construction of Route A at this time would interfere substantially with our productive war effort by reason of its necessary diversion of machinery, labor, supervision, and strategic materials. . . . " See letter, Stimson to Cartwright, undated (in NA, Diplomatic, Legal, Fiscal Branch, Bureau of the Budget—hereinafter DLFB and BB—file entitled, "To Authorize the Construction of a Military Supply Highway to Alaska," 6-23-42, folder A204 [3]).

For the documents of the critics see especially two memos from Gruening, 27 Feb. 42, and 16 Apr. 42; See also "Paul Woodbridge Interviews Governor Gruening," 13 Mar. 42 (in NA, Social and Economic Records Division—hereinafter SERD—9-1-55, file 372). Senator Langer's accusatory speech on the Senate floor may be found in "The Alaska Highway," *Congressional Record—Senate*, 21 May 42, pp. 4569–71. Langer proposed a Senate investigation—S. Res. 253—but a Foreign Relations Subcommittee assigned the task said that such a review "would be futile, a waste of vitally necessary time and an unwarrantable interference with the strategic efforts of the army." See "Report of Subcommittee of Foreign Relations Committee Having under Consideration Senate Resolution 253," 18 June 42. Congressman Magnuson also spoke in a critical manner on the House floor. See "Alaska-International Highway; Extension of Remarks of Hon. Warren G. Magnuson, of Washington, in the House of Representatives," *Congressional Record - Appendix*, 9 June 42, pp. A2310–11.

The differences between the army's chiefs on the one hand and the critics of the Edmonton route on the other seem to have been irresolvable. "Not only the Corps of Engineers but also the General Staff and Air Staff were consulted in the selection of the route," Secretary of War Stimson wrote to Secretary Ickes in May, "and they were unanimous in their decision." He continued:

> This country has unhesitantly made graver decisions based on advice from these same sources, and while this advice is, of course, not infallible, it is undoubtedly better under the urgent circumstances than could be obtained from any other single source. Personally, I concur in the necessity of building the supply route along the air-line, as we could not rely on winter tractor road supply of these vital staging fields. [The army chose the Edmonton route largely because it would link together the air bases across northern Canada known as the Northwest Staging Route.] "Furthermore, I do not believe that military necessity exists for duplication of effort in constructing another road from Fort St. James to the vicinity of Whitehorse paralleling this "C" route, a task which would present many construction problems of its own, including greater snowfall. Perhaps I am unduly optimistic, but I do not share Governor Gruening's apprehension.

See letter, Stimson to Ickes, 12 May 42 (in NA, MMRD, OPD 611 Alaska 2-26-42). A brief comparison of the alternative routes and a summary of the army's reasons for selecting the route from Edmonton are given in Major Shelby A. McMillion, "The Strategic Route to Alaska," *The Military Engineer*, **34** (November 1942), 546–53.

CHAPTER 3

Much of the information in this chapter is from the *Edmonton Journal*. Articles on the highway appeared almost daily in that newspaper after the announcement that the road would follow the prairie route.

The army authorized the Haines Military Road, the connecting link between the Alaska Highway and the port of Haines, in November 1942. The purpose was to provide an alternate route to the vulnerable railroad from Skagway to Whitehorse, to open another access point for construction on the highway, and to provide a way of minimizing the "rehandling" of supplies bound for the Alaska Highway north of Whitehorse. Workmen began construction on January 16, 1943 and opened the road on December 31, 1943 at an estimated cost of $13,176,000. Construction included a base at Haines and relay stations along the road. A year later the Americans ceased winter maintenance of the Haines Road as a part of the winding down of United States military operations in the North. For historical information on the Haines Road, see Dziuban, pp. 226–27, and a memo, by Major General W. D. Styer, 6 June 44 (in NA, MMRD, OPD 611 Alaska [Section II], cases 42–59, box 1633). In a typescript Richard Finnie gives an interesting firsthand account of the Haines Road under construction. "Richard Finnie's Report on Whitehorse, Skagway and Haines, June 28–July 8, 1943," pp. 1–9 (in FRC, NSC, box P51830).

At the end of February 1942 an incident occurred which threatened for a few days to slow down American entry into the North. On February 20 an American commercial firm, Northwest Airlines, signed a contract with the Air Corps Ferrying Command to fly supplies and men for the U.S. Air Corps projects along the proposed Alaska Highway and in Alaska. Before the application for permission to use Canadian facilities reached the Dominion government through the Permanent Joint Board on Defense, Northwest Airlines flew its first mission into western Canada on February 27. The Canadian authorities immediately grounded the aircraft and its crew for investigation. The Dominion's Deputy Minister of Transport notified C. D. Howe, Minister of Munitions and Supply and Acting Minister of Transport, that the Northwest Airlines flight represented an American attempt to compete with Canadian aero companies. Mr. Howe, however, discussed the problem with General Olds of the Air Corps Ferrying Command by telephone, then recommended that his government grant the necessary permission.

At about the same time, American journalists got into the affair with inflammatory articles in the *Washington Times-Herald*. When the Canadian Minister in Washington reported the journalism to Ottawa, Dominion officials, and especially Mr. Howe, were rightly outraged, but they did not hold up the permission for Northwest Airlines to fly across northern Canada.

The incident revealed, among other things, a lack of effective communications channels between the two governments at this early stage of the war. It also revealed the longstanding Canadian suspicion of American commercial motives, a fear which had already played an important part in the inability of the two countries to cooperate in the authorization and construction of the Alaska Highway in the 1930s (see Chap. 13 of this book).

For a brief account of the Northwest Airlines incident and the reasons why Northwest and other aero companies were hired, see Conn and Fairchild, pp. 395–96; and Wesley Frank Craven and James Lea Cate, eds., *The Army Air Forces in World War II, Vol. One, Plans and Early Operations, January 1939 to August 1942* (Chicago: University of Chicago Press, 1948), pp. 357–58.

Primary sources are the memo, Deputy Minister of Transport C. P. Edwards to C. D. Howe, 27 Feb. 42; and a teletype, Canadian Secretary of State for External Affairs to the Minister in Washington, 15 Mar. 42 (both in the Canadian Public Archives in Ottawa—hereinafter PA—C. D. Howe Papers, M.G. 27, III B 20, Vol. 84). Relevant newspaper articles are Drew Pearson and Robert S. Allen, "Washington Daily Merry-Go-Round," *Washington Times-Herald*, 7 Mar. 42; and Frank C. Waldrop, "Canada's Chances," *Washington Times-Herald*, 14 Mar. 42. For a Canadian journalist's view of the whole matter see Grant Dexter, "The Alaska Highway," *Winnipeg Free Press*, 25 Mar. 42.

CHAPTER 4

Secondary historical sources for the reconnaissance and surveys as well as interesting photographs made in 1942–1943 may be found in Dod, pp. 308–09; Colonel Albert L. Lane, "The Alcan Highway: Road Location and Construction Methods," *The Military Engineer*, 34 (October 1942), 492–99; Harold W. Richardson, "Alcan—America's Glory Road, Part I: Strategy and Location," *Engineering News-Record*, 129 (Dec. 17, 42), 81–96; K. H. Siddall, "Planes Blaze Trail for Alaska Highway," *Flying*, 30 (September 1943), 54–56, 94, 99; and Brig. Gen. C. L. Sturdevant, "The Alaska Military Highway," *The Engineering Journal*, 26 (March 1943), 117–21.

Company D of the 29th Engineer Regiment (Topographic) operated over the Northern Sector of the highway from Lower Post to Slana between April 10, 1942 and May 1, 1943; an advance detachment of the 29th had arrived in Whitehorse under Maj. Frank H. Pettit as early as March. Soon after arrival, the officers divided Company D into several survey platoons and one headquarters platoon. The purpose was to furnish one survey platoon to each engineer construction regiment working on the Northern Sector. Each survey platoon was then divided into a front and rear party, the front to locate, the rear to map. The work of the front and rear parties consisted of trailblazing and mapping for the engineer Cat skinners who were supposed to follow the survey parties. For the Southern Sector of the highway, a company from the 648th Engineers (Topographic) performed a service equivalent to that of Company D on the Northern Sector. For primary sources, see "Co. 'D', 29th Engineers, Historical Information"; and a typescript entitled "History of the Whitehorse Sector of the Alcan Highway, 10 June 1943" (both in FRC, NSC, box P51823, folder 314.7 entitled "Military Histories, 1943").

The PRA performed its own surveys for the improved road. PRA surveyors began arriving in Whitehorse in early April, and by the end of the month several parties were in the field. F. E. Andrews was Northern Division Engineer for the PRA division headquartered in Whitehorse. He was assisted by J. B. Reher, Chief Location Engineer. Under Reher were C. G. Polk (Alaska locations) and H. A. Stoddard (Canada locations). J. H. Brannon, D. H. Cadmus, John McGillivray, and E. N. Moore were Supervising Engineers of various field sections within the Northern Division. An equivalent structure performed the PRA surveys on the Southern Division of the Alaska Highway. For primary sources see two type-scripts, "The Alaska Highway, First Year"; and "The Alaska Highway, Second Year: A Report by R. E. Royall, Senior Highway Engineer" (Federal Works Agency, Public Roads Administration: Washington, 1944). Both documents are in FRC, OCE 611 Alaska A52-434, file 30.

The typed reports of the early reconnaissance trips made by dog team and packhorse, the reconnaissance trips which preceded the organization of actual PRA survey parties, may be found in the Bureau of Public Roads Library in Washington—hereinafter BPR—(in TE4265, U66A5, 1942a, b, c, d, and e). The Willesen, Curwen, and McGillivray reports quoted in Chap. 4 are available in this BPR file.

Another interesting firsthand account was written by Southern Division engineer C. F. Capes. The army and PRA leaders in 1942 had a great deal of difficulty deciding precisely what route to follow between Fort Nelson and Lower Post. In late April the commanders in the field, General Hoge for the army and C. F. Capes for the PRA Southern Division, flew over the terrain to attempt to resolve the troubles. Hoge and his assistant, Major Pettit, accompanied Capes by aircraft over both routes under consideration—the Trout River route (which the highway eventually followed) and the more northerly Crow River route. The three men could not agree as to which route was best, although Capes was convinced of the superiority of the Trout River line. Capes telegraphed his recommendation that it be followed to the Edmonton office on the twenty-sixth. A rapid decision was of crucial importance at the time since the 35th Engineer Regiment could not begin construction west from Fort Nelson until they knew which route to follow. See "Report 1942c" (in the BPR file cited above).

Further extensive ground and aerial surveys were necessary before the leaders decided whether to follow the north or south bank of the Liard even after they had selected the Trout River route. Siddall describes the aerial reconnaissance in "Planes Blaze Trail."

Over parts of the North where airplanes could be made available, they were of great service in locating highway line. General Sturdevant speaks of the important contribution of pioneer air reconnaissance, especially of the country in the area of the Yukon-Mackenzie River Divide (Sturdevant, "The Alaska Military Highway"), and Huntley reports that Les Cook pointed out the route the highway followed through a pass some eighty miles east of Teslin near the headwaters of the Swift and Rancheria rivers ("The Alaska Highway, First Year").

Precise aerial mapping with specially equipped aircraft of the whole country traversed by the Alaska Highway came somewhat later. Although it was begun in 1942, it could not be completed and the results made available to PRA and army field units in time to help a great deal with the location of the pioneer road. Siddall's article "Planes Blaze Trail" gives a detailed account of the methods and equipment used on the early aerial mapping expeditions. Huntley suggests the extent of the communications problem which existed with the field units in 1942. The fact that these parties were largely cut off from one another and from headquarters increased the difficulties of making the results of precise aerial mapping available to them. "There were no communications of any kind between headquarters and field parties," Huntley writes, "except by runners or planes, and at times weeks passed with no word from men in the field" ("The Alaska Highway, First Year," p. 42).

226

The section of road between Fort St. John and Fort Nelson was an exception. Here aerial photographs were completed early enough to be able to help the pioneer PRA and Corps of Engineers survey parties. On this part of the highway two planes were in use. The first, equipped with pontoons, flew over the terrain and spotted what appeared to be the best for road building. Often this plane landed on lakes or rivers so that the reconnaissance party could walk over the areas in question. Then the second plane, equipped with camera equipment, flew over at altitudes of from 7,000 to 12,000 feet and photographed the landscape. The photographs had 60 percent forward overlap and about 8-mile coverage on either side of the centerline of the proposed route. The information gained from the study of these photographs was then furnished to the location parties in the field. See Colonel Lane, "The Alcan Highway: Road Location and Construction Methods."

Much of the information about the country came from Canadian guides and trappers in the spring of 1942. Reports as to the reliability of the information gathered from these local people differ. Huntley remarks: "It is an interesting commentary on the final location of the highway that it follows so closely in general direction the trails long used by Indian trappers and prospectors. The Indians and trappers particularly know the country better than anyone else could know it" ("The Alaska Highway, First Year," p. 13). Huntley adds, however, that the winter trails used by the local people were not suitable for the year-round highway. In contrast, K. H. Siddall observes: "The location information gathered from trappers, guides and Indians proved to be practically useless. Advice from such sources showed a surprisingly limited knowledge of the areas and could be very misleading" ("Planes Blaze Trail," p. 56). Siddall cites an example in which Indian guides were wrong in the attempt to locate the road along the Liard. One must conclude that there were both competent and incompetent persons attempting to guide in 1942. Overall, Huntley's assessment is probably more nearly accurate than Siddall's.

The Garrett Mattingly quotation is taken from the Bernard DeVoto–Garrett Mattingly correspondence quoted in Wallace Stegner, "On the Writing of History," *The Sound of Mountain Water* (New York: Doubleday, 1969), p. 218.

Most of the PRA engineers who took part in the pioneer reconnaissance and who led the surveys in 1942–1943 came from the Denver and Portland offices of the Public Roads Administration. Men from the Portland office operated the Northern Division from Whitehorse, while men from the Denver office established and ran the Southern Division from Fort St. John. The Denver men were called into the PRA office on a Friday in early March 1942 and told to pack up and be ready to leave for the Alcan Highway within four days. On the following Tuesday morning, March 11, twelve men left the Denver office together driving a convoy of six Chevy panel trucks. This pioneer group included Van Buskirk, Cheatham, Curwen, Willesen, Ambos, Warren, and others (from a taped conversation with O. D. Van Buskirk, 13 Apr. 75).

CHAPTER 5

Much has been written on the American and Canadian frontiers and frontier people. A full list of useful sources here is out of the question.

The Turner quotation is from the famous paper Turner read at a meeting of the American Historical Association in Chicago in 1893. The paper is "The Significance of the Frontier in American History," *Frontier and Section: Selected Essays of Frederick Jackson Turner* (Englewood Cliffs, N.J.: Prentice-Hall, 1961). Modern historians have criticized Turner's thesis, but it remains suggestive and to some extent valid.

Bernard De Voto's *The Course of Empire* (Boston: Houghton Mifflin, 1952) is a very readable introduction to the subject of the Spanish, French, and Anglo frontiers in the New World. Modern critical readings on the subject are to be found in the multivolume series *Histories of the American Frontier* edited by Ray Allen Billington and originally published by Holt, Rinehart and Winston. An excellent bibliographical guide to the study of the frontier in America is Nelson Close, *A Concise Study Guide to the American Frontier* (Lincoln: University of Nebraska Press, 1964). Henry Nash Smith's *Virgin Land: The American West as Symbol and Myth* (Cambridge, Mass.: Harvard University Press, 1950) is a brilliant, seminal study of the idea of the West in the American mind and literature. Roderick Nash's *Wilderness and the American Mind* (New Haven, Conn.: Yale University Press, 1967) deals with, among other topics, the dark and "real" aspect of the West and wilderness in American life. Nash makes it clear that the paradise myth—the haunting notion that hope lay somewhere to the west—was rapidly undercut by the hard realities of life in the western back country, that in fact many early diarists on the frontier characterized the wilderness as an enemy to be conquered rather than as a new Garden of Eden.

I taped Nan and Barney Streeper's voices at the Streeper home in Fort Nelson, British Columbia, in the summer of 1970.

CHAPTER 6

In the summer of 1970 I met Jack Baker, Bill Blair, George Nelms, and Norman Harlin in British Columbia and the Yukon Territory. Norman Harlin died very shortly after I recorded his voice, and Bill Blair was placed in a home in Dawson City. George Nelms has since retired from the Canadian Department of Public Works, and Jack Baker spends all the time he can afford flying the North for pleasure in his private plane during the short summer months.

CHAPTER 7

The story of the construction of the pioneer road and bridges and many of the problems that went with that construction task may be pieced together from the following secondary sources: Arthur E. Buckley, "The Alaska Highway," M. Sc. thesis, University of Alabama, 1956; Dod, pp. 300–15; Harold J. McKeever, "10,000,000 Trees: The Building of Alcan Highway," *Roads and Streets*, 86 (January 1943), 34–60; Harold J. McKeever, "Bridges on the Alaska Highway," *Roads and Streets*, 87 (January 1944), 47–54; Froelich Rainey, "Alaskan Highway an Engineering Epic," *National Geographic*, 83 (February 1943), 143–68; Harold W. Richardson, "Alcan—America's Glory Road, Part I:

Strategy and Location"; Harold W. Richardson, "Alcan—America's Glory Road, Part II: Supply, Equipment, Camps," *Engineering News-Record*, **129** (Dec. 31, 1942), 35–42; Harold W. Richardson, "Alcan—America's Glory Road, Part III: Construction Tactics," *Engineering News-Record*, **130** (Jan. 14, 1943), 131–38; Theodore Strauss, "Alcan Cold Numbs Men and Machines," *The New York Times*, 31 Dec. 42; Theodore Strauss, "Alcan Road Booms Vast Untamed Area," *The New York Times*, 1 Jan. 43; Brigadier General C. L. Sturdevant, "The Alaska Military Highway"; and Brig. Gen. C. L. Sturdevant, "The Military Road to Alaska: Organization and Administrative Problems," *The Military Engineer*, **35** (April 1943), 173–80.

For the problems of permafrost and icing, see A. C. Clark, "Alaska Highway: Problems in Roadway Design," *Western Construction News*, **18** (March 1943), 105–09; William L. Eager and William T. Pryor, "Ice Formation on the Alaska Highway," *Public Roads*, **24** (January–March 1945), 55–74, 82; and Stephen Taber, "Some Problems of Road Construction and Maintenance in Alaska," *Public Roads*, **23** (July–September 1943), 247–51. Taber writes:

> Over large areas the surface of Alaska is covered with a dense growth of mosses, grasses and other small plants which grade downward into a peaty layer. This plant material is like a sponge in its absorption of water and thus prevents rapid run-off. It also acts as an insulating blanket so that slow thawing through the summer helps to keep the soil wet. Most of the precipitation in central Alaska occurs in the form of light showers during summer and early fall. Since water does not percolate downward through the frozen subsoil, and surface drainage is slow, the soil is usually saturated close to the surface when seasonal freezing occurs. Removal of the vegetal cover in the construction of roads results in deeper thawing.

I am aware of histories of two of those seven engineer regiments which worked on the highway in 1942. These are very interesting for their photographs as well as for their texts. See *Lower Post or Freeze: 340th Engineer Regiment on the Alaska Military Highway, 1942–1943* (Charlotte, N.C.: Herald Press, 1944); and *The Long Trail: 341st Engineers on the Alaska Military Highway, 1942–1943* (Charlotte, N.C.: Herald Press, 1943). These were privately printed volumes available only to the members of the regiments, and they are very difficult to find. The Library of Congress has a copy of *Lower Post or Freeze*, but they were not able to locate *The Long Trail*. Boyd Howard, a friend of mine who was a sergeant in the 341st Engineers, does have a copy and has graciously loaned it to me.

Primary historical documents for the army engineers' work on the Alaska Highway in 1942–1943 are located in FRC and NA, MMRD. The files of the AG (Adjutant General), OCE (Office of Chief of Engineers), and NSC (Northwest Service Command), all in the Federal Records Center at Suitland, Maryland, contain hundreds of interesting items. The World War II operations reports in the AG file, for instance, contain a typescript from the 35th Engineers entitled "Historical Information," 24 Feb. 43. The typescript gives detail of various construction projects and the methods by which the unit organized its work. The OCE file contains, for example, historical notes from the 35th and the 93rd regiments and progress reports sent from the field to the Chief of Engineers.

One of the fullest files at FRC is that of the Northwest Service Command, the command in Whitehorse which was in charge of the army's work on the

Alaska Highway and elsewhere in the Canadian north. Most of the NSC records were stored until recently at the Federal Records Center in Kansas City, but they have now been moved and made available at the main FRC at Suitland. The materials from Kansas City contain typed "Weekly Progress Reports" from both the 340th and the 341st Engineer regiments in the field. These are stored in boxes 566961 (340th) and 5669567 (341st). The NSC records also contain day logs of the 35th, 93rd, 97th, 340th, and 341st regiments, and records of the main office in Whitehorse itself. Examples of main office records are transcripts of staff conversations held at regular intervals, and typed NSC historical notes. FRC also has the files of the Northwest Division Engineer (both Edmonton and field offices), CANOL records, copies of the contracts and the reports of the civilian contractors hired by the PRA, Task Force 2600 records, Richard Finnie's reports, and many other items of interest, such as the results of the investigation of the Charlie Lake drowning of several men from the 341st Engineer Regiment.

In preparing this chapter I have used items from the files outlined above and the following typescripts: "The Alaska Highway (1 June 1945)," an unsigned document giving a historical report on the highway (in NA, MMRD, ASF CG 611 Alaska 1945, file 30); "Alaska Highway Completion Report . . . 6 April 1945," a brief history of the highway with very useful appendixes containing copies of important letters and orders relating to major decisions; "History of the White-horse Sector of the Alcan Highway"; and "Road Log, Alcan Highway, Dawson Creek, British Columbia to Whitehorse, Yukon Territory," a printed report of a reconnaissance of the highway made in October 1942 by engineers of the firm of Bechtel-Price-Callahan (in FRC, NSC, box P51835).

Little has been said anywhere in secondary materials of the work of black soldiers on the highway in 1942, and little in the primary sources refers specifically to the work of the blacks. Of the seven engineer construction regiments, three—the 93rd, 95th and 97th—were black units commanded by white officers. This setup followed the military's policy of segregating black from white units throughout World War II. Lt. Col. Lewis of the 93rd Engineers carefully observed the work and the special problems of his black soldiers and wrote a sixteen page assessment of their difficulties and their performance. He was pleased with his men. One of their problems, he writes, was that most of them were not trained technicians, so that whites often had to give on-the-job training or supervise the black soldiers at work. However, Lewis maintains, his men showed a greater interest in learning than did unskilled white soldiers from other commands.

The main problems of the black soldiers were racial. Lewis reports that recreational opportunities were more limited than they were for whites due to the suspicion felt by the Canadians, most of whom had never even seen a black man. Loneliness, Lewis believes, was the root of all the unrest his black troops felt. There were, of course, few enough girls for the white soldiers, but none for the blacks.

Lewis's black soldiers also deeply resented the lack of publicity given their work. "Most of the news articles in magazines about the construction of the Alaska Military Highway," he writes, "failed to give negro regiments much credit for their share of the completion of that project. Enlisted men of this regiment feel this deeply and their friends back home ask them why this is true" (p. 12). Colonel Lewis concludes:

> Since most negroes have a persecution complex from years of discrimi-
> nation against them, it is inevitable that this subject should be

important to all of them. . . . Treatment of negro soldiers by the civilians has not always been conducive to high morale or good feelings. The unfortunate assignment of unqualified officers has provoked some racial feelings. Most negro soldiers acknowledge the situation exists and take a realistic view that they are soldiers in the Army of the United States and that winning the war and getting home again are more important. . . . [p. 16].

See "Notes on Service with the Ninety-Third Engineer Regiment (GS) in Extreme Cold and Wet Climates, Prepared by James L. Lewis, Lt. Col., 93rd Engrs" (in FRC, AG, World War II Operations Reports, ENRG 93–3.0). Overall, insofar as the records show, black soldiers in the North performed their work as efficiently as anyone else, and in some cases better than anyone else.

CHAPTER 8

Sources of information on supply problems in the North may be found in several primary documents. "History of the Whitehorse Sector of the Alcan Highway" contains an outline of the problems facing the Northern Sector; the quotation about the boatload of coal and slabwood arriving in Skagway is from that document (pp. 11–13). Historical notes in FRC, NSC files, cóntain references to supply matters. Most useful are the typescripts, "Mission and Functions of Northwest Division and Branches" (in FRC, NSC, box P51835); and "Report on the Supply Activities of the Northwest Service Command" (in FRC, NSC, box P51829). For historical sources on the use of the White Pass and Yukon Railway for supplying Whitehorse, see FRC, NSC, boxes P51826 and P51828. Primary sources for Task Force 2600, the name for the military organization which prepared the Mackenzie River waterway for the use of United States forces on the CANOL project, may be found in FRC, NSC, box P51832. General Hoge's orders to Major Bedell in Seattle are to be found in a memo, M. Dawson to Bedell, 19 May 42 (in FRC, OCE A52-434, file 29).

Secondary sources for supply problems are as follows: Dod, p. 302; both Dod, pp. 318–39, and Dziuban, pp. 228–35, discuss the CANOL project; Dziuban, pp. 225–26, discusses the White Pass and Yukon Railway's part in the supplying of the Alaska Highway; see also Joseph Bykofsky and Harold Larson, *United States Army in World War II, The Technical Services, The Transportation Corps: Operations Overseas* (Washington, D.C.: OCMH, Department of the Army, 1957), pp. 55–56. Bykofsky and Larson have, in addition to their discussion of the White Pass and Yukon, a short section on supply and transportation of the whole Alaska Highway project; see pp. 57–64.

For information on Elliott's tiny fleet of boats and barges, see "Small Boats Helped Build the Alaska Highway," *Pacific Motor Boat*, **35** (March 1943), 16–18, 64. Samuel Eliot Morison discusses "Parker's Navy" in *History of United States Naval Operations in World War II, Vol. IV: Coral Sea, Midway and Submarine Actions, May 1942–August 1942* (Boston: Little, Brown, 1950), pp. 164–65. This volume and *History of United States Naval Operations in World War II, Vol. VII: Aleutians, Gilberts and Marshalls, June 1942–April 1944* (Boston: Little, Brown, 1962), provide important background to a study of Alaska defense projects and the Alaska Highway.

CHAPTER 9

J. Frank Willis and Peter Stersberg broadcast the official opening ceremony over CBC in Canada, and the program was heard simultaneously over the Mutual Network in the United States. The voices quoted in this chapter are on a recording of the broadcast made by CBC. For a description of the condition of the pioneer road at the time and of the ceremony itself, see Lorne Bruce, "Alaska Road Traffic Starts: Official Opening Ceremony Attended by Canadian, U.S. Envoys," *Edmonton Journal*, 20 Nov. 42; and Don MacDougall, "'Impossible Task' Is Done as North Road Constructed," *Edmonton Journal*, 20 Nov. 42. "Alaska-Canada Highway, Dedication, Kluane Lake - Yukon - November 20th 1942" is the title of the program and dinner menu for the ceremony (in NA, MMRD, ASW 611 Alaska, file 8.0).

CHAPTER 10

De Voto's book *The Course of Empire* is an excellent introduction to the early fur trade in the North and western Canada. For additional reading on the Hudson's Bay Company, the Northwesters, the fur industry, and early exploration in western Canada, see Majorie Wilkins Campbell, *The Saskatchewan* (New York: Holt, 1950), p. 31ff.; G. P. de T. Glazebrook, *A History of Transportation in Canada, Vol. I, Continental Strategy to 1867* (Toronto: Ryerson, 1938), p. 24ff.; and T. H. MacDonald, ed., *Exploring the Northwest Territory: Sir Alexander Mackenzie's Journal of a Voyage by Bark Canoe from Lake Athabasca to the Pacific Ocean in the Summer of 1789* (Norman: University of Oklahoma Press, 1966). Mackenzie's own account of his voyages, Sir Alexander Mackenzie, *Voyages from Montreal . . .* (London: Cadell and Davis, 1801), is available in reprint.

A fine book on the Klondike gold rush is Pierre Burton, *The Last Great Gold Rush, 1896–1899: Klondike*, rev. ed. (Toronto: McClelland and Stewart, 1972). The trails of early man across the North are covered by Dan Cushman, *The Great North Trail: America's Route of the Ages* (New York: McGraw-Hill, 1966); and Peter Farb, *Man's Rise to Civilization, As Shown by the Indians of North America from Primeval Times to the Coming of the Industrial State* (New York: Dutton, 1968). Ernest Gruening, *The State of Alaska* (New York: Random House, 1968) covers briefly the gold rush in Alaska.

Two articles in the *Edmonton Journal* describe the attempts of parties to travel from Edmonton to the Klondike around the turn of the century: C. H. Stout, "Terrors of Klondike Recalled: Highway Follows Trail of 98," *Edmonton Journal*, 18 July 58; and W. P. Walker, "Forerunners of Alaska Road," *Edmonton Journal*, 8 June 42. The story of the Mounted Police trail to the Klondike may be found in "March Marks Anniversary of Two Routes to Yukon," *Edmonton Journal*, 7 Mar. 46.

CHAPTER 11

For a brief account of early air transportation across Canada, see G. P. de T. Glazebrook, *A History of Transportation in Canada, Vol. II, National Economy*,

1867–1936 (Toronto: Ryerson, 1938), pp. 256–64. Gruening sketches the history of flying in Alaska in *The State of Alaska*. Ronald A. Keith, *Bush Pilot with a Briefcase: The Happy-Go-Lucky Story of Grant McConachie* (Toronto: Doubleday, 1972) is a readable study of the man who opened the air route from Edmonton to Whitehorse on a regular basis. Other information in this chapter, especially on Les Cook and the bush flyers, was provided by Norman Harlin and by Jack Baker who worked for Grant McConachie in the early days. The account of Les Cook's night flight to carry doctors and operating equipment to the White River camp is from Theodore Strauss, "Alcan Cold Numbs Men and Machines." There is a picture of Les in *Lower Post or Freeze*. The picture is reproduced in this book.

CHAPTER 12

The information on northerners and their dogs is from the many old northerners and mushers with whom I have talked over the past twenty years.

CHAPTER 13

Political efforts to build the Alaska Highway may be said to have made their mark for the first time with President Hoover's appointment of the first of the Alaska Highway Commissions, and with the attempt of Premier Tolmie of British Columbia to bring the American and Dominion governments into a mutual accord on the matter of the international highway. The U.S. Congress passed the first of the international highway bills; it was signed into law on May 15, 1930. The President then appointed three members who soon began a study of the feasibility of constructing the highway to Alaska. In the meantime Premier Tolmie tried to persuade the Canadian government to appoint a body of commissioners, but without success. He then invited the American commission to a meeting in Victoria with three Canadian "representatives" whom he also invited. Even though two of these "representatives" happened to be Dominion officials, Ottawa made it clear that she would have nothing to do with the meeting. After the meeting in Victoria, the American commission continued its study without the official cooperation of Canada, and, in 1933, published the report which so enraged Canadian editors and Dominion officials.

The primary documents telling the Hoover Commission–Tolmie story may be found in NA, State Decimal File 842.154; and NA, DLFB, BB, file entitled "Subject: Alaskan International Highway Commission, 1929–1938." The reactions of Canadian journalists to these doings are told, of course, in the newspapers. See especially, "Caravan of Fifty Autos Starts Trip, B.C.–Alaska Highway Boosters Are Off for Hazelton, Premier Tolmie Leads Tourists," *Vancouver Daily Province*, 4 June 30; "Important Disclosure on Alaskan Highway," *Prince George Citizen*, 20 Nov. 30; editorial in *Stewart News*, 21 Nov. 30; "International Highway Not Feasible Present Time, Economic Conditions Will Not Permit Building of System," *Juneau Daily Alaska Empire*, 22 Oct. 31; editorial in *Stewart Northern*

Argonaut, 8 Nov. 34; and an editorial in *Prince George Citizen*, 13 Nov. 34, which argues that "in the light of current world finance the Alaskan highway is altogether too fantastic," that the whole idea of Canada's putting up $12 million to America's $2 million (the figures given out by the Hoover Commission's report) is absurd. Premier Tolmie, the editorialist says, "fell for the ballyhoo of the promoters of the Alaskan Highway in 1930, when nothing was known as to its probable cost."

For British Columbian Premier T. D. Pattullo's efforts to deal directly with the United States government over the proposed highway, there are, so far as I know, no secondary sources except some newspaper articles and a paper read by David A. Remley, "'Energy and Enterprise': Aspects of Canadian-American Relations over the Alaska Highway in the 1930's," Rocky Mountain American Studies Association Conference, University of Idaho, spring 1974. In the newspapers see especially "Canada and U.S. May Link Up B.C. Highway with Alaska-Yukon Road," *Vancouver Sun*, 9 Feb. 38; and "The Alaska Highway," *Vancouver Sun*, 6 May 38.

Primary documents on Pattullo's activities and their results, including the appointment of the Canadian Commissioners, are as follows: letter and enclosure, Pattullo to President Roosevelt, 4 Mar. 38; letter, Secretary Ickes to Secretary of State, 25 Mar. 38; letter, Pattullo to Gruening, 20 Apr. 38; memo, Gruening to Secretary of Interior, 20 Apr. 38; memo, Gruening to Secretary of Interior, 29 Apr. 38; and a letter, Gruening to Pattullo, 23 May 38. All are in NA, SERD, 9–1–55, box 372.

President Roosevelt himself showed an interest in the proposition to loan money to Canada for the construction of the highway. When Alaska's Delegate Dimond wrote the President asking support for a House amendment to loan the money to the Canadians, Roosevelt replied that although the Canadian government had shown "no favorable response" to American approaches about the highway, "I, nevertheless, feel that the amendment should be supported and am glad to so state. As drawn, it would become effective only in the event we were able to get the Canadians to agree. Since we expect to continue our efforts in that direction, it would be useful to have the funds available should we obtain their consent." See letter, Roosevelt to Dimond, 2 June 38; and memo, Dimond to the President, 25 May 38 (both in NA, SERD, 9–1–55, box 371; other pertinent records are in the same box).

The President was interested enough in the proposed highway to discuss it with Prime Minister King at their meeting in Washington in April 1937, and even, apparently, to suggest that he thought it would "pay for itself" within thirty years. The State Department wrote to Ernest Gruening soon after the President's meeting with the Prime Minister to say that King had come away from the talks with Roosevelt with the impression that the Alaska Highway would be a paying proposition and that the Prime Minister had "now become very interested in the matter as a result of a conversation with the President while here." State also had no idea where the thirty-year pay notion had come from and wondered whether Gruening, who was at that time Director of the Division of Territories and Island Possessions, knew anything about it. See letter, J. Dunn to Gruening, 19 Apr. 37 (in NA, SERD, 9–1–55, box 372). Gruening didn't. A careful search was made in the Division of Territories and Island Possessions and in the Bureau of Public Roads, but no statistics could be found to support the idea that a highway to Alaska would pay back the investment in thirty years. See memo, P. Gordon to the Secretary of Interior, 8 Oct. 37 (in NA, SERD, 9–1–55, box 372).

But the President's interest had been aroused. In the summer of 1937 he suggested to various people that Canada and the United States should establish an international park running on both sides of the border between the Alaska Panhandle and British Columbia, and at about the same time he discussed with Gruening and probably also with Delegate Dimond and perhaps others the idea of making Skagway a free port as an inducement to the Canadians to build their part of the international highway to Alaska. "I have discarded as undesirable," he wrote the Secretary of State on August 4, "the suggestion that Skagway be ceded to Canada. But I believe that the ends which the Canadians seek, namely an outlet to the sea in northwestern Canada, may be secured by making Skagway a free port. Such an inducement might tend to encourage and interest the Canadians in building their part of the international highway." See memo, P. Gordon to the Secretary of Interior, 8 Oct. 37 (cited immediately above); and letter, Roosevelt to the Secretary of State, 4 Aug. 37 (in NA, DLFB, BB file entitled "Alaskan International Highway Commission, 1929–1938").

General Ashton, Chief of the Canadian General Staff, emphatically expressed his views about the importance of keeping American economic and military power *out* of Canada to the Dominion's Minister of National Defense and to the Department of External Affairs. Ashton's views may be found in a memo, "Alaska–B.C. Highway," 24 Aug. 35 (in PA, WLM King Papers, M. G. 26, J4, Vol. 171).

Congressman Magnuson introduced H. Res. 8177 in August 1937 to authorize the President to establish a commission of five members for communication with a similar Canadian commission, should it be established, and for the "study" of survey, location, and construction possibilities as well as the problems of financing the construction and maintenance. By May 1938, both the House and Senate had passed the Alaska International Highway Commission Act. In December 1938, Mackenzie King announced that a similar Canadian commission was to be appointed. Members of that Commission were Charles Stewart (chairman), Brig. Gen. Thomas L. Tremblay, J.M. Wardle, Arthur Dixon, and J. W. Spencer. Members of the American commission were Congressman Warren G. Magnuson (chairman); Donald MacDonald, locating engineer for the Alaska Road Commission and a long-time proponent of an Alaska highway; James W. Carey, a Seattle consulting civil engineer; Thomas Riggs, former Governor of Alaska and member of the International Boundary Commission; and Ernest Gruening, Director of the Division of Territories and Island Possessions of the USDI.

Description of Routes A, B, and D—the routes proposed by various people but turned down when the army chose Route C—may be found in various places. For Route A, see Hon. Warren G. Magnuson, "The Alaskan International Highway, Extension of Remarks in the House of Representatives," *Congressional Record—Appendix*, 30 Oct. 41, pp. A5235–36. For a brief description of Route B, favored by the Canadian commission, see "Periodical Report on General Conditions in Canada, no. 42," 3 June 39 (in NA, State Decimal File 842.154). For Route D, the Mackenzie River route favored by Vilhjalmur Stefansson, see Hans W. Weigert and Vilhjalmur Stefansson, eds., *Compass of the World: A Symposium on Political Geography* (New York: Macmillan, 1944), p. 233ff. For a comparison of the routes, see "The Alaska Highway," House Report 1705, 79th Cong., 2nd Sess. See also Conn and Fairchild, p. 393.

For Magnuson's position and his efforts in support of the choice of a western route for the Alaska Highway, see his letters to President Roosevelt, 16 Apr. 40; 19 Apr. 40; two letters, both of 31 July 41; and one of 14 Aug. 41 (in "Papers of Franklin D. Roosevelt Pertaining to the Alaska Highway," Roosevelt Library, Hyde Park, N.Y.). Copies of memos stating Roosevelt's responses are also available at Hyde Park. Magnuson also wrote to Cordell Hull on 7 Apr. 41, and 8 May 41 (two letters in NA, State Decimal File 842.154), and to Chief of Staff, Gen. George Marshall. To Marshall, Magnuson argued the military value of a western route. He spoke of the "isolation" of Alaska, the problems of supplying the Territory by sea, and the difficulties of air supply along the coast. A western highway, he asserted, would permit "transportation . . . to Fairbanks from Prince George in three or four days, most of the year." See letter, Magnuson to Marshall, 17 Apr. 41 (in NA, State Decimal File 842.154). Magnuson also wrote to or talked with officials of the Canadian Department of External Affairs and to Mayor La Guardia, Chairman of the American Section of the Permanent Joint Board on Defense (see letters to President Roosevelt cited immediately above). Congressman Magnuson discovered that officials of the Canadian government were not especially sympathetic to the construction of the highway and probably would not become interested unless they could be assured that its construction was in the interest of national defense and unless the matter could "be given a definite priority by the P.J.B.D." (letter, Magnuson to Roosevelt, 14 Aug. 41, cited immediately above).

Although the American commissioners showed a willingness to compromise on the precise line of the western route so long as it went through Whitehorse rather than Dawson City, the high Dominion officials in Ottawa remained generally uninterested in a highway following any route. The Canadians stated their position at a meeting in Canada in August 1941 between Magnuson, Thomas Riggs, J. Pierrepont Moffat (the American Minister to Ottawa), and three high officials of the Department of External Affairs. Moffat noted that the Canadian officials showed "a complete lack of interest unless and until" the Permanent Joint Board on Defense might first approve the project. He also noted that the Canadians had said that when their section of the Permanent Joint Board had attempted to bring up the subject at a recent meeting of the board, "the American Service members had indicated that they were not prepared to discuss the project." "My own impressions are," Moffat wrote, "that unless our defense authorities give the highway a high priority, and convince the Permanent Joint Defense Board of the importance of the road there is little hope of obtaining Canadian collaboration during the war." The Canadians had also indicated during the meeting that Canada's problems were both financial and had to do with "the allocation of the available labor supply." One of the Canadian officials had told Moffat over lunch after the meeting, however, that he believed Dominion opposition would "automatically disappear" if the American service members of the Joint Board "really went to the mat for it" in the board's meetings. See letter and attached memo of conversation, Moffat to the Secretary of State, 7 Aug. 41 (in NA, State Decimal File 842.154). Magnuson also made a memo of the meeting, which he sent to A. A. Berle, Jr. He observed about the same things as Moffat had, but added that it appeared "from necessity the United States would have to put up most of the money." See memo, Magnuson to A. A. Berle, Jr., 13 Aug. 41 (in NA, State Decimal File 842.154).

Mackenzie King's enthusiasm for the highway, which he had revealed after talking with President Roosevelt in April 1937, had collapsed under the pressures of financial and other concerns. When Secretary of State Hull himself spoke directly to King about the proposed highway in the spring of 1941, the Prime Minister showed little interest. Mr. King "was not entirely favorable," Hull noted, "in holding out hope for immediate cooperation." See memo of conversation, Secretary Hull and Prime Minister King, 17 Apr. 41 (in NA, State Decimal File, 842.154).

Before Pearl Harbor the War Department showed little interest in the Alaska Highway as a defense measure. See Conn and Fairchild, pp. 391–92, and Dziuban, p. 217. In the late 1930s plans for the defense of the Pacific side of the Western Hemisphere were based upon a theoretical structure called the "strategic triangle." The points of this triangle consisted of Alaska, Hawaii, and Panama; they were to serve as the bases for the defense of the western half of the continental axis. The planners believed that naval and air power would have to be the main means of supplying and protecting the vast area within the triangle, and they played down the importance of a land line to Alaska in this scheme of defense. They simply could not believe that air and sea lanes to Alaska might be cut off. Much of their planning was based upon the assumption that the Japanese, if they went to war, would strike southward and westward into the islands and along the coast of Asia, rather than eastward into the Aleutians and toward the west coast of America. This assumption in turn was based upon the well-known fact that Japan had long wanted to control China and other parts of Asia and that she would have to grab for the supplies of oil in the islands, especially the Netherlands East Indies, if she declared war and the Western powers cut off her shipments of oil and other critical matériel for the Japanese had no oil at home. The military planners turned out to have been correct, of course. The Japanese did throw the main body of their forces southward into the Pacific islands. The brief sea and air thrust at Kiska and Attu and onto the Alaska coast was no more than a feint.

For discussion of the planning for the defense of the western half of the hemisphere before Pearl Harbor, see the appropriate references in Conn and Fairchild; Craven and Cate, *Plans and Early Operations*; Samuel Eliot Morison, *History of United States Naval Operations in World War II, Vol. III, The Rising Sun in the Pacific, 1931–April, 1942* (Boston: Little, Brown, 1948); and Louis Morton, *United States Army in World War II, The War in the Pacific, Strategy and Command: The First Two Years* (Washington, D.C.: OCMH, Department of the Army, 1962). The letter in which Secretary of War Stimson set forth his reasons for thinking the value of a highway to Alaska was negligible is to Chairman Cartwright of the House Roads Committee, 2 Aug. 40 (in NA, DLFB, BB, file entitled "Authorizing the Construction of a Highway to Alaska," A204 [2], "Alaskan International Highway Commission").

CHAPTER 14

Throughout most of the 1930s Canada and the United States refrained from making mutual defense arrangements and focused upon overcoming the depression at home. John Bartlett Brebner discusses that broad subject in *North Atlantic Triangle: The Interplay of Canada, the United States and Great Britain* (New Haven: Yale University Press, 1945), p. 304ff. See also Donald Creighton, *Dominion of the North: A History of Canada* (Toronto: Macmillan, 1957), pp.

486–505. The quotation about Canadians being profoundly unmilitary is from Creighton, pp. 506–07. For the Rainbow 4 plan, see Conn and Fairchild, p. 367. Conn and Fairchild also give the statement by the Canadian leaders, members of the Institute of International Affairs, p. 368. For the meetings between President Roosevelt and Prime Minister King in 1937, see Conn and Fairchild, pp. 365–66.

The establishment of the Permanent Joint Board on Defense began at the Ogdensburg Conference on August 17 and 18, 1940. For a description of the conference and its results, see Conn and Fairchild, p. 370ff. This passage also contains the quotation from Stimson's diary, an entry for August 17, 1940. For a lively account of Prime Minister King and his relations with FDR, see the appropriate references in Bruce Hutchison, *The Incredible Canadian, A Candid Portrait of Mackenzie King: His Works, His Times, and His Nation* (Don Mills, Ontario: Longmans, 1952).

The joint board held its first meeting on August 26, 1940. Accounts of this and the subsequent board meetings were kept in the *P.J.B.D, Journal of Discussions and Decisions*, copies of which are located in PA, C. D. Howe Papers, M. G. 27, III B 20, Vol. 50. Besides Fiorello La Guardia, whom Roosevelt had appointed Chairman of the American section, the American contingent was made up of two U.S. Army members, two U.S. Navy members, and a secretary, J. D. Hickerson of the State Department. The Canadian section was similarly structured, with a civilian chairman, members representing the Canadian General Staff, the Royal Canadian Navy, the RCAF, and a secretary, H. L. Keenleyside of the Department of External Affairs.

Histories of the Northwest Staging Route, the chain of air bases which largely determined the choice of route of the Alaska Highway, may be found in the following works: Maj. Edwin R. Carr, "Great Falls to Nome: The Inland Air Route to Alaska, 1940–1945," Diss. University of Minnesota 1947 (Carr's dissertation is the most thorough piece written on the subject); Craven and Cate, *Plans and Early Operations*, pp. 303–04, 357ff; Wesley Frank Craven and James Lea Cate, eds., *The Army Air Forces in World War II, Vol. Seven: Services Around the World* (Chicago: University of Chicago Press, 1958), pp. 152–72; and Dziuban, pp. 200–13. The shocking state of air defense at the time of Pearl Harbor and in the immediately succeeding months is suggested by General Buckner, and also by General DeWitt, head of the Western Defense Command at the time. DeWitt wrote that the Commanding General of the Alaska Defense Command had notified him that "the Navy has approximately 9 planes with which to patrol a band of water several hundred miles wide and several thousand miles long." See letter, DeWitt to A. G., 20 Mar. 42 (in NA, MMRD, AG 611 Alaska 3–20–42). This state of affairs is especially unsettling when one remembers the concept of the "strategic triangle" and the plan to have aircraft, operating from bases in Alaska, reach out to defend the northerly sweeps of the sea and island spaces within the triangle. These nonexistent Alaska-based aircraft were supposed to be able to prevent the establishment of enemy bases in Alaska or the Aleutians, and they were to cover the northern flank of Hawaii.

The story of the formation of the Special Cabinet Committee is interesting. At a meeting of the Cabinet on January 16, 1942, Secretary of Interior Harold Ickes suggested that new consideration be given to the construction of the road to Alaska. The matter had been brought to his attention when Ruth Hampton, Acting Director of the USDI, had noted to Ickes that "a matter affecting national defense which occurs to me to be worthy of Cabinet consideration is the construction of the so-called international highway. . . . " Because, as she saw it, "the war in the Pacific . . . places such a heavy responsibility upon ocean-borne commerce . . . a land connection between the States and Alaska takes on an entirely new and possibly critical importance." See memo, Hampton to the Secretary of Interior, 14 Jan. 42 (in NA, SERD, 9–1–55, box 372).

Perhaps as a result of Hampton's suggestion, Ickes apparently did bring the matter to the Cabinet's attention. In a letter to Bruce Bliven several months after the decision to build the highway had been reached, Ickes recalled that, "Last January, after we found ourselves at war with Japan, I began to worry about getting gasoline and army supplies to Alaska, to say nothing of civilian supplies. I conceived of the possibility of heavy sinkings of our ships by Japanese submarines and surface vessels during the summer when the fogs are frequent and heavy along the Pacific Ocean from Seattle to Juneau." Following Ickes' suggestions to the Cabinet, the Special Cabinet Committee was formed and took immediate action with the Corps of Engineers. See letter, Ickes to Bliven, 19 May 42 (in NA, SERD, 9–1–10, Records of Div. of Territories and Island Possessions— hereinafter T and IP—box 3).

Governor Gruening, on the other hand, remembered Ickes' part in the formation of the Special Cabinet Committee quite differently. "I can relate the facts of my personal knowledge," he wrote to Sen. Warren Magnuson several years after the war had ended.

> I arrived in Washington toward the end of January 1942. I went to see Secretary Knox (having been unable to get any action out of Ickes) and suggested to him the obvious necessity of building a highway since our sea lanes across the Gulf of Alaska might be cut. As a result of that, the matter was brought up at the next Cabinet meeting and a Committee consisting of the Secretaries of War, Navy and Interior was appointed by President Roosevelt to consider the highway.

See letter, Gruening to Magnuson, 4 Feb. 48 (in NA, SERD, 9–1–55). Gruening's failure to "get any action out of Ickes" can probably be understood when one remembers that Gruening, along with the other members of the Alaskan International Highway Commission, was an unbending supporter of a western route for the Alaska Highway and one of the critics of the route from Edmonton after the army and the Special Cabinet Committee had selected it. There is little doubt that when he talked with Ickes in late January 1942 he was doing what he and the other members of the AIHC always did with so much vigor, that is, promote the western route as the only really sensible route for the international highway. Ickes, aware of the heated controversy going on over Routes A, B, and D, probably stayed aloof on purpose. Probably too, he believed it the army's job to select the route and did not wish to seem to commit himself to any particular one at the time.

For the reasons why the army selected Route C from Edmonton and for a reading of the consideration they gave the other proposed routes, see a report, J. Amberg to J. Mead, 18 Apr. 45 (in NA, MMRD, OCS 611 Alaska 1944–45). Hon. James Mead, Chairman of the Special Senate Committee Investigating the National Defense Program, had requested an explanation of the choice of route from the War Department, and Amberg, a Special Assistant to the Secretary of War, replied. Amberg pointed out that the army chose Route C essentially because of the already established line of Northwest Staging Route air bases.

"None of the various routes proposed," he wrote, "would have served the Army's purpose or fitted into its plans as well as the route finally selected. The selection of the final route was governed by purely military considerations. . . ." Amberg summarizes the reasons why each of the other routes—A, B, and D—was rejected.

Colonel Tully's case for Route C, presented at the special Cabinet committee's meeting on February 2, is reported in a memo, R. Gilles to Secretary Ickes, n.d., but filed with letters of February and March, 1942 (in NA, SERD, 9-1-10, T and IP, file entitled "B.C.–Alaska Highway, Part 2, March 25, 1938, to March 19, 1942"). Secretary Stimson wholeheartedly supported the choice of Route C made by his Department, even though the members of the Alaskan International Highway Commission believed that choice a blunder. See letter quoted in notes to Chapter 2, Stimson to Ickes, 12 May 42 (in NA, MMRD, OPD 611 Alaska 2-26-42).

The War Plans Division did make a comparative study of the proposed routes and listed the advantages and disadvantages of the "western" route from Prince George through Whitehorse and the "eastern" route from Edmonton via Dawson City. The War Plans Division's study concluded that "a route combining the advantages of both routes should be selected if practicable. Superficial surveys indicate that the route Ft. St. John–Ft. Nelson–Watson Lake–Whitehorse–Fairbanks is practicable and will include the best features of both Eastern and Western routes." See memo, Generals Gerow and Crawford to the Chief of Staff, n.d., but filed with early 1942 documents (in NA, MMRD, WPD 4327-21-39, box 249). The western route, supported by the members of the Alaskan International Highway Commission, would have gone north by a more westerly line than the route finally chosen, but it would in any case have gone through Whitehorse to Fairbanks as did the army's route, Route C. Thus the army believed that their route combined the advantages of both eastern and western routes. Theirs was an "eastern" route from Edmonton to Whitehorse, but beyond Whitehorse was the same route as that supported by the AIHC.

I have made many references in this book to the controversy between the members of the AIHC, the War Department, the PJBD and others over the selection of the route of the Alaska Highway. I believe that the army, given the circumstances of the day, made the correct choice. Certainly the records in MMRD prove that they did consider the alternative routes and looked at the advantages as well as the disadvantages of each before they selected Route C. So far as I can discover, there is no evidence that special interests influenced their choice of route, as their critics—especially Senator Langer—suggested. Beyond pointing out what is clearly correct, that the western route would have served the interests of the Alaska Panhandle towns and cities and would have put Seattle and the west coast of the United States on a more direct line to Alaska trade and defense, I have purposely avoided questioning the motives of the other side. Such questioning would have to be the subject of considerable additional study and writing for which there is not the space here. A concise, point-by-point summary of the AIHC reasons for believing the western route the best one may be found in a letter, Magnuson to Secretary Hull, 8 May 41 (in NA, State Decimal File 842.154).

As soon as the newspapers announced that the highway to Alaska would be built, suggestions began to come in from imaginative people. A Major Howard Coleman of the Air Corps wrote a paper on the problems of building an "Alaskan-Siberian Highway"—with a road from Fairbanks to Nome and a wooden barge bridge across Bering Strait. In Russia, the road was to hook up with the Trans-Siberia Railroad. Major Coleman requested that he be placed on special duty to supervise the project. See SOS Form No. 1, 30 May 42 (in NA, MMRD, SP 611 Alaska 5-27-42). Another man suggested using aircraft-engine-propelled sled barges on the Bering Strait in the wintertime. These barges, he believed, would be inexpensive to build, they could be constructed up to two blocks in length, and they could attain speeds of 200 miles per hour on smooth ice. Their use, he thought, would make it possible to transport freight into Russia via the North Pacific and thus avoid the submarine menace of the North Atlantic route. See letter, S. Silver to (Senator) L. Hill, 7 Aug. 42 (in FRC, OCE A52-434 611 Alaska, file 30). Still another man suggested laying railroad tracks along the side of the new Alcan Highway so that "Truck-Locomotives" could pull short strings of railroad cars loaded with freight. See letter, E. Ogon to Chief of Engineers, 11 Oct. 42 (in FRC, OCE, A52-434 611 Alaska, file 30). Finally, an Ohioan named Philip Verplanck designed a suspended high-speed railroad-highway-monorail combination which was to be constructed of treated-timber pile bents. The War Department did consider Verplanck's idea, but decided that his structure would be "highly vulnerable" to "aerial bombardment, fire or other enemy action." See telegram, Verplanck to Secretary Ickes, 20 Feb. 42; and letter, R. Patton (Acting Secretary of War) to Secretary of Interior, 5 Aug. 42 (both in NA, SERD, 9-1-10, T and IP, file 3).

The Canadian government and the joint board approved the Alcan Highway soon after the Cabinet Committee's decision.

CHAPTER 15

The accounts of early Christmases and Christmas memories on the highway are from the oral informants.

CHAPTER 16

The information in this chapter is from the Calverleys and Jack Baker.

CHAPTER 17

For accounts of the first car to travel the full length of the highway, see Lorne Bruce, "Alaska Road Traffic Starts," *Edmonton Journal*, 20 Nov. 42; and William Gilman, "Army Truck Started at Dawson Creek," *Fairbanks Daily News-Miner*, 23 Nov. 42. "Richard Finnie's Report on the Alaska Highway" and other reports by Finnie are in FRC, NSC, box P51829, file 3, folder B. Gail Pinkstaff's photographs of the Alcan Highway in the early days are located in the Audio-visual Division of the National Archives.

For the organization and operation of the PRA forces in 1942–43, see Buckley, "The Alaska Highway"; "The Alaska Highway, First Year"; "The Alaska Highway, Second Year"; and McKeever, "10,000,000 Trees." See also Clark, "Problems in Roadway Design"; and MacDonald et al., "Organizing $30,000,000 Job."

Bridges and bridging are covered in "The Alaska Highway, Second Year"; "The Liard River Bridge," an undated seven-page typescript (in FRC, AG, Operations Reports, ENRG—35—0.3.0); McKeever, "Bridges on the Alaska Highway"; "Peace River Bridge," *The New York Times*, 1 Sept. 43; and John A. Roebling and Sons Company, "Short Cut to Tokyo: Building of the Peace River Bridge," a printed monograph by Roebling.

For PRA contributions on the Alaska Highway during the second year, besides "The Alaska Highway, Second Year," see Harold J. McKeever, "Second Year on the Big Road: The 1943 Alcan Construction Job," *Roads and Streets,* **86** (October 1943), 45–61; and W. H. Spindler, "Second Year of Building the Alaska Military Highway," *The Highway Magazine* (November–December 1943), 124ff. "The Alaska Highway, Second Year" describes the standards to which the highway was completed in 1943 and tells the story of the closing of PRA operations in that year.

CHAPTER 18

For maintenance on the Alaska Highway after the end of October 1943, see an unsigned typescript, "The Alaska Highway (1 June 1945)" (in NA, MMRD, ASF CG 611 Alaska, 1945, box 30). Also see Buckley, "The Alaska Highway."

For problems with icing and permafrost, see especially Eager and Pryor, "Ice Formation on the Alaska Highway"; and Taber, "Some Problems of Road Construction and Maintenance in Alaska." See also McKeever, "10,000,000 Trees." For a brief account of heavy equipment maintenance in the subzero temperatures, see James Montagnes, "Ingenious Makeshifts Beat Alaska Highway Truck Servicing Ills," *Transport Topics,* **17** (May 17, 1943), 20. For overall estimates of cost and other vital statistics, see *House Report 1705,* 79th Cong., 2nd Sess. Also see *P. J. B. D. Journal of Discussions and Decisions* for 6–7 Sept. 44. This document records the 'Thirty-third Recommendation' of the board, the recommendation having to do with the disposal of United States matériel in Canada (see Chap. 19).

CHAPTER 19

There were and are countless oral reports of waste and corruption, especially concerning the civilian contractors and construction workers laboring on the Haines Road, the Alaska Highway, and the CANOL project. For instance, Richard Finnie was told while he was photographing CANOL installations at Whitehorse in 1943: "Overtime could be 'fixed' and so could travel approvals. For a consideration a man could quit and be given a release without prejudice and a recommendation, and have his fare paid back to the States. . . . Everybody,"

242

someone told Finnie, "wants a car, a stenographer and a raise." See the typescript, "Richard Finnie's Report on Whitehorse to Norman Wells," pp. 3–4 (in FRC, NSC, box P51830).

For demobilization of the United States forces on the highway at the end of 1943 and the categorization of matériel which had to be removed or destroyed, see "The Alaska Highway (1 June 1945)."

For a period of several years the *Edmonton Journal* carried articles on waste and salvage along the Alaska Highway. A selection of the articles from the *Journal* follows in chronological order: "Charge Waste in Northland: 'Not True,' Says U.S. Army," 6 July 44; "Writes of Waste on Alaskan Road," 11 July 44; "Senior Army Men Go to North after Equipment Said Wasted," 12 July 44; "Waste on Northern Projects," 12 July 44; "Officer Unaware of North Wastage," 14 July 44; "Coast Firm to Buy Salvage in North," 19 July 44; "Prepare Dispose Highway Stores," 20 July 44; " 'Horrible Wastage' in North Charged," 24 July 44; "Sure There Was Waste in the North," 24 July 44; "U.S. Army Handing Salvage on Alaska Road to Dominion," 25 July 44; "U.S. Officials to Prosecute Salvagers in North, Report," 25 July 44; "Northern Salvage Up to Canada," 26 July 44; "Crown Firm Selling Agency for Surplus U.S. Equipment," 27 July 44; "Much Drugs Said Wasted in North," 28 July 44; "Seek Agreement Sell U.S. Goods," 29 July 44; "Disposal U.S. Goods Is Not Completed," 26 Aug. 44; "U.S. to Give Up Canadian Assets," 31 Jan. 45; "Sell War Goods at Dawson Creek," 7 June 45; "Thefts Rife on Alaska Road, Shots Stop Two Suspects," 11 Jan. 46; " 'War' on the Alaska Highway," 12 Jan. 46; "U.S. Search Fails to Confirm Valuable Machines Abandoned," 19 Feb. 46; "Trucks for Disposal on Alaska Road," 19 Feb. 46; "No Waste Found in Alaska Highway," 22 Mar. 46; and "No Corruption in Alaska Highway," 23 Mar. 46.

The *Journal* articles for March 23 and 24, 1946, describe an investigation carried on by the House Roads Committee into the charges of corruption. "Rumors of abandoned equipment, wild extravagances, fraud and corruption were not borne [out] by the committee's detailed studies," the chairman of the committee announced, according to the *Journal's* report. The committee had concluded that, under the circumstances, the highway had been built as " 'economically as could be expected.' " In the editorial "No Corruption in Alaska Highway," the *Journal* commented:

> The phrase "as could be expected" undoubtedly covers a lot of what civilians here and in the north described as "waste." The explanation is a valid one. It is to be found in the reminder of the committee that this military highway was built during a period of great stress, that it was an urgent priority job, and that none knew, when the bulldozers were pushing their way through wilderness, brush and muskeg, whether they or the Japanese would get to Alaska first.

The House Roads Committee report, HR 1705 (cited in notes to Chap. 13), is an excellent secondary source for information on the Alaska Highway. It is a 323-page study containing valuable appendixes, maps, and statistics. Those who made the study concluded that "there was no evidence of graft or corruption on the part of any official," but that "much larger quantities of materials were brought into the area than were needed for the construction project" (p. 68). The cost estimates for the construction and maintenance of the highway which the House Roads Committee provided in its report are probably more nearly accurate than are various other estimates for the same task. The committee estimated the total of both the PRA and the army expenses for building the pioneer road at $19,744,585, and the total of PRA and army expenses for the improved highway at $94,079,635. One is sobered by the thought that $19 million, the amount needed to build the pioneer road, would not buy much more than two fancy fighter aircraft today.

CHAPTER 20

The ceremony held when the Canadian army took over the maintenance of the highway from the Americans in 1946 is described in the following articles in the *Edmonton Journal*: "Notables to Attend Northern Ceremony," 27 Mar. 46; "Site Is Selected for Historic Act," 30 Mar. 46; "Officials Fly to Whitehorse for Road Transfer Ceremony," 3 Apr. 46; and "Canada Takes Over Alaska Highway," 5 Apr. 46. For a description of the nature of the task the Canadian army faced at the time of takeover in 1946, I have used a typed manuscript given me by Brig. Gen. J. R. B. Jones (Ret.), of the Canadian army; the manuscript, written by General Jones, is entitled "The Alaska Highway." General Jones elaborated on the problems his men faced when I tape recorded a talk with him in 1970. See also Buckley, "The Alaska Highway," pp. 55–62.

The *Edmonton Journal* describes travel regulations and travel difficulties in the following articles: "50 Letters Daily Seek Word on Alaska Road," 12 Feb. 47; "Accommodations Greatly Increased, Alaska Highway Restrictions May Be Relaxed this Year," 26 Jan. 48; "End Restrictions on Alaska Road," 14 Feb. 48; and "Deposit Required, Customs Rule Seeks End Abandonment of Cars," 21 June 49. See also "Canadians Clamp Down on Alaska-or-Bust Adventurers," *Vancouver Sun,* 25 Aug. 59. For descriptions of the travelers themselves and their problems, see the following articles in the *Edmonton Journal:* "Complete Fast Trip on Alaska Highway, Three Drive 2,162 Miles, Reach Here in 59 Hours," 31 Aug. 49; "Truck Is Carrying Meat to Fairbanks," 9 Nov. 46; "Family Driving Five Buses on U.S. to Alaska Trip," 19 Aug. 47; "Nine U.S. Tourists End Alaska Highway Bus Trip," 26 July 47; "Fast-Talking American Fails to Secure Permit to Take Strange Vehicle over Alaska Highway," 9 Aug. 47; "North Protesting Highway Stories," 26 Jan. 47; "Officials Defend Travel Suggestions," 21 Jan. 47; "A.M.A. to Probe Northern Protests," 22 Jan. 47; and "Dude Trapline Is Latest Wrinkle for Attracting Tourists to North," 4 Sept. 45.

Bridging the rivers and streams the Alaska Highway crosses has been since the beginning one of the most difficult and tricky of the construction and maintenance problems. There are several articles in the *Edmonton Journal* on bridging the Donjek: "Long Stored Girders Will Bridge Donjek," 9 Jan. 51; "Army Engineers Brave Frost on Far North Donjek Bridge," 27 Feb. 51; "New Alaska Highway Bridge Ready for Opening in June," 23 Apr. 52; and "$2,500,000 Donjek Bridge Will Open on June 15," 3 June 52. For the problems with the Roebling-built Peace River suspension Bridge, its collapse, and the construction of the new bridge, see in the *Edmonton Journal:* "Peace River Bridge Starts to Collapse," 16 Oct. 57; "North Highway Bridge Has Troubled History," 17 Oct. 57; "Thunderous Roar Marked Span's Fall," 17 Oct. 57; "Ice Takes Out All of Bridge," 11 Dec. 57; "Detour Span over River Is Victim of Heavy Ice," 10 Dec.

57; "Contract Let for Bridge," 1 Aug. 58; and "New Peace Bridge Ready for Duty," 27 Jan. 60.

For the Canadian Army's effort to get rid of the maintenance responsibility for the Alaska Highway and for the changeover in 1964 to management by a civilian department of the Dominion government, see in the *Edmonton Journal:* "Group Tours Alaska Highway to Report on Administration," 25 Aug. 54; "Anyone Want a Highway?" 19 Aug. 59; "Alaska Highway in Canada Going to Public Works," 26 Oct. 63; "Highway Changes Will Take Time," 28 Feb. 64; "Alaska Highway Control Changed," 1 Apr. 64; "Public Works Get Highway Custody," 2 Apr. 64; and "Army Says Farewell to Yukon," 27 June 64.

CHAPTER 21

For accounts of the twenty-five-year anniversary ceremony, see in the *Edmonton Journal:* "Highway Celebration May Be Lonely Affair," 10 Nov. 67; "The Date: Nov. 20, 42—Historic Highway Opened," 18 Nov. 67; and "Wintry Ceremony Recalls Alaska Highway Opening," 21 Nov. 67.

Since World War II probably the greatest controversy over the Alaska Highway has been whether or not to pave it. A great many articles in the *Edmonton Journal* have described the controversy and reported the different points of view. See the following: "Would Have Canada Improve Share of Alaska Highway," 16 May 50; "Alaska Highway Paving Project Obtains Support," 31 May 63; "More Benefit Seen for U.S. in Alaska Road," 12 Sept. 63; "Delegates Back Alaska Highway Paving Program," 13 Sept. 63; "U.S. Prepared to Pay Share," 14 Sept. 63; "Alaska Highway Dust to Promote Paving," 6 July 64; "Bennett Offers Union to Yukon and N.W.T.," 15 Sept. 64; "Improved Highway Sought," 23 Sept. 64; "Mansfield Discusses Highway," 8 Oct. 64; "Ottawa to Study Alaska Highway," 23 Oct. 64; "Highway Could Be Panhandle Lever," 26 May 65; "Alaska Highway Paving Said Losing Proposition," 22 June 66; "Ottawa Needs Prod on Alaska Highway," 4 May 67; and "Taylor Says Canada Should Initiate Top-Level Talks on Alaska Highway," 10 Aug. 67.

INDEX

INDEX

INDEX

248

INDEX

INDEX